OUT THERE

OUT THERE

The Batshit Antics of
the World's Great Explorers

PETER ROWE

SUTHERLAND
HOUSE

Toronto, 2023

Sutherland House
416 Moore Ave., Suite 205
Toronto, ON M4G 1C9

Sutherland House and logo are registered trademarks of The Sutherland House Inc.

First edition, October 2023

If you are interested in inviting one of our authors to a live event or media appearance, please contact sranasinghe@sutherlandhousebooks.com and visit our website at sutherlandhousebooks.com for more information about our authors and their schedules.

We acknowledge the support of the Government of Canada.

Manufactured in China
Cover designed by Lena Yang and Jordan Lunn

Library and Archives Canada Cataloguing in Publication

Title: Out there : the batshit antics of the world's great explorers / Peter Rowe.
Names: Rowe, Peter, 1947- author.
Description: Includes index.
Identifiers: Canadiana (print) 20230457703 | Canadiana (ebook) 20230457711 | ISBN 9781990823336 (hardcover) | ISBN 9781990823435 (EPUB)
Subjects: LCSH: Explorers—Europe—Biography. | LCSH: Discoveries in geography—History. | LCGFT: Biographies.
Classification: LCC G200. R69 2023 | DDC 910.92/2—dc23

ISBN 978-1-990823-33-6
eBook 978-1-990823-43-5

A portion of the story told in the Northwest Passage section of this book was originally published in *Canadian Geographic* as "Vilhjalmur Stefansson, Ada Blackjack and the Canadian Invasion of Russia."

The story of the discovery of petroglyphs near the Caño Cristales River in Colombia was originally published in *The Explorers Journal*, Vol 95, No 4.

Cover: From the September 19, 1909 edition of Le Petit Journal, illustrating the battle between Robert Peary and Dr. Frederick Cook over which of them was the first to reach the North Pole

Out There
adj.

1. crazy, mentally deranged, loony.

2. so extremely individualistic as to appear mentally unstable.

3. not conforming to mores, accepted norms, or standards.

—*The Urban Dictionary*

TABLE OF CONTENTS

PREFACE

The crazy idea was to cross Baffin Island on skis, snowmobiles, and mostly by dogsled. In March. One of the coldest months of the year. I organized the trip. Four of us southerners joined two Arctic guides, three Inuit rangers, and twenty dogs for the expedition. We set off from Pangnirtung, traveling through the Auyuittuq Pass, heading north. At night we camped under the northern lights in unheated tents that were dwarfed by the towering cliffs of Mt. Asgard and Mt. Thor.

The temperature fell to −42° C, cold enough, as the expression went in the period we'll be examining in this book, to freeze the balls off a brass monkey.

One of our campsites was on a frozen piece of water called Windy Lake. There are lots of "Windy Lakes" in Canada, nearly as many as there are "Trout Lakes" and "Owl Lakes." I've never caught a trout in a "Trout Lake," nor have I ever seen an owl on an "Owl Lake," and until that trip I'd never experienced much wind on a "Windy Lake." That night, a spectacular hurricane-force storm blew through the night, ripping our tents right out of the snow and ice and collapsing them. At daybreak, we set out to find sleeping bags and camping gear that had been blown to God knows where. Most were never found.

I had a small, wind-up shortwave radio with me. The last item I heard on the newscast of Radio Canada's Northern Service that stormy night was that a volcano had erupted in Tonga, in the South Pacific, creating a brand-new island. I resolved right there and then that once we got out of the godforsaken Arctic, we should go look for it.

Three weeks later we were on a flight to New Zealand. We learned that a typhoon was crossing the Pacific. Normally we'd be up for some storm-chasing, but this time we didn't want to be distracted. While waiting for the typhoon to blow through, we rappelled into a wet cave that was lit only by thousands of glow worms hanging from the ceiling. A cool experience, but not what we'd come for. Eventually I made it to Tonga with my expedition partner, George Kourounis. We boarded a rust bucket boat and headed toward the new island. I had imperialist ideas of planting the Canadian flag, claiming it for Canada, and naming it "Candy Island" after the rotund comedian John Candy, with whom I'd shared a few drinks back in the SCTV days. The Tongans cheerfully told me to shove that idea. The island already had a name—Hunga Ha'api. They didn't feel it needed a new one.

We had a few misadventures along the way, including a broken engine, a leaking bilge, a Coast Guard radio operator furiously shouting at us that we were not to land on the island (we told him we couldn't hear him and turned the radio off), and a flying piece of boat gear that sliced open George's eyebrow and sprayed blood across the deck. When we finally got alongside the new island, the fuckery continued. An unreliable outboard motor (is there any other kind?) meant we had to swim in through the surf. A leaking dry bag flooded a camera and a microphone.

Nonetheless, we made it! The pair of us were the fourth and fifth people to stand on the newest land on earth. It was still warm to the touch. We had to step around puddles of water that were close to boiling. The sun was sinking in the west (as the old travelogue narrations used to say), so after photographing the hell out of the new island, it was time to return to the outboard motorboat and head to our mothership. We swam back to the surf line. Our boatmen sensibly wanted us to board the boat one at a time, so I hung back while George clambered aboard. At that point the outboard stalled once again, and the little boat began to drift away from me. For the next twenty minutes the boatmen pulled on the starter cord, swearing in Tongan. The boat floated toward Fiji, 600 kilometers to the southwest, while I was being swept toward the Wallis and Futuna Islands, 800 kilometers to the north. Darkness set in.

At this point I began thinking about sharks. The Tongan waters are famous for their substantial shark population. Sharks like to feed at dusk. Sharks are attracted by noises—volcanic explosions, for instance. And perhaps guys trying to start outboards.

You know the outcome, so I won't prolong it. There may have been sharks, but I didn't see them, and there were certainly no shark bites. The boatmen finally got their crappy outboard going, came and searched for me in the dark, finally found me, and pulled me in. We all made it back to the rusty mothership and, with only one engine working, made our way through the night back to the capital of Tonga. Twelve hours later.

It was on that long bumpy boat ride back to Nuka'alofa that I began thinking about exploration and about writing a chronicle. Not a story of my adventures, but rather one of the insane misadventures of the nuttiest period ever of exploration—the years 1800–1940. The period when independent exploration peaked, when madcap adventurers charged off to the unknown parts of the world hell-bent on testing themselves against the worst that nature could throw at them.

And so, some years later, here is that chronicle.

INTRODUCTION

THE HEROIC ERA OF EXPLORATION BEGINS

There were four eras of exploration, only one of which, the craziest and most interesting one, concerns us in this book.

First was the ancient period, in which now largely forgotten explorers—Harkhuf of Egypt, Zhang Qian of China, Marco Polo of Italy, Leif Ericson of Norway—went off to exotic lands on ambitious, adventurous, but under-documented expeditions.

Next was the so-called Great Age of Discovery, from about 1400 to 1800. In this period the much-ballyhooed explorers Christopher Columbus, Ferdinand Magellan, Francis Drake, Jacques Cartier, James Cook, George Vancouver, and others captured, at least in broad strokes, how the world really looked. Most of us learned of these explorers in grade school. What we weren't told was that many of them were arrogant, exploitative numbskulls, which is why there has been a revisionist movement in recent years to reexamine their legacy.

Christopher Columbus

Columbus, for instance, has been absurdly lauded for having discovered North America, a ridiculous claim on three counts. First, all the Americas, from Alaska to Tierra del Fuego, from the deserts of California to the islands of the Caribbean, had been extensively explored and lived in by indigenous people for over 10,000 years. Second, Europeans from Scandinavia and possibly also Ireland had made it to North America years before Columbus set sail. Finally, Columbus explored the Caribbean and (briefly) Central America. He never once set foot anywhere in North America. Regardless, the Admiral of the Ocean Sea has been slavishly lionized over the past three centuries, with the District of Columbia, Columbia University, British Columbia, the Columbia River, Columbus Day, the adjective pre-Columbian, Columbus, Ohio, Columbia Records, the Columbia space shuttle, and the country of Colombia, all named for him. Not so much today. He may have been a decent navigator, but his dickish, violent, and genocidal activities, including forced labor and slavery, mean that it is very unlikely that his name will be attached to anything more in the future.

If anything, Portugal's Vasco de Gama was worse. He infamously burned alive 400 Muslim pilgrims on a ship sailing from India to Mecca. However, on his next trip to India, karma caught up with Senhor de Gama, and he succumbed to the locals' best weapon against European imperialist conquest, the malaria-carrying mosquito. He was merely the first in a long line of explorers who would be killed by the pest.

Pope Nicholas V

It is little wonder Columbus and de Gama acted the way they did. They were following the guidance of the most powerful institution of the day, the Roman Catholic Church. Pope Nicholas V laid down the rules in 1452 in a despicable document known as the Doctrine of Discovery—in Latin, *Dum Diversas*. It proclaimed:

Explorers who come upon inhabited lands are instructed by the Pope to invade, search out, capture, vanquish, and subdue all pagans whatsoever and to reduce their person to perpetual slavery. These explorers must appropriate and give to the Pope and his successors all the inhabitants, kingdoms, dominions, possessions, and goods, and to convert these pagans to his use and profit.

Not even, you'll note, "convert these pagans to Christianity." Rather, "convert these pagans to his use and profit." You might assume this archaic order would have been rescinded by the period covered in this book. Nope. The nineteenth-century explorers chronicled here were still taking their marching orders from this fifteenth-century Papal Bull. In fact, as recently as 2005 it was used to defeat a motion from a New York State tribe by the berobed judges of the U.S. Supreme Court. After well over 500 years, the Bull was finally rescinded on March 19, 2023 by the Vatican, following pleas to Pope Francis by Indigenous people protesting the church's role in the scandalous tragedy of the Canadian residential school system.

The second era of discovery typified by explorers like Columbus and De Gama ended in the late eighteenth century. Jumping ahead, the fourth or modern era, from the end of World War II to today, has been grandly called by some "The Great New Golden Age of Exploration." In this period mankind has explored not only space but also the depths of the oceans, the subterranean world beneath us, and hitherto unimagined mysteries of life on earth.

But forget all that. This book focuses only on what was the wildest, nuttiest era in the history of exploration, the wacky third period from 1800 to 1940, a period often described as the heroic era of exploration. The adjective "heroic" could easily be swapped out for "fucking maniacal."

The exotic exploits of explorers in this period fascinated the public, especially in Victorian Britain, where the adventurers were the popular equivalent of sports heroes or rock stars today. Exploration in this period is distinguished by the high number of independent, DIY travelers in the field. Explorers in the Age of Discovery almost always led large expeditions sponsored by kings, queens, rich merchants, or emperors. Similarly, the most famous exploration of our modern era has been financed by billions from US, Soviet, or commercial programs. The maverick explorers of the nineteenth and early twentieth centuries were frequently true independents, beholden to no-one and following their own, often hare-brained inspiration. There were exceptions, of course. Some had official or semi-official sanction of one sort or another, but even these explorers tended to do their own thing once they got out there—in the wilderness.

One of the most important of our era, Alexander Von Humboldt had it both ways, sometimes traveling independently and other times as part of sanctioned expeditions. A well-educated German of a prominent family, he was a serious geologist and geographer connected to some of the most important scientific societies of his day. By the end of his career, he had published many volumes of important work and was credited with an enormous range of scientific achievements. But he is typical of many of the explorers we'll meet ahead for a number of reasons, starting with the fact that he seemed an unlikely candidate for the calling.

Von Humboldt was a chubby, entitled German. His education at the University of Frankfurt was in finance, although you wouldn't know it by the rate at which he squandered his considerable inheritance. In 1799, he became fixated with the idea of heading off to explore the remote jungles of South America. Along with one of his many BFFs, the handsome young French doctor Aimé Bonpland (Humboldt was probably gay), he charmed the Spanish king, Carlos IV, into helping him and his pal get there. He needed the king's stamp of approval to travel through Spanish-controlled South America but not his funds to pay for it. A true independent, Von Humboldt financed many of his own travels and was obligated to no-one.

On February 7, 1800, he and his bud set out from Caracas on an adventurous voyage up the Orinoco River. They were beset with all manner of issues, including bad weather, wild animals, and giant hordes of insects. Humboldt, nonetheless, managed to collect over 12,000 new plants and animals in his travels through Venezuela. Among them was an eel that he named *Electrophorus Elicticus*. The 600-volt current it could produce was enough to kill a horse. Crazy bastard Von Humboldt volunteered to have the fish give him a jolt so that he could experience and describe the phenomenon.[1]

A small (or sometimes large) dose of insanity was also typical among explorers in the era we are examining. Another commonality is the near-death experience, or, for that matter, actual death. Before returning home, Humboldt caught typhoid fever, almost *de rigueur* for nineteenth-century explorers in warmer climes. It came closer than the eel to killing him. Good thing it didn't, because his explorations and writings led to his becoming one of the most respected and original scientists of his era, a man who was later described as "the last man who knew everything."

*

James Holman, son of an Exeter apothecary, was another explorer at the dawn of our era, not as high-minded as Humboldt but more ambitious, at least in terms of mileage. While most of our explorers stick to one particular stomping ground (Humboldt to South America, Livingstone to Africa, Franklin to the Arctic), Holman explored the whole world, visiting every continent and dozens of countries. He did it on his own. He did it with very little money and with no outside help. And he did it while he was totally blind. He lost his eyesight at the age of twenty-five while serving in the British Royal Navy. Holman is typical of the wild characters we'll be examining in this book in that

---

1 Mind you, I once did more-or-less the same thing myself in a Venezuelan stream, intentionally swimming not with an electric eel but with a large school of piranhas. Humboldt did it for the sake of science. My nutty dip was for the sake of art (or more accurately, for the sake of cable television). Both of us survived the experience.

exploration, for him, was a compulsion. "I have been conscious from my earliest youth," he wrote, "of this desire to explore different regions to trace the variety exhibited by mankind under influences of different climates, customs and law." Nothing would stand in his way—not lack of finances, lack of preparation, or lack of sight.

Holman began close to home by exploring France, Italy, Switzerland, and Germany. He took on challenges that would be considered madcap and often illegal today. He decided to climb to the very pinnacle of St. Peter's Basilica in Vatican City. He was only stopped on the last part of this dangerous stunt by Vatican police, not out of concern for his blindness but rather because a sighted nutjob previously had made it to the top of the dome and unfurled a Union Jack on top. They worried Holman might do something similarly stupid.

After his European tour, Holman wrote a book about his travels, using a secretary to transcribe his memories when he could afford one and a newfangled mechanical device called a noctograph when he could not. He then settled on a much grander plan, a circumnavigation of the world. Other than professional sea captains, whalers, and a handful of missionaries and diplomats, few had ever accomplished the feat. It was rare among independent travelers, and certainly no-one had done it blind.

In the 1820s, it was virtually impossible to circumnavigate the globe by heading east to west. Almost no-one other than Alexander Mackenzie, Meriwether Lewis, and William Clark had yet crossed the North American continent. Holman said screw it, I'll go the other way, and started by crossing Russia. The fact that no foreigner was known to have crossed Russia didn't seem to worry him. Nor did the fact that he had only a very modest income, a sort of disability pension of 84 pounds a year. He got no encouragement from his friends. "Everyone," he wrote, "made it his business to demonstrate the madness and absurdity of attempting so dangerous and uninteresting a journey."

Off went Holman. He was hit with his first misadventure before he had even crossed the English Channel. His ship, the *Saunders-Hill*, crashed into a coal barge. Blind Holman had to take the helm while the captain and crew dealt with the emergency. He couldn't see the obstacles ahead of him, but he knew what to do when the captain screamed "Port!" and "Starboard!"

Holman made it to Russia and then, sometimes walking, sometimes on horse cart, ventured as far as Siberia. Then, as now, Siberia was a bleak, frigid landscape, sparsely populated mostly by desperadoes and forced exiles.[2] The authorities wondered why anyone would go there voluntarily, unless they were a spy. Holman made it as far as the village (now city) of Irkutsk before he was captured by the Czar's feared military police and forcibly returned to the Polish border.

Holman banged out a book about his Russian adventures. It was well received, although some in the British critical establishment couldn't get beyond Holman's affliction. "There is something incongruous and approaching the absurd," whined one, "in supposing the scenes described by a journalist so imperfectly fitted to conceive them." As we'll see, controversy and conflict are common features of this acrimonious era of exploration.

While a true indie traveler himself, Holman was on close terms with several of the establishment-approved explorers of his time. One of these, William Fitzwilliam Owen, although himself also an unorthodox character, was highly regarded by the British Admiralty. Owen was authorized to undertake a number of important mapping expeditions around the globe. If you have ever explored the Thousand Islands of eastern Ontario and upstate New York, you may have wondered who gave the 1,768 islands their peculiar names: Bloodletter Island, Astounder Island, Cold Bath Shoal, Horsethief Bay, Deathdealer Island, Dumfounder Island, The Spectacles. It was James Holman's bud, William Owen.

After his dandy job of charting and naming the Thousand Islands, the British gubmint gave him two new assignments. First, he was to

---

2   I traveled over a swath of eastern Siberia in the winter of 2015, heading for Oymyakon, considered the coldest inhabited place on earth. Siberia is one of the most undeveloped and sometimes disgusting places in the world. Challenging today, it was far more difficult when Holman chose to explore it.

chart the entire coast of Africa. Then he was to set up a new British colony on the island of Fernando Po off the Guinea coast. For the latter task, Owen thought that he would take along his pal James Holman. Like Homer (Greek King of Poets, not Simpson), the blind bard's task was to chronicle the mission. The exploration of Fernando Po was yet another disaster, of which this era saw many. It was believed that the island might become an idyllic outpost of the Empire. Instead, wrote the *Times*, it was "the most pestiferous land which the universe is known to contain."

At first, Owen and his bard were enthusiastic. "Luxuriant foliage of various tints and hues," wrote Holman, "blending with the scarcely ruffled bosom of the ocean, and the retiring clouds . . . formed such a variegated picture of natural beauty, that we unanimously hailed it as the land of promise." Their opinion soon changed. Although geographically it was ideally suited to fight the slave trade to America, the buggy island soon got the nickname of being the "White Man's Grave." As many as 40 percent of Europeans in West Africa died annually from what they then thought was "mal air"—the bad air thought to cause malaria. Of the 135 men in the ship's crew, only twelve, including Owen and Holman, survived. The mission was doomed. The Royal Navy recorded it as the deadliest expedition of all time. Yet Holman not only survived—he thrived. He became the translator/contact man with the island's natives. In a small sloop, he and Owen circumnavigated the island to survey and chart its coast. Holman made himself so useful that Owen named one of the island's rivers after him. However, he had not forgotten his goal of rounding the world, and so, typical of his highly adventurous spirit, he eventually jumped from Owen's ship, while under sail, to a Dutch vessel, the *Young Nicholas*, which was heading for Rio de Janeiro.

His very unlikely exploration of the world continued. The blind traveler explored Brazil on horseback, where he was attacked by Marabunda wasps, jiggers, and pneumonia. The goofy cure for pneumonia at the time, at least in Brazil, was a blistering plaster that intentionally covered the chest with open sores. Doctors believed these would drain the fluid from the lungs. Holman also ran out of money. He tried, unsuccessfully, to get royalty payments on his bestselling books from his British publishers, who in those days were notoriously slow in settling their author accounts.

Onward Holman traveled, from Brazil to South Africa, which he explored extensively, to Madagascar, Zanzibar, and Ceylon (now Sri Lanka), where he participated in an elephant and crocodile hunt, using his ears to determine where to shoot. From there he moved on to Australia, where he traveled with a group of Aborigines. It was in Australia that he learned of the death of his king, George IV. Holman and the colony mourned the monarch, who died an obese opium addict and an alcoholic suffering from dementia, convinced he was a soldier fighting in the battle of Waterloo.

From there, Holman sailed around South America and back to England. Then out with another book, then back on the road: Spain, Portugal, Malta, Moldavia, Syria, Turkey, Palestine, and Tunisia. In all, a quarter of a million miles of sightless exploration, making him the most accomplished traveler alive. What distinguishes Holman from the rest of the travelers we will meet is that he managed to avoid the tunnel-vision maniacal geographic preoccupations of the era. He journeyed far and wide and never got bogged down in the dead-ends that obsessed so many others.

Five nutty geographic quests preoccupied explorers in the 1800–1940 period. To our twenty-first-century eyes, it seems somewhat unbelievable that so much effort, so much goddamn blood, sweat, and tears were expended on these somewhat quixotic goals, for today, not one person in a thousand cares much about any of them. Nonetheless, back then, they were thought wildly interesting and important.

The five fascinations were the search for mythical, mysterious Timbuktu; the attempt to find a Northwest Passage through the frozen Canadian Arctic; the quest to discover the source of the Nile River; the race to the North and South Poles; and the search for the legendary lost cities of Latin America.

At the time, these were thought to be missions of crucial importance, although it was not always clear why. Reputations and fortunes were to be made in their pursuit. Horrific loss was more often the outcome. Today? Who thinks much about Timbuktu or frets about the exact source of the Nile? How little does the Northwest Passage contribute to world trade, even though today it has now largely melted and is thus much more navigable? How little do the mostly meaningless North or South Poles matter? How generally forgotten are the mysterious cities of Xanadu and Z? No matter. These quests produced such extraordinary stories of almost impossible-to-believe suffering, bravery, hubris, and idiocy that made them fundamental to the batshittery of this entire era.

CHAPTER 1

TIMBUKTU—*LA CITÉ MYSTÉRIEUSE*

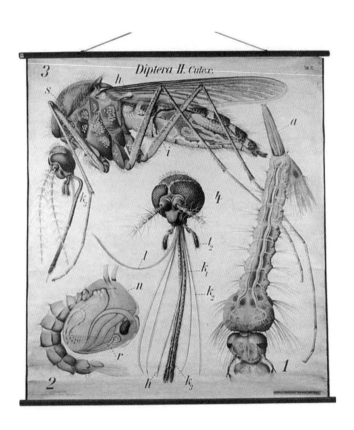

Asked what they knew about Timbuktu in a 2006 survey in England, 34 percent of the recipients claimed they did not believe the place existed at all, and most of the others described it as "a mythical place." It does exist, it is not merely "mythical," and at one time, albeit a long time ago, it was the center of an empire, probably the largest and arguably the most important city in all of Africa. Most of the gold that was traded in Europe came from Timbuktu. By the thirteenth century, it had a population of over 100,000, many of them scholars attached to the town's universities. By 1800, it had gone into steep decline, but even as it seemed to disappear back into the dusty Sahara, it held a mighty spell over European geographers and explorers. No European had been able to visit the mysterious city for 500 years. Now, English and French wannabe explorers, with visions of gold and fame in their addled skulls and egged on by explorers of the armchair variety, took up the quixotic quest to be the first to rediscover the fabled, hidden, and often dangerous town.

The first of the explorers to get on the road to Timbuktu was a courageous but somewhat unprepossessing Scotsman named Mungo Park. With such a bizarre name, how could he have become anything other than an African explorer, amirite? Park's travels in Africa were disastrous in the extreme, but the public's response to them was exuberant.

Mungo Park

Born in Selkirkshire, Scotland, Park was the seventh in a brood of thirteen. At the age of fourteen he was apprenticed to a local surgeon, after which he was able to study both medicine and botany at the University of Edinburgh. Following a successful voyage as a surgeon on an East India Company vessel sailing to Sumatra, Park managed to get himself the gig of exploring West Africa. He was bitten by many bugs during his travels, the first of which was the widespread obsession with trying to discover the source and the mouth of the Niger River. At the time, Europeans did not know in which direction the river flowed, let alone where it started or where it ended. Many geographers had the mistaken notion that it emptied into the Nile, which is over 3,000 freaking kilometers away. So, groups like the African Association were enthused to hear that twenty-four-year-old Mungo Park would take on the monstrously difficult task of getting the scoop on this major African thoroughfare.

The African Association was an interesting organization, a spin-off of London's celebrated and notorious Saturday's Club. The members (all male, white, and upper-crusty) met monthly. They would drink, dine, and listen to one African explorer or another regale them with stories of the Dark Continent. When they tired of listening, they would dismiss the windbag and invite a waiting group of the best-looking, best-dressed (and undressed) whores in London into their chambers, lock the doors, and have a ball.

Notwithstanding his support from the African Association, Park set out from England like an amateur. He packed as if he were going on a holiday to the French Riviera. Unlike many exploration missions of the past, he carried only the bare minimum of navigational equipment and protective armaments. He sailed to The Gambia and headed on horseback into what he called the "boundless forest." His party included only two others, a slave named Johnson and a Mandingo interpreter named Demba. He soon discovered a bitter truth about sub-Saharan Africa that others who followed would learn in turn. Horses do not do well in Africa. They are susceptible to African Horse Sickness and African Sleeping Sickness when bitten by tsetse flies. Park's steeds were soon dead.

White men were viewed with extreme antagonism by most of the Africans and Arabs in the lands traversed by Park. He was captured and taken prisoner on several occasions. A paranoid dipstick named Sheikh Ali was particularly upset about Park entering his territory. He took the interpreter Demba into slavery and nearly starved the explorer to death. Park only survived because Ali's wife Fatima had a notion she might convert to Christianity. She sent some of her attending women to his jail cell to find out more about the strange habits and rituals of Christians. Mostly, they wanted to know if Park was circumcised. He would later recount how he had to give an "ocular demonstration" to one particularly beautiful and curious female.

Park eventually escaped Ali's encampment and stumbled along on his journey through the wilderness. Like many of the explorers we'll be considering, he had a mighty dose of courage and determination, even if he knew the square root of fuck-all about what he was doing. As he continued on his kooky quest, he was robbed, besieged by mosquitoes, and, on numerous occasions, close to death. Finally, six months after he set out, he found the celebrated Niger. He deliriously plunged in and began drinking from it, adding a few more parasites to the many coursing through his body.

Having reached the Niger, Park considered indulging his related obsession with the fabled city of Timbuktu, thought then to be on its banks. It is actually 20 kilometers north. Why it was built there and not on the river is a mystery, but they do call it *La Cité Mystérieuse*. When the Muslims along the river proved as antagonistic as the ones encountered coming overland, Park realized he was not going to make it to Timbuktu. He said, "Fuck it," or something like that, and began his nightmarish, 1,200-kilometer, eleven-month return trek to The Gambia. Once again, Park was captured by marauding bandits. He was stripped naked and taken to their chieftain, who ordered that his right hand be cut off, his eyes plucked out, and his life ended. Again, Park escaped by the skin of his teeth.

It took him almost a year to get home—by American slave ship to Antigua and then a packet back to England. London welcomed him as a sensation, even if society types considered him socially maladroit and a gauche personality. His accomplishments and adventures, disastrous in the extreme, made for good reading. His journeys as described in his best-selling book were considered (and still are) among the greatest in the annals of African exploration. Park singlehandedly invented a new and illustrious heroic archetype—the lone, brave explorer, battling the elements, the natives, the wild animals, and the deadly insects all in the effort to seek out what were, from a European perspective, new lands.

Park retired to a career as a Scottish country doctor but, glutton for punishment, returned to Africa in 1805 for another go at Timbuktu and the Niger. This time, he took a much larger team, including forty soldiers from the Royal African Corps. It sounds impressive, but in reality, the corps consisted of soldiers considered to be scum—those who opted for service in malarial West Africa rather than facing floggings in their own regiments. The men were dressed, in typical British military fashion, in inappropriate and stifling outfits, and commanded by a drunken Irishman. The party was attacked by bees, lions, wild dogs, crocodiles, and, more lethally, fever-bearing mosquitoes. Within fourteen weeks both all their beasts of burden and almost all the Europeans were dead.

Park and three others commandeered a pair of rotting canoes, tied them together to create a makeshift catamaran that he grandiosely named the HMS *Joliba*, and headed down the Niger. Unwittingly passing by Timbuktu, they ended up at a spot named Bussa, where they opened fire on some Africans for reasons they would no doubt describe as self-defense. What happened next depends on whose account you are reading. According to the rah-rah Boys Own-style exploration books, the brave British fought until they ran out of ammunition, linked arms, and made a suicidal leap together into the water and drowned. According to African accounts, they escaped the battle *that they had fucking instigated*, continued down the river, then, ignoring the advice of their African guides, entered a set of rapids, capsized, and... drowned.

The British love a tragic, failed hero, so when the story of Park's second expedition got back to England, his reputation was gilded some more. Not everyone approved, however. Alexander Gordon Laing, another explorer with the Timbuktu bug, utterly disapproved of his predecessor's behavior. "How imprudent, how unthinking; I may even say, how selfish was it of Park to attempt making discovery in this land at the expense of the blood of its inhabitants," he wrote. "How unjustified was such conduct! What answer am I to make to the question which will be often put to me? 'What right had your fucking countryman to fire upon and kill our people?'" [Note – He didn't really say "fucking". Back then, writers had some manners.]

*

By 1820, the distinguished members of the African Association, cosseted in the comfortable armchairs of their London club, had to admit they were no closer to the answers about either the river Niger or the equally mysterious city of Timbuktu than they had been fifteen years earlier. Various explorers they sponsored on the chimerical quest were total busts. The AA members were jazzed about Jean Louis Burckhardt, who spent a couple of years learning how to dress as a Muslim, then promptly died from dysentery before he even got out of Cairo. Their next Great White Hope was Henry Nicholls, who kicked the bucket from malaria as soon as he arrived on the swampy coast of West Africa. In 1815 Sir John Peddie was sent out, who once again let the members down by dying very soon after he arrived in Senegal. The difficulties of travel in West Africa—disease, distance, Islamic fanaticism, parched landscapes, wild animals, insects—were now plain to the AA's muckety-mucks. A new approach was needed.

In the first fifteen years of the new century, the British were preoccupied with fighting two wars—the Napoleonic War in Europe and the War of 1812 in North America. The latter is stupidly named. It lasted until 1815. It was that year, when both wars were over, that the new age of exploration really got going. Suddenly, there were thousands of soldiers and sailors released from duty and actively seeking new forms of adventure, along with hundreds of ships released from military service and available for other purposes.

It also helped that the Barbary Wars between Tripolitania (now Libya) and the United States were also over. They had been fought over the issue of piracy off North Africa and would be entirely forgotten today if not for that jingoistic tune played by marching bands at US college football games: "From the halls of Montezuma to the shores of Tripoli/We will fight our country's battles on the land and on the sea." Sailing to North Africa via the Mediterranean was once again a safe activity, and the notion of reaching Timbuktu by traveling south from Tripoli caught on. Though crossing the Sahara was no picnic, it seemed preferable to the plainly dangerous route across central Africa.

Three unlikely companions volunteered for the first foray across the Sahara to the city of mystery. Joseph Ritchie was a frail and introverted twenty-seven-year-old surgeon, completely unsuited for African exploration. George Lyon was a naval officer, ultimately blackballed by the British Navy for his various failed expeditions in Africa and the Canadian Arctic. John Belford was a Scottish boatbuilder who came along to build them a boat should they have the good fortune to reach the Niger (which they did not).

The three were thrust into a controversy that dogged the whole of nineteenth-century exploration. Should explorers dress and act like European gentlemen, or should they rather disguise themselves as Africans, usually Arabs, in an effort to blend in with the locals? The Ritchie-Lyon party chose the latter course. They not only studied Arabic and adopted full Arab dress but also shaved their heads, grew beards, adopted new Arab names, studied Arab mathematics, and adopted the customs of mameluks—mercenary Muslim soldiers. They even went so far as to have themselves circumcised, without anesthetic, in order to pass close inspection as believers. Their dick-snipping charade probably fooled no one.

They bought twenty-two camels and an assortment of items no local would consider carrying, including a great supply of corkboard to preserve insects, two large chests of arsenic, and 600 pounds of lead (purpose unknown). They joined a caravan of 200 men and 200 camels heading south and made it as far as the Saharan slave-trading town of Murzuk. It was infested with mosquitoes, which meant they all came down with dysentery and "bilious fever" (probably, again, malaria) and were virtually bedridden for months. Belford became deaf and unable to walk. Ritchie began to act like a zombie. Having run out of money, they could not get any food and were slowly starving to death.

In November 1819 Ritchie died. Belford used his carpentry skills to build him a coffin. They secretly gave him an Anglican funeral and then, publicly, a Muslim one. Eventually, the two remaining travelers, both still sick, were able to continue south toward Timbuktu. The caravan had carried on without them, so they were almost on their own, traveling by horseback with a diminutive camel boy as a guide. "We more resembled two men going to the grave than fit persons to travel over strange countries," wrote Lyon. They made it as far as the oasis town of Tegheri, where they lived with the Tebu people—a subset of the Tuareg, the fierce "blue men" of the Sahara.[3]

Belfort became too sick to continue, so the pair headed back, eventually joining a slaving caravan, taking a huge group of slaves north to Tripoli (and from there on to Turkey and Tunis). Mounted overseers whipped the slaves to keep them moving. Those that stumbled were just tossed aside to die in the desert. Lyon was shocked by the brutality but could do little about it.

The explorers were so ravaged by disease and exhaustion that they were not even recognized on finally returning to Tripoli. They made their way back to London and reported their findings to the African Association. Lyon and Belfort announced that they had discovered that the Niger flowed into a giant lake and on from there to become a tributary of the Nile. This was bullshit or, at best, hearsay, as they had never made it to the river or discovered where it went. Regardless, it was exactly what the African Association wanted to hear. The report was received enthusiastically. The only tangible product of their expedition, other than the usual ceremonial swords and other Saharan knick-knacks, was an ill-tempered camel, which they presented to

---

3   Tuareg means "the abandoned of God" in Arabic. Apparently, these people had their own notions of the proper way to be Muslim. Inevitably, other Muslims were always wanting to kill the Tuaregs for being irreligious. Lyon and Belfort had to watch their asses in this dangerous town.

King George IV. The animal, apparently anti-monarchist, spat upon the king and was banished to the stables of Windsor Castle.

Lyon, like Park, was a bear for punishment and pestered the British Admiralty to return to Africa, but the medal-draped nobs had other ideas and rejected him in favor of a team that would prove more colorful but even less successful than Lyon and Ritchie's.

*

Hugh Clapperton

Throughout the nineteenth century, the British managed to come up with some spectacularly mismatched exploration teams. They really outdid themselves this time. Sir John Barrow offered the next kick at the Niger to Scottish doctor Walter Oudney. History recalls the doc as "quiet, short, self-effacing, with a weak constitution unsuited to the rigors of African travel." Oudney made matters worse by choosing Hugh Clapperton and Lieutenant Dixon Denham to accompany him. Both had just been released from British military service, after the wrap-up of the Napoleonic War and the War of 1812. Oudney would spend the next two years trying to prevent the two from killing each other.

Hugh Clapperton had been press-ganged, a fancy nineteenth-century euphemism for kidnapping and forced servitude, into the Royal Navy at the age of seventeen. He ended up commanding a schooner on Lake Huron, lost most of a thumb in a battle with the damned Yanks, and got himself engaged to a Huron princess. In typical imperialist fashion, once he had canoodled with her for a while, he promptly ditched her and returned to England.

Lieutenant Dixon Denham had fought in the Peninsular Wars and was now kicking around London, mostly retired from the army and looking for adventure. He had some skills as a soldier, an artist,

10

and a writer. He was also a prig, a snob, and a martinet with a mean streak. In short, he was an asshole.

The ill-fated trio of Oudney, Clapperton, and Denham met up in Tripoli early in 1822, where the blowhard British consul, Colonel Hanmar Warrington, claimed he "had never seen men better calculated for the undertaking." This was nonsense. The three were at each other's throats before they'd even left town. Denham already said of his new partner Clapperton, "so vulgar, conceited, and quarrelsome a person I have scarcely ever met."

The three men made an unspeakably difficult crossing of the Sahara. The distances are vast, the heat ridiculous. They reported temperatures as high as 150° F. They were desiccated, tortured by thirst, their eyes so bloodshot and swollen they could not close, and both acting crazy.[4]

Denham, always the interfering dumbfuck, got himself involved in violent skirmishes with the locals. In one instance he was captured

---

4   The Sahara can unhinge you. On my overland expedition to Timbuktu in 2009, our driver resolutely refused to turn on the air conditioning, believing that using it burned additional gasoline. I didn't bother arguing with him, since in that heat, the sputtering AC was mostly futile and since, unlike Dixon Denham, I felt it important to stay on good terms with all my traveling companions. One day, it became so hot and I became so crazed that I took to the backseat, stripped off all my clothes, removed my turban, and wrapped it vaguely around my waist. The water in our drinking jugs was so hot it could barely be consumed, so instead I poured it over my body in an attempt to cool down. The water leached the blue dye from the turban, and I was soon as streaked as the Tuareg "Blue Men" of the Sahara, who become blue from exactly the same cheap indigo dye that was staining me. At this point, our driver, also now suffering from heat-dementia, drifted off and managed to get our Land Cruiser stuck in the soft sand. It seemed we were in the middle of nowhere, but typical of Africa, a group of boys spotted us and appeared out of the desert haze to investigate. They were eventually joined by others—old men, women, even young girls. Everyone, including my travel companions, began pushing and digging to free the Toyota. After considerable lack of progress, I deigned to join them, emerging from the back seat with the flapping, flimsy turban barely covering my blue-stained body. I began to shriek unintelligible commands at them, certain that my many times stuck in Canadian snow drifts qualified me to tell them how to get the vehicle free. My loud, dotty imprecations not only shocked the Africans but seemed to inspire them to push harder, if only to get away from the mad, blue-skinned foreigner. Eventually, we all pushed it free. I climbed back in and immediately fell back into my delirious heat-stroked sleep.

and almost killed, except that his captors fancied his European clothes and did not want to ruin them by sticking him full of spears. They first stripped him naked. Before they could then kill him, he somehow got away and ran through the night to rejoin his team.

Besieged by insects, the Oudney team all caught malaria. Sick or not, Clapperton and Denham continued their absurd, never-ending dick-swinging contest and were on such bad terms that for months of travel they refused to speak to each other and only communicated by passing each other snippy letters, copies of which eventually made their way back to London, so that the Admiralty eventually learned all the sordid details of their petty squabbles and enmity.

The tensions between the men were not helped by the fact that while Oudney and Clapperton were bedridden with fever for weeks on end, Denham seemed to be bursting with good health. Indeed, while they suffered, he enjoyed the blandishments of gorgeous young Black women who gave him what he called "shampoos"—full body massages with oil. These were complete enough that he crowed to the others that "verily I began to think that I not only deserved to be a Sultan, but that I had already commenced my reign."

The battle between Denham and Clapperton descended to a level that could have sent Clapperton to prison, if not the gallows. Denham accused him of what was then called buggery—having homosexual relations with one of his Arab servants, a man named Abdullahi. The "infamous, vile, diabolical insinuation" made its way back to Tripoli and from there to London. Denham later retracted his accusation but did not reveal this to Clapperton, leading historian E.W. Bovill to observe that "in the checkered history of geographic discovery, there is no more odious man than Dixon Denham."

The trio did make their way down to Lake Chad, becoming the first Europeans to make a north–south crossing of the Sahara and the first to see this giant but previously hidden (at least to the pale-faced crowd) body of water, which is the size of Switzerland. However, they had still not found the Niger. They continued searching. Walter Oudney, the nominal leader of the sorry team, his body stricken with fever and wracked by the hot days and cold nights of the desert, died in January of 1824. He did manage to get a genus of African plants he had collected on the expedition named after him, *Oudneya*, which, I suppose, is something.

After Oudney's death, the expedition split up for a while, with Clapperton spending time with local leader Sultan Bello, whom he grew to admire. He admitted to the Sultan that "my people had hitherto supposed yours devoid of all religion and not far removed from the condition of wild beasts," but that he now found the African people "civilized, learned, humane, and pious." However, Clapperton did not approve of the slave trade that both Arabs and Americans were still heavily involved in. Like many Brits of that period, he did what he could to fight Arabic and American slave trading and slave transport. Eventually, he and Denham linked up again and made a 133-day crossing back north to Tripoli. Though their camels in the daytime and their tents at night were only a few feet from each other, they did not share a single word for the entire long journey. Only scowls.

One might think that Hugh Clapperton would now be done with the rigors of African exploration, but that was not the case. On his arrival in Tripoli, he was about to demand Consul Warrington open a formal inquiry into Denham's charges against him of homosexuality when he learned of an even bigger problem. Lord Bathurst, British secretary of the colonies, was hedging his bets and planning to send yet another explorer to Africa to find Timbuktu. Clapperton was livid. Like so many others, he had become obsessed with exploration and felt the Timbuktu beat was exclusively his. Suddenly, the issue of buggery faded beside the much more pressing concern of who was going to be the first cauliflower-colored man to make it to Timbuktu. If there was another explorer now in the mix, Clapperton needed to head back into the desert to beat him to the prize.

*

The next nutter to go looking for the fabled city was yet another Scotsman, Alexander Gordon Laing. What's with all these Celts? If it weren't for all the Scots and Irishmen charging off to Africa, northern Canada, and Antarctica, we wouldn't have a book here. But among all the many other Edinburgh-born, home-schooled, military-trained nineteenth-century explorers, Laing's story is utterly unique. If one happened to want a model of a dashing, tragic hero for an old-fashioned, Harlequin-style, bodice-ripping paperback romance, Alexander Gordon Laing would be your man.

Laing's first go at Timbuktu was a solo trip north from Sierra Leone, where he was serving with the Royal African Corps as a major. Unpopular with the troops under his command, he convinced the governor of the colony to let him leave his grouchy soldiers behind and wander off to look for Timbuktu. He got close to the Niger but finding the inland tribes even more hostile than he expected—they pelted him with spears—Laing turned back and eventually headed home. Once back in London, he linked up with the relentless Lord Bathurst, who decided Laing would be the perfect candidate for another go at Timbuktu, this time from North Africa.

Maybe we should blame cartographer Gerardus Mercator for the British naiveté about the size of Africa. Mercator maps, by far the most common projection used, notoriously inflate the size of Europe and distort Africa and the other southern continents, making them look much smaller than they really are. In fact, you can fit the land masses of all of Europe, plus all of China and India, into the giant continent of Africa and still have land to spare. Greenland is not nearly as big as all of Africa, as it ridiculously appears on some Mercator maps, used back then and still in use today. Instead, it's about the size of just one African country—Algeria. The long, meandering land route from Tripoli to Timbuktu is nearly 4,000 kilometers across one of the most parched, difficult desert landscapes in the world. Nonetheless, Bathurst thought it was the smart route to take, and Laing was all like, "Sure, boss, piece of cake," and off he went. Laing prepared for his arduous travels by teaching himself how to write with his left hand and later by holding a pen with his toes, in case of an emergency. It was a highly prescient move, for during the journey he indeed did have his right hand chopped off by a group of Arabs.

While Laing was prepping for his arduous journey in Tripoli, Clapperton was back in London, trying to convince Lord Bathurst to get him on a ship to take him back to Africa. Bathurst thought, "Why not?" Two British explorers battling to be the first might double the odds of at least someone getting to Timbuktu. He didn't care who it was, as long as it wasn't a goddamn Frenchman. He arranged passage for Clapperton on an antislavery patrol ship headed for Badagry on the Bight of Benin. He instructed Clapperton to write a letter to his competition. Clapperton duly recommended that Laing be "kind and patient with the natives" and that he carry many gifts to distribute along the way. Laing found the letter haughty and supercilious and was right-pissed to learn that he was not alone in his quest for *La Cité Mystérieuse.* No hated rival was going to "snatch the cup from my lips." He was now in a race, just as idiotic as the ones that would follow ninety years later between Cook, Peary, and then Amundsen, Shackleton, and Scott for the North and South Poles, and 140 years later between the Americans and Soviets for the moon.

Laing especially did not appreciate Clapperton's advice that he should "not meddle with the local women," for he was already meddling with the local women or, in particular, one woman, Emma, the second daughter of his patron, the consul of Tripoli, Colonel Hammer Warrington. The convoluted and romantic story of this ill-timed love affair, which seems as if it was penned by one of the most famed novelists of the era, Jane Austen, is one of the most unusual preludes to an expedition in the long, wacky history of exploration.

Although trying to organize the complex expedition and doing his best to learn Arabic, Laing had time on his hands. He devoted it to Emma, whom he described as "a delicate flowerlike girl" with "haunting, shadowy eyes" that made his heart "contract every time he looked at her." As he fell madly in lust with her, she too fell head over heels for the dashing explorer. They became inseparable, riding together on the beaches, strolling among the jasmine and almond trees of Tripoli's gardens. Laing decided to propose to young Emma.

Colonel Warrington wasn't sure what to think. He liked Laing, but he also knew he was heading off on a dangerous mission. What if he never came back and his daughter, no longer a virgin, became a teen widow or, God forbid, a pregnant teen widow? On the other hand, Emma's competing suitor was the loser son of the French consul to Tripoli. A marriage to him, felt Warrington, would damage his own political prestige. The consul's novel solution was to perform the marriage ceremony himself and insert a clause into the marriage contract that there could be no hanky-panky between the couple until Laing had returned from Timbuktu.

Laing and Emma were married amidst the blossoms of Warrington's English Garden on July 14, 1825—Bastille Day, just to rub it in to Emma's unlucky French paramour. The couple promised they would follow the rules and avoid any horizontal tangoing. Of course, who knows if they did? Warrington duly sent off copies of the certificate to England, one of them for the new king, George IV. Not that the obese, drunken monarch cared for the proprieties of marriage. He ran through two wives of his own, sired a great number of illegitimate children, and kept at least six mistresses on the royal payroll.

Two days after the wedding, Laing left his virgin bride behind and headed out into the desert. The route south was not hard to find—the caravan simply had to follow the path of the thousands of skeletons of dead slaves who had succumbed on their forced marches north. Laing was disgusted by the grisly sight, but his mind was mostly back with the pretty girl he had left behind. He shipped dozens of love letters back to her by desert couriers.

As Laing headed south, Clapperton was in West Africa, preparing to head north. Included in his party were a young servant/friend of Clapperton's, Richard 'Lemon' Lander, two doctors, and their servant, George Dawson. Having European doctors participate in expeditions in 1826 was about as useful as carrying monkey penis fetishes provided by local witch doctors. Perhaps less. The medical community had yet to discern the connection between mosquitoes and malaria, or that quinine would help combat the disease.[5]

All of the Clapperton party succumbed to the sickening dangers of West Africa. Only two weeks out of Badagri, the young Lander had come down with fever. "I bled in the temple," he wrote, "but the doctor who was himself suffering from fever, being unable to hold the instruments steadily, inadvertently thrust it into my skull. The accident occasioned the most excruciating agony and made me shriek with pain." Lander became delirious from both the fever and sunstroke, and had a violent fit, attacking his boss and the doctors. Surprisingly, he recovered and would eventually become the only survivor of the ill-fated expedition. Both doctors succumbed to the deadly fever, and their servant George Dawson flipped out in a most violent manner and in his delirium swallowed a handful of drugs from the medicine chest, which killed him.

Clapperton remained remarkably healthy and continued north to Borgu. He had been warned that it was inhabited by "the craziest and most untrustworthy gang of cutthroats in all Africa," yet he was welcomed by Yarro, the king, who formally met Clapperton while surrounded by his six youngest wives, all of them stark naked and gorgeous. Yarro offered Clapperton his nubile twenty-five-year-old daughter. The explorer accepted and lived with her for six days. Although he found the village charming, full of cheery people of all ages with both sexes indulging in hedonistic and merry activities that would have shocked most Brits of the day, he eventually pushed on. Timbuktu and the goal of beating that goddamn Laing still called.

---

5 Even when it became available many would refuse it, as on its own, the taste is very bitter. Only when tonic water was created in 1870 and the Gin and Tonic cocktail the following year did travelers to Africa begin regularly consuming enough quinine to combat malaria. Today, the most popular drink in explorers' hangouts such as the Royal Geographical Society and The Explorers Club is probably Scotch whisky. It really should be the G&T, for this is the drink that helped protect explorers against the scourge of the tropics—the tiny but often deadly malaria-bearing mosquito. A successful vaccine against malaria was not created until 2022. Thank researchers at Oxford University and vaccine manufacturers in India for this long overdue breakthrough.

Both exploration teams had their challenges. Malaria continued to plague the Clapperton party, killing another European and several African porters. In Wawa, a rich, corpulent widow named Zuma ("Honey" in Arabic), whom Clapperton described as "a walking water-butt," decided she wanted to marry either him or Lander and pursued them tirelessly.

Laing had a different kind of problem. For some reason the locals mistook him for Mungo Park, the early explorer on the Timbuktu trail who had been dead for twenty years. It was a dangerous case of mistaken identity, for the Africans had not forgotten or forgiven Park's bloodthirsty ways. It took all of Laird's persuasive skills to convince them that he was not Park and had no interest in emulating him.

Both teams were utterly dependent on finding oases in the vast desert. On approach, there would inevitably be a shitshow, with men, women, camels, donkeys, and zebus surging forward to get to the precious water. Children were often trampled to death in the stampede. On arriving, they often found the oasis was polluted with green scum, animal droppings, and carcasses of dead, drowned camels. The choice was either to risk illness by drinking the swill as it was or wait hours while men dug a new well nearby, hoping it would produce fresh water.

In one such squalid oasis Laing was betrayed by his guides and viciously attacked by Tuareg mercenaries. While he was sleeping, he was shot, then viciously slashed with sabres. He took a total of twenty-four cuts—many of them extremely serious. Laing was somehow saved from near certain death by his porters and servants. Forced to recuperate from the dreadful wounds, he was abandoned by the merchants attached to the caravan. After two weeks rest, he was tied to his camel, and his now depleted party continued toward Timbuktu.

Both teams were closing in on the fabled city. Both were severely disabled. The wounded Clapperton was not only feverish again but a victim of the byzantine politics of the desert. Powerful King Bello, his former friend, had determined, accurately, that these European explorers wandering around Africa were just the thin edge of the wedge.

If allowed to continue to keep snooping around, they would soon be followed by armies, traders, and other *nasranis* who would colonize Africa just as, he knew, they had done to India. Bello's suspicions landed on Clapperton, who was arrested and held in a miserable hut. Besieged by heat, insects, and disease, getting weaker by the day, the Scotsman survived for several weeks and on April 13, 1827, drew his last breath.

Clapperton's faithful friend Lander organized a funeral out in the desert. It was as cursed as the rest of the brave but futile expedition had been. Lander valiantly tried to read an Anglican burial service but was totally drowned out by the slaves who had brought out the casket and body, shrieking—not from grief, but rather about how the fee for their porter services would be split.

It was an unfortunately appropriate end to Hugh Clapperton. History has not been kind to this energetic explorer of Africa. Unlike the famous names who would follow him, such as Livingstone, Speke, Stanley, and Burton, his travels have largely been consigned to oblivion.

Young Lander had slightly more luck. Never as prepossessing a figure as Clapperton or Laing, he used his wits to make it back to Badagri, navigate among the Brazilian gangsters and American slave-traders of that hellhole, and get rescued by a British anti-slaving ship. He returned to England. There, he edited and published what remained of Clapperton's journals (although most had been destroyed in the attack by the Tuaregs). In 1830, he would return to Africa and successfully navigated the Niger to its mouth. Of all the explorers who had been assigned the task, it is somewhat ironic that the least promising of all of them pulled it off. Nevertheless, Lander, too, would die in Africa. In 1834, seven years after Clapperton's death, he, too, was attacked by angry Africans and fatally wounded by a musket ball.

On Sunday, August 13, 1826, after a brutal year of hardship, heat, illness, and bloodshed, Alexander Laing finally stood at the gates of Timbuktu. Throwing off his Muslim disguise, he bravely entered the town "as a Christian envoy of the King of England." He was the first Briton and the first European since the Middle Ages to see the fabled city reputedly built of gold, jewels, and ivory.

There was both good and bad news for Laing. The bad was that Timbuktu, a destination for which so many had given their lives, was a shithole. Hundreds of years earlier, at the height of the Malian Empire, the city had been spectacular, its population 100,000, including black Africa's greatest university with 25,000 scholars. It was now a crumbling mess, reeking of stale dung and urine, populated by unwashed people and sick animals. The good news was that Laing was well received by Timbuktu's governor, Othman bin Boubakr, who set him up in a little house inside the town.[6]

Timbuktu was a dangerous place in 1826, but more importantly to Laing it was an unsatisfying one. He had hoped to write a book about his discovery of the mysterious lost city, thought of in the same way as the mythical lost cities of South America like El Dorado, Z, and Machu Picchu, which we'll examine in a later section of this book. Instead of a rich golden town, he'd landed in a collection of neglected hovels. The once-great city was in fatal decline. Who wanted to read that?

Nonetheless, a milestone had been reached in exploration. There was no longer a question of whether Timbuktu was a real place or an imaginary one. It was quite real, even if disappointing. Laing stayed in the city for thirty-five days and sent some letters by couriers back to Tripoli and England. One of them he described as "the First Letter ever written from Timbuktu by any Christian." He was careful to temper his disappointment about the state of the town, for fear of diminishing the value of his planned memoirs. At first, he felt safe there, but increasingly he began to hear rumors about the Fulani warriors, who

---

6   The house is still there, now with a small plaque on it commemorating his visit. On my expedition to Timbuktu, I visited it to pay homage to the explorer. Visiting the fabled city is now virtually impossible. There was a CIA travel advisory about Timbuktu when we visited, but it is now much more serious. As of this writing there is an advisory against all travel to Mali, due to crime, terrorism, and kidnapping.

were encamped around the city and on the Niger River, who he heard might be preparing to attack and kill him.

Laing also used subterfuge to get out of town. Instead of heading back north to Tripoli, he headed west, hoping to get to the Atlantic coast. He was betrayed by his guide, a villainous fuck named Sheikh Ahmadu El Abaya. Thirty miles out of town, El Abeyd had two of his slaves seize Laing and plunged a spear into his chest. He then burned all of Laing's papers and other possessions because "he had come to poison the land, and we held our noses as we burned them." Laing's corpse was left to be consumed by vultures. El Abeyd had the cockamamie belief that the bodies of Christians were "unclean," and that to bury them would render the earth unfertile.[7]

Laing's death was a tragedy for his young bride Emma Warrington, an embarrassment for her father, another frustrating failure for the British exploration establishment, and a mystery of great interest to the French, who were themselves becoming increasingly interested in Saharan Africa and Timbuktu.

*

In December 1821, 217 smarty-pants French scientists came together to create the world's first association dedicated to world exploration,

---

7   On the day before my planned departure from Timbuktu, our driver/guide learned that bandits had taken an interest in us and were planning to follow us out of town into the desert, hijack our vehicle, steal our filming gear and money, and conceivably kill us. We pulled a Laing, putting out word that we would be leaving late the next morning and heading north towards the Algerian border. Instead, we quietly left town at the crack of dawn, before even the first morning prayers rang out, heading in the opposite direction—south toward the Niger River, Mopti, and eventually Bamako. We were looking over our shoulders for the first few hours but saw no sign that we were being pursued. We did pass long caravans of salt-laden camels crossing the desert. Notwithstanding my interest in getting closer to photograph the exotic sight, our worried Malian driver allowed only the briefest of stops, and at a distance. He knew the territory, and he wasn't about to lose his life for some shots for a TV show.

the *Société de Géographie*. One of its first actions was to offer a 10,000-franc prize for the first person to make his way to Timbuktu and return. That caught the attention of a poverty-stricken young Frenchman who had already caught the Timbuktu bug and who most certainly could use the money.

René Caillié

René Caillié was born in the French village of Mauzé-sur-le-Mignon in 1799. He suffered a difficult start on life. Four months before his birth his father was charged with stealing 6 francs and sentenced to twelve years hard labor in the godawful Rochefort penal colony. His mother died when he was twelve. Inspired by a French translation of *The Life and Adventures of Robinson Crusoe,* the highly popular book of South Seas adventure considered by many to be the first English novel, Caillié ran off to join a flotilla of ships running along the African coast. One of them, the *Medusa*, was wrecked. The famous painting of the aftermath, Géricault's "The Raft of the Medusa," is powerful enough to convince anyone with a lick of sense to stay away from both Africa and the Atlantic, but Caillié apparently had none and so carried on to various maritime escapades off Senegal, then Gambia, and then Guadeloupe before returning to France.

In 1824, he caught wind of the 10,000-franc Timbuktu prize and scraped up enough money to return to Senegal. He didn't have the cash to mount a proper expedition so determined to go it alone. Having read the accounts of previous Timbuktu searchers, he determined the main impediment was the threat posed by the many desert marauders. He planned to try to avoid them by traveling as inconspicuously as possible. He dressed as a Muslim, worked hard to learn Arabic, and studied the Koran, hoping to convince any Arab skeptics that he came across that he was a true believer.

Once he had nailed the Muslim Penitent act, he set out to the Niger River. The cloak-and-turban bit seemed to work for the people he met, but of course did little to dissuade the mosquitoes. Caillié was soon as feverish as all the explorers who had preceded him on the road to Timbuktu. He did reach the Niger, however, and lay sick and hidden in the bottom of a thirty-five-meter canoe as the leaky boat crept down the river at the painfully slow snail's pace of 3 kilometers an hour. Finally, he made it to Timbuktu's port town of Kabara and was transported by a party of slaves to the fabled city.

Caillié was just as disappointed by the state of Timbuktu as Laing had been and just as pleased to have made it there. He, too, realized the dangers of the place and after just a two-week stay found a caravan heading north. He joined it to return to his idea of civilization. By the time the caravan reached the mid-Sahara entrepôt town of Araouane, it had grown to 1,400 camels and 400 men. Still feverish, Caillié endured heat, thirst, sandstorms, dreadful food, and bullying, yet stuck with the caravan all the way to Fez, Morocco. From there he made it to Rabat and Tangier. Still in disguise, he slipped into the French consul's residence, removed his turban to reveal his identity, and was hailed like a prodigal son.

On his return to France, he was greeted as a hero. He received the 10,000-franc award and was additionally given a pension of 3,000 francs a year. Like so many of the explorers of this period, he was tormented by enemies, skeptics, and critics. Some doubted he had ever been to Timbuktu, others claimed he had only discovered Laing's lost journals and used them to cook up his own yarns. Caillié declared these accusations were more painful to him than all the aching thirst and illness he had endured in the Sahara. He died of tuberculosis, then called consumption, at the age of thirty-eight.

So ended the weird quest to find Timbuktu. The British, beaten to the punch by the French in West Africa, shifted their sights to an even more hostile and inhospitable part of the world.

CHAPTER 2

THE NORTHWEST PASSAGE— KNUCKLEHEADS AND GUTSY WOMEN

In April 1845, the London docks were the scene of preparations for what was expected to be the grandest expedition of all time. Moored there were the *Erebus* and the *Terror,* two Hecla-class bomb ships originally designed for warfare. The *Terror* was the ship that fired those bombs "bursting in air" during the War of 1812 at the Battle of Baltimore, described in Francis Scott Key's poem that was later turned into the American national anthem.

Now, the ships were being readied for an anticipated conquest of the Northwest Passage across Arctic territories then in possession of the British crown, now belonging to Canada. To light the ships during the long, dark winter, or maybe even winters, stevedores loaded 2,700 lb of candles. To feed the officers and crew, the *Erebus* alone was stocked with 16,416 lb of beef, 16,320 of pork, 18,355 of biscuits, 69,888 of flour, 11,928 of sugar, 4,822 of chocolate, and 612 of pemmican. The supplies also included 3 tons of tobacco, 200 gallons of wine, and 4,500 gallons of 140-proof Jamaican rum. Also loaded were 8,000 cans of tinned meat, later to become suspects in the mystery of what happened to the doomed men in what would become the most disastrous expedition in history. To prevent scurvy, the scourge of polar exploration, the Navy provided 4,750 lb of lemon juice. British sailors, and later all Englishmen, became known as limeys, although lemons, not limes, were the preferred citrus fruit used to try to ward off the disease.

The ships each displaced over 370 tons. To make their way through the ice-clogged channels, the ships were outfitted with twenty-horsepower steam engines and propellors. Today, twenty-horsepower engines are seen on very modest aluminum runabouts weighing less than a hundred pounds and not expected to push through ice. Modern icebreakers typically have 40,000 horsepower diesel engines. Still, a twenty-horsepower steam engine was better than trying to break through ice flows under sail.

The leader of this dangerous and difficult expedition was John Franklin. He was not the first choice. He was not even the second or the third. He was widely thought to be, at fifty-nine, too old for

Sir John Franklin

the task, too soft, and too fat. He also had a very checkered résumé. The bilious, opinionated Arctic expert Dr. Richard King thought it likely that Franklin would end up forming "the nucleus of an iceberg," which he eventually did. However, Franklin had several powerful supporters, including his formidable wife, Lady Jane Franklin, who told the Admiralty she "dreaded the effect on his mind of being without honourable and immediate employment." Sir Edward Parry, who had made five more modest attempts to navigate the elusive passage between 1818 and 1827, seconded this, saying, "if you don't let him go, he will die of disappointment." So, Sir John got the gig, as some said, out of pity.

Franklin already had one botched Arctic adventure on his C.V. He began his search for the passage in 1819 by sailing into Hudson's Bay and then striking out across the land. While ostensibly the leader of the expedition, he became a virtual prisoner of the French-Canadian voyageurs and native Cree, who led him across the tundra. They were alternately baffled, amused, and contemptuous of Franklin and his British naval officers setting off in their buckled shoes and cocked hats.

The party traveled on foot and by canoe. The naval officers, of course, would not deign to paddle, nor would they drag sledges or schlep packs, but only carry their own belongings. Franklin had wildly unrealistic travel goals and argued with Chief Akaitcho, the leader of the native guides, who could plainly see that the explorers were out of their depth. Two of the young midshipmen, Robert Hood and George Back, fell in lust with a pretty fifteen-year-old Copper Indian girl named Greenstockings. In the style of the day, they decided to fight a duel over her. Only the removal of ammunition from their guns by a third party prevented blood from being spilled in the snow.

The doomed expedition was an utter debacle. Franklin, while exerting himself the least, was the first to faint from lack of food. Others soon followed. The travelers were down to chewing on old shoes, scraps of leather, and bits of lichen to satiate their hunger. The diet weakened even the hardened voyageurs, two of whom died from diarrhea. At the nadir of the trip, two of the Iroquois went off hunting. Only one, Michel Teroahauté, returned, bringing with him some fresh meat. At first, the midshipmen thought it was deer, but they later came to believe it was human flesh. Cannibalism? If so, it was a harbinger of what would happen on the infamous 1845 Franklin expedition.

Teroahauté became erratic and hostile to the Brits. Finally, John Richardson, with the agreement of the others, convinced that Teroahauté was going to kill them, took his pistol, and shot the Iroquois through the head. Richardson couldn't believe the shitshow he was in. "No words can convey any idea of the filth and wretchedness . . . the ghastly countenances, dilated eyeballs, and sepulchral voices were more than we could at first bear." Franklin lost half his men on the expedition, although most of these were French Canadians and natives who, to the British, scarcely mattered.

George Simpson, then head of the Hudson's Bay Company's Athabasca district, and an experienced wilderness hand, was appalled at the recklessness of the Franklin crew:

> It appears to me that the mission was projected and entered into without mature consideration and the necessary previous arrangements totally neglected; moreover Lieut. Franklin, the Officer who commands the party, has not the physical powers required for the moderate voyaging in this country; he must have three meals per diem, tea is indispensable, and with the utmost exertion he cannot walk eight miles in one day.

By comparison, Simpson's favorite arctic explorer (and mine), John Rae, averaged 40–50 miles a day, and once managed 65 miles.

Nevertheless, Franklin was lauded on his return to England for his "dauntless resolution and indomitable will; that useful compound of stubbornness and endurance which is so eminently British." He gained fame as "The Man Who Ate His Boots," and his new renown attracted him one of the most influential women in the history of exploration. She would become his wife, and after he was knighted, Lady Jane Franklin.

Lady Jane Franklin

Jane was a far more interesting person and a far more accomplished traveler than her corpulent, stubby, ponderous husband. By her thirties, she had already explored Russia, Egypt, Palestine, Turkey, and Greece. She had cruised the Nile and climbed Mt. Olympus, among other adventures. Even Sir John admitted to her, "You have completely eclipsed me, and almost every other traveler—females certainly." By the end of her life, she had visited virtually every corner of the globe. (Of course, a globe has no corners, but that is the idiotic phrasing we use.) Ultimately, Lady Jane Franklin would contribute far more to filling in the empty spaces of the northern territories than did her hapless husband, one of the great ironies of this testosterone-packed era of exploration. Writes Arctic historian Ken McGoogan, "It can fairly be said, without exaggeration, that of all individual contributions to Arctic discovery, hers was the greatest."

Of course, in the hyper-sexist society of nineteenth-century England, Lady Jane could not act on her own and was certainly not eligible to lead the enormous undertakings for which her husband is known—Admiralty-sponsored journeys that owe more to previous eras of exploration than to this one, even if the batshittery was novel and extreme. But Sir John's adventures, for which his wife worked backstage, giving advice and pulling strings, made possible an abundance of independent exploration by her and others.

Before getting her husband back in harness as an Arctic explorer, Lady Jane's machinations helped gain him a knighthood. She also found him a not-insubstantial interim gig as lieutenant governor of what was then known as Van Diemen's Land and today is called (largely due to efforts by Jane, who got the name changed) Tasmania, the island state of Australia. The island was a horrible British penal colony that had recently been opened to settlers from England. The very conservative colonial establishment on the island quickly recognized that Sir John was a bit of a bumbler, "a vain, good-natured weakling," with a dangerously powerful wife whom they took to calling "a man in petticoats." Colonial Secretary John Montagu called her "a relentlessly ambitious busybody . . . puffed up with the love of fame and the desire of acquiring a name by doing what no one else does."

Not only was Montagu offended by Jane's active participation in the politics of his little island fiefdom but outraged at her adventures and explorations. While Sir John idled in Hobart (then called Hobarton, until Jane campaigned to have the name abbreviated), his wife became the first woman to climb Mt. Wellington, the snow-covered mountain that towers over the city. She then proceeded to commission the construction of a 35-ton yacht and badgered her husband to teach her the rudiments of navigation so she could explore the coast of the island. Sir John was not a part of the expedition. At this point, he weighed 300 pounds and was described as "an enormous mass of blubber and wind."

The following year, she set out on her overland transit from Melbourne to Sydney. The misogynist culture of Van Diemen's Land and New South Wales lost its shit over this junket. This "errant lady," undertaking a madcap trip through a land populated by snakes, runaway squatters, and half-naked Aborigines, was plainly a "perversion of ordinary female qualities." Had she no sense of decency? Besides, whined *The Australian*, "Who is going to pay the expenses of this freak of Lady Franklin?"

The rigorous expedition—traveling on horseback, sleeping under canvas—was a success. On her arrival in Sydney, she was likened to Queen Sheba visiting Solomon. After lingering to further explore the Blue Mountains, she sailed back across the often-stormy Bass Strait to Hobart, a lengthy and difficult passage of five weeks.[8]

Returning to the Tasmanian capital, Jane discovered that her husband's reputation there was worse than ever. The *Cornwall Chronicle* was denouncing the "imbecile reign of the Polar Hero." Franklin fired his colonial secretary, John Montagu, believing him responsible for the bad press. Montagu sailed for England, vowing revenge: "I'll persecute him as long as I live."

Lady Jane knew that Montagu hated her and had total contempt for her husband, whom, in the crude vernacular of the twenty-first century, he considered to be pussy whipped. She worried that Montagu would mount a campaign against her husband and considered returning to the mother country herself to set the record right. Ultimately, she was convinced things would settle down and so decided to instead go off on another expedition. She wanted to explore the penal colony islands off the rugged western coast. The *Colonial Press* called it "a wild goose chase through the bush, a scheme to obtain false praise . . . a dereliction of duty, and a foolish expedition at an unpropitious time of year."

It *was* an unpropitious time of the year, rainy season, and the expedition was dogged by storms and flooded rivers. The group came close to running out of food, was trapped in the bush, and was weeks overdue. Two ships were enlisted to search for them, one the famous *Beagle* with Charles Darwin onboard. Not everyone, by any means, was sympathetic to Jane's plight. The *Launceston Advertiser* sniffed that "unexpected deprivations and difficulties are the penalties justly due to so wild and senseless a freak."

---

8 By contemporary comparison, the annual Sydney–Hobart sailing race, taking the same route, is now usually done in about three days. The record is thirty-three hours.

Safely back in Hobart, Lady Jane learned that a group of six convicts had been sent out to search for her and now they were lost. She offered to cover the costs of finding the men. "How gladly, oh how gladly, I would bear the costs of finding the men. It is horror itself to think of leaving those poor gallant fellows to perish." Search parties were sent out, and the men were found, emaciated but alive. It was a small-scale precursor of the massive search parties Lady Franklin would send years later to look for her husband.

Montagu did mount a devastatingly successful campaign against the Franklins, writing that "Franklin is a perfect imbecile . . . unable to put two sentences together in correct English so as to be intelligible . . . the tool of any rogue who will flatter his wife, for she is in fact Governor." The Colonial Office bought all of Montagu's slanders and, without waiting for rebuttal, informed Franklin that he was relieved of his duties and should return to England in disgrace. "Glorious News!" reported the *Colonial Times*.

The Franklins returned to England in 1844 and worked without much success to restore John's reputation. The colonial office was through with them. The pair transferred their attentions to the Admiralty, which was once again enthused by the idea of finding a Northwest Passage through the ice-clogged archipelago over North America. It offered 10,000 British pounds for the team that discovered it. There was considerable backstage politicking in the decision of who would lead the expedition, exactly the kind of court intrigue at which Lady Jane excelled. By 1845, her husband had the gig, notwithstanding his reputation as a fat, aged imbecile who had left his last post in public disgrace.

Had she commanded the expedition herself, one imagines it might have been a modest success or at least an unremarkable but unlethal failure. But that was impossible in the England of 1845 (or 1945, for that matter). Lady Jane had to content herself with waving off her husband from Greenhithe, England, on May 19, 1845. As a parting gift she gave the crew an odd present to keep them entertained on the long jaunt—a pet monkey. There is no record of how long the monkey lasted, but a gentle reminder, Lady Jane: monkeys live in the tropics, not the Arctic. Perhaps she had a little sweater knitted for it. With Curious George aboard, the crusade set off.

The expedition sailed to Scotland, then Greenland. On July 28, they were seen by whalers anchored to an iceberg in Canada's Lancaster Sound. It was the last time the ships would ever be seen afloat, at least by Europeans, even though dozens of search parties would be sent to look for them. Everyone—129 officers and men, and one monkey, perished.[9]

Lady Jane did not sit at her hearth waiting for John to return. Instead, she went off on her own travels and explorations—first to France, then to Madeira, the West Indies, and the United States, where she climbed yet another mountain—New Hampshire's formidable Mt. Washington. At 6,288 feet, it is the highest peak in the northeastern United States.[10]

In the meantime, not a peep was heard from the doomed expedition. By December 1846, Lady Jane began to worry. She convened a meeting at her London home of the men she considered the foremost Arctic experts of the day, including explorer James Clark Ross but not his irascible uncle Sir John Ross or the eccentric Arctic boffin Dr. Richard King. Both of those men were of the heretical view that exploration through the Arctic passages could only be conquered using much smaller, shallower-draft boats than the British Navy favored. The seventy-four-year-old Sir John learned of Jane's machinations. "Unknown to me, a meeting was held at Lady Franklin's residence,

---

9 Were they really all men? Recent DNA analysis of the recovered bones of the crew of the Franklin expedition has shown in four cases no Y chromosome, indicating that they were from European women. Women did serve in disguise in the British Navy in this era—at least one was known to have been wounded in the Napoleonic Wars. Is it possible some of the crew of the Erebus and Terror were female?

10 I have spent several days in the dead of winter at the summit of Mt. Washington, photographing what is famously considered to be the world's worst weather. It is mightily impressive that in 1845, with the crappy climbing gear of the time, a fifty-four-year-old woman chose to challenge the mountain.

at which all my proposals were sneered at, and my opinions scouted, while I was represented to be too old and infirm to undertake such a service."

Following Jane's meeting, the Admiralty sent Sir John's nephew, James Clark Ross, on two ships, the *Enterprise* and the *Investigator*, to look for Franklin. These were the first of dozens of vessels that would search in vain for the *Erebus* and the *Terror*. After Ross' expedition found nothing, the Admiralty decided to take a different tack. They appointed John Richardson, Franklin's second in command on his 1819 overland expedition, to lead a land-and-river expedition through Northern Canada to search for Franklin's ships. As his second-in-command, Richardson brought on John Rae, probably the most skilled explorer ever to travel the Arctic, but also, as things turned out, the most maligned and the most controversial. Absolutely the least batshit of any who grace these pages.

Rae grew up in the town of Stromness, at the very northern tip of Scotland in the Orkney Islands. The Vikings used Stromness harbor. The buccaneering explorer Martin Frobisher called in many times en route to the Arctic, as did Henry Hudson, as did Captain Cook. Rae had a good training ground. He became a skilled sailor as a teenager aboard a 6-meter yawl called the *Brenda*. With Rae at the helm, he and his brothers raced and beat all comers, even the old salts who sailed fast pilot boats out to meet incoming ships transiting from southern England to the north.

Rae put his sailing skills to use when, at twenty, and already trained as a doctor, he began working for the Hudson's Bay Company, exploring the wilderness of northern Canada.[11]

On one occasion, while Rae was posted to the HBC at York Factory, he agreed to a challenge by an experienced sloop captain "with a by no

---

11 The Hudson's Bay Company, begun in 1670 as a fur-trading company, is the oldest corporation in the world. Today, it is the largest department store chain in Canada, with an annual revenue of over $9 billion (CAD). It sells many upscale items but no longer carries furs.

means poor opinion of his own efficiency as a boatsman" to test two York boats that had been built in the outpost. Rae gave the captain his choice of boats and then beat him soundly. When the skipper complained that the first boat was obviously faster, Rae switched boats with the man, and in a second contest won again.

Rae could not only out-sail but also out-hike, out-hunt, out-track, out-snowshoe, out-canoe, out-smart, and out-survive any man in North America—certainly any white man. For his third trip north to try to find Franklin, he built two boats, and then successfully sailed them for hundreds of miles in uncharted waters, navigating through ice flows, rocks, storms, and past polar bears. He did this basically alone, for the natives and voyageurs he traveled with, while strong, skilled watermen, were not sailors, and the naval ratings he was saddled with were lazy and incompetent knuckleheads, quite unskilled in small boats.

Ernest Shackleton's lifeboat voyage across the Drake Passage to South Georgia Island is frequently described as "the greatest small boat voyage ever made," but Rae's voyages in small boats in the Arctic were far more perilous and took far more skill. Shackleton had an almost entirely downwind run with very little to potentially bump into, and he had a professional captain (Frank Worsley) to navigate and steer and a professional ship's carpenter (Harry McNish) to look after repairs. Rae was in Hudson's Bay, a hellish place to sail—winds from all directions (or none at all), shallow, littered with rocks, with a tidal range that can leave a boat grounded miles from shore. Not to mention *Ursus Maritimus*—polar bears—that can swim at a speed of six knots, faster than nineteenth-century boats.

It is amazing that Rae was able to successfully navigate, chart, and sail these waters while at the same time solving the twin mysteries of the Northwest Passage and the lost Franklin expedition, but then Rae, unlike most of the travelers we've been discussing, was not only an experienced wilderness hand but a trained surveyor. In January and February 1844, he snowshoed 2,000 kilometers from the Red River settlement (present-day Winnipeg) to Sault Ste. Marie and from there to the Toronto Magnetic and Meteorological Observatory to improve and update his surveying skills.

Driven by his own curiosity and egged on by Lady Franklin, Rae continued mapping the coastline of the Northwest Passage while keeping his eyes open for signs of the *Erebus* and *Terror*. He covered vast distances in the summers of 1850, 1851, and 1853, hunkering down for the winters in near total darkness. After initially traveling with tents and building huts out of rocks, he became one of the few European explorers to adopt the igloo as a far warmer and superior form of shelter. He not only used these "savage" structures but learned to build them himself, becoming self-sufficient in the snow. An expert hunter, he was confident that he could capture enough food and thus could travel much lighter, faster, and further than other Europeans traveling above the treeline. He did not blast away with boomsticks for the pleasure of killing wildlife like some others did.

The north was now crawling with search missions. Over fifty ships sailed in the search for Franklin's frozen, possibly by now sunken pair of bomb ships. The weird obsession to find a Northwest Passage was replaced with a new obsession to find Franklin. Many used the northern expeditions to follow their own passions—especially killing animals. Robert McCormick was ostensibly looking for the remains of Franklin, but his journals are more frequently focused on the wildlife of the Arctic. Hunting and exploration are always inextricably linked during this period. Explorers like McCormick would marvel at the new species of wildlife they had discovered, then kill it. Another of the Lady Franklin-sponsored expeditions, this one led by Edward Inglefield, shot sixty muskox just for the hell of it.

Lady Franklin herself volunteered to join the 1848–1849 Rae-Richardson expedition. Richardson, no surprise, turned her down, convincing her that her presence would place the men "in a number of disagreeable situations during long and rough voyages." They were indeed long and rough voyages. In 1853, Rae headed north once again. He overwintered in Repulse Bay, and in spring 1854 pushed north to Pelly Bay, where he met a group of Inuit hunters.

One of them was wearing a cap with a gold band. It was the first discovered relic of the Franklin expedition. Rae bought it. The Inuit then told him about the skeletons of thirty-five *kabloonas* (white men) they had found, wearing torn British naval uniforms, lying beside a battered lifeboat at a site 12 miles to the west. They also showed him telescopes, watches, guns, and compasses, many inscribed with the crests and initials of officers on Franklin's two ships. Lest there be any mistaking their provenance, there was even a small silver plate engraved, "Sir John Franklin, K.C.H."

Then Rae heard the explosive story. Through an interpreter, the Inuit described bodies with arms and legs cut away and cooking pots that had contents that were shocking to them and would be even more shocking when the news got back to England. "From the mutilated state of many of the bodies, and contents of the kettles, it is evident that our wretched countrymen had been driven to the last dread alternative as a means of sustaining life." In short, the lads ate each other.

Rae felt he had to share the news in England. First, he pushed west, crossing the Boothia Peninsula, named twenty years earlier for Sir Felix Booth, the largest distiller in England and maker of Booth's Gin. About the size of Belgium, the peninsula is probably the largest geographic feature in the world named for a brand of liquor.[12]

After crossing the Boothia Peninsula, Rae discovered the waterway running between it and King William Island. This, finally, was the missing link in the long serpentine route running from the Atlantic to the Pacific, and John Rae could finally and accurately claim to have

---

12 Gin-maker Sir Felix was accused of homosexual activities and tried in one of the most famous court battles of Victorian England. He was found innocent. His accuser was found guilty of blackmail and, ironically, sentenced to twenty years in the Franklins' old stomping grounds, Van Diemen's Land. More recently, Booth's Gin, still being manufactured, has enjoyed royal approval. It was reportedly the favorite late-afternoon drink of both Queen Elizabeth II and the Queen Mother.

completed the discovery of the Northwest Passage. The channel is now named Rae Strait.

After the pack ice finally cleared in August, Rae sailed for home. Little did he know that he was about to suffer the most onerous ordeal of his life. As the only traveler with hard evidence of the Franklin expedition's fate, Rae presented his findings to the Admiralty. Typically, the Naval nobs might have resisted contentious information like this from an independent explorer attached to the Hudson's Bay Company like Rae. Now they found it convenient to accept his report. They were sick of pouring vast amounts of money and risking men's lives into Franklin searches, especially as they were also now pouring vast amounts of money and manpower into the Crimean War with Russia. Lady Franklin was still pestering them to continue the search for her husband, calling their reluctance "indecorous, indecent, and presumptuous in the sight of God." They hoped perhaps Rae's discoveries might finally shut her up. The Admiralty released Rae's findings to the *Times*, including the shocking revelation about cannibalism that he had assumed was for their eyes and ears only.

The *Times* report horrified England and, according to one report, the whole of "the civilized world." The now sixty-three-year-old dowager Lady Franklin, following Tammy Wynette's dictum of standing by her man, led the charge against Rae. She called the explorer to a very frosty meeting in the drawing room of her London home.

"How could you," she began. "That is what I do not understand. How could you make such terrible allegations against my husband?"

Rae responded, "Madam, I have made no allegations. I did have a responsibility to report what I learned to my superiors at the Hudson's Bay Company, and also the British Admiralty."

"That report, Dr. Rae, was shameful."

"I did not write the report for public consumption. And I deeply regret that the Admiralty chose to publish it in full."

Lady Franklin hissed back at him: "Such allegations, Dr. Rae, should never have been committed to paper in the first place. You speak only of what you heard from Esquimaux savages."

Rae found it hard to contain his Victorian manners as Lady Franklin's permanent aide-de-camp Sophia Cracroft showed him the door, repeating her mistress' epithet: "The word of savages. Oh, you shall pay for this, Dr. Rae. For this, you shall certainly pay."

She was correct. Rae did pay. Lady Franklin enlisted the London newspapers in a vicious campaign against him. The *Times* accused the Inuit of killing the explorers. "Like all savages they are liars . . . and although they are a harmless race little given to violence, they might have been tempted by the emaciation and weakness of the white men to attack them." There are British historians in the twenty-first century who still buy this racist nonsense and who have told Inuit representatives as much to their faces.

The *Sun* joined the campaign against Rae's report: "The more we reflect upon the fate of the Franklin Expedition the less we are inclined to believe that this noble band of adventurers resorted to cannibalism. No—they never resorted to such horrors . . . Cannibalism! The gallant Sir John Franklin a cannibal? Such men as Crozier, Fitzjames, Stanley, Goodsir, cannibals?"

Daily newspapers were not enough for Lady Franklin. She wanted Rae eviscerated by the best writer of the age. Charles Dickens' popularity was beyond compare in the nineteenth-century English-speaking world. When New Yorkers learned that a steamship was arriving with the latest installment of *The Old Curiosity Shop* aboard, the ship was greeted before it was even tied up with anxious shouts of "Is Little Nell dead?" But Dickens had also shown himself to be a racist and an antisemite. Fagin, the evil villain of *Oliver Twist*, was originally described many times as "The Jew." (Under pressure, Dickens excised the references in later editions.) *Bleak House* has numerous vicious slags in it against visible minority residents of London. In response to the Indian Mutiny of 1857, Dickens went far beyond the most extreme views of British military commanders, proclaiming that if he had the power, he "would do my utmost to exterminate the race [of Indians]."

When Lady Franklin presented him with her views on Rae's report, he enthusiastically took up her cause in his *Household Words* magazine, accusing the Inuit of murdering the starving sailors of the Franklin expedition and of concocting the story they told Rae to hide their guilt. "It is impossible to form an estimate of the character of any race of savages, from their deferential behaviour to the white man while he is strong . . . we believe every savage to be in his heart covetous, treacherous and cruel . . . with a domesticity of blood and blubber." Dickens finished his devastating screed by reporting that "the word of a savage [regarding cannibalism] is not to be taken—firstly because he is a liar, secondly because he is a boaster." He ended by pronouncing that the Inuit savages had likely killed and eaten the sailors themselves as "offerings to their barbarous, wide-mouthed, google-eyed gods."

His ugly but effective words together with Lady Franklin's continuing bilious efforts worked to destroy Rae's reputation. The British Hydrography Department removed credit to Rae on their Arctic maps. The Hudson's Bay Company withheld his pay. The British government delayed the award for his discoveries, although, ultimately, it did capitulate and give it to him. Unlike every other Arctic explorer, Rae never received a knighthood or any other honors, nor did he receive a fraction of the attention given to the ersatz Arctic explorer Sir John Franklin.

The Franklin expedition can be seen as a prime example of Britannic hubris, much like the sinking of the *Titanic*, sixty years later. Franklin himself was thought of in the nineteenth century as a hero of self-sacrifice. He and many of the other explorers who make an appearance in this book were then the equivalent of sports heroes. Trading cards with their images were distributed as bonus giveaways in cigarette packages, with Franklin the king of the cards.

*

Five years after Rae delivered his findings to the Admiralty, a man who would confirm portions of Rae's report decided that he was destined by God to travel north and search for John Franklin. An American, Charles Francis Hall, was an unlikely candidate for heroic exploration—a high school dropout, former blacksmith's apprentice, and proprietor of the tiny *Cincinnati News*. He had no marine, wilderness, or navigation training, but he did have boundless energy and an appetite for all things Arctic. To the amusement of his fellow Cincinnatians, Hall trained for his quixotic search by setting up a tent in the city and sleeping in it for a few cold nights in February 1860.

After selling his little rag of a newspaper, he went off to New York, his head full of Arctic and Inuit lore. He saw many new sights in the Big Apple, including his first Chinese person. He immediately accosted the man and asked if *he* was an Eskimo. Moving on to the whaling port of New London. Hall contacted Lady Franklin about his plans. Usually one to react positively to any proposed scheme, however harebrained, to search for her husband, she was cool to Hall. Her snooty friends and advisors in the United States and England considered him a rube and a crackpot.

Hall raised enough money to mount his expedition but then found himself in an angry wrangle familiar to many explorers in this period. He thought that he had secured a commitment from experienced Arctic whaler John Quayle to take him north but was dismayed to discover that another would-be Arctic explorer, Dr. Isaac Hayes, had stolen Quayle's services from under his nose. "Here I am, devoted to the rescuing of some lone survivor of Sir John Franklin's men," wrote Hall, "and yet within their hearts must lurk deep damnation. I pity Hayes. I pity his cowardice and weakness. I spurn his trickery—his devilry!" With his navigator lost to Hayes' devilry, he had to find himself another ship.

Hall eventually booked passage on the *George Henry*, a whaling ship out of New Bedford. His plan was not simply to explore the north but to live with the natives, learn their language, and study their ways in order that they might lead him to any clues about Franklin's fate. In this respect Hall distinguishes himself as perhaps the first Arctic explorer interested not just in Franklin or in the geography of the Arctic but also its people.

During his first winter aboard the now-icebound ship off Baffin Island, Hall heard a voice addressing him, "Good morning, sir." It was "a soft, sweet voice," a female voice "musical, lively and varied." This was Taqulittuq, one of the important and largely forgotten characters of Arctic exploration. Along with her husband Ipirvik, she would become a constant companion and supporter of Hall till the day of his violent death.

The pair spoke English. A few years earlier, they had been taken to England by whalers as curiosities. They created a sensation and were even invited to have tea with Queen Victoria and Prince Albert. The monarch later wrote of them in her diary, saying, "They are my subjects, very curious and quite different to any of the southern or African tribes, having very flat round faces with a Mongolian shape of eyes, a fair skin, and jet-black hair."

After their experiences in Victorian England, the adventurous pair returned to the Arctic, where they met Hall, and threw in their lot with the Yankee explorer. Taqulittuq taught him how to speak Inuktikut. Hall taught her how to read English. He became the first *kabloona* to totally identify with the natives and the first to refer to them by the name they usually called themselves—Inuit (although many, to this day, still refer to themselves using the name the Cree Indians gave them—Esquimaux). Hall was particularly impressed by Taqulittuq, writing that she had "a degree of calm and intellectual power about her that more and more astonished me."

At the height of the winter of 1861, Hall left for a forty-two-day dogsled trip with Taqulittuq and Ipirvik on the first of his searches for the remains of the Franklin expedition. The three lived in igloos in close quarters. Hall reported he was so cold at night that Taqulittuq had to massage his bare feet with her own. While Inuit custom was that wives and husbands were shared, and while there is certainly much evidence of cross-cultural intimacy between Arctic explorers and Eskimo women (descendants of Robert Peary still live in Greenland today), the picture Hall painted of his relationship with Taqulittuq, at least in his edited memoirs, is platonic.

Hall did not immediately find relics of the Franklin expedition but did instead find the remains of the sixteenth-century Martin Frobisher expeditions. "Great God!" he shouted, "Thou has rewarded me in my search." It was an odd reward, since he was searching for Franklin, not Frobisher, but it was something, and it certainly validated his claim to be a bona fide explorer. Even more important than the relics was his geographic discovery that Frobisher Inlet was indeed a dead-end bay, not, as many in the British Admiralty still believed, a route potentially leading to the Northwest Passage.

The indefatigable Hall again wintered over with his native friends into 1862. Once sunlight returned in April, he set out on another overland trip across Baffin Island. This time Taqulittuq could not accompany him, as she had just given birth to a son, Tuqerlikto ("Little Butterfly"). Hall was disappointed that she didn't at least see him off, but miles out on the ice, he looked back and saw a figure running toward him. Stopping the dogs, he waited until the runner caught up. It was Taqulittuq, who gasped, "I wanted to see you before you left to bid you goodbye." Hall asked her what she had done with her newborn. She rolled down the hood of her parka to show him the baby, tucked inside. Imagine carrying a 12-pound baby and running across deep snow for several miles, fast enough to catch up with a dog team. As Hall would learn again and again, this was one tough woman.

Hall lived on the land with the natives for fifty days, eating the Inuit food that few other whites could stomach and sleeping in rough igloos built every night after a day of travel.[13] On August 9, 1862,

13 In a modest way, I have duplicated the sort of trek Hall made in 1861, traveling in the Arctic by dogsled and skidoo on two occasions. While modern clothing and motorized transportation make it a much different experience than it was in the nineteenth century, it is still a wild and bitterly cold environment. After you've careened across the ice hanging onto the back of a dogsled or a komatik and slept under canvas in minus 40° temperatures, you find it hard to believe that anyone can have done it wearing the pathetically inadequate clothing of Hall's era.

he sailed south, taking Taqulittuq and Ipirvik with him. In St. John's, Newfoundland, he learned to his shock that his homeland was enmeshed in a massive Civil War. In New York, he exhibited the two Eskimaux, in their native dress before the American Geographic Society and as an attraction in P.T. Barnum's Museum of Oddities. The *New York Times* wrote of Taqulittuq's "mild, amiable, and even ladylike expression . . . when she turned her small but sparkling black eyes upon her Arctic flower—the baby on her breast—the beholder began to discover a very pretty and engaging woman, on whose clear, broad brow innocence and goodness sat enthroned."

The trip south turned sour when Taqulittuq's baby grew sick and died. For a time, she was lost to grief. The Civil War meanwhile threw a wrench into Hall's attempts to raise money for a new Arctic expedition. He resorted to collaborating with the irascible and difficult explorer William Parker Snow on a book about his Arctic travels. The pair quarreled and ended up in a New York courtroom fighting over credit and ownership.[14]

Hall now had the support of the iron-willed Lady Franklin. Although she was originally contemptuous of the amateur American explorer, his tenacity had won her over, and she wrote to him calling him "brave and adventurous" and encouraging him with the words,

---

14 Massive but fragile egos are endemic to exploration, even in the modern era. In 1980, canoeist Don Starkell undertook an expedition to paddle 19,600 kilometers from his hometown of Winnipeg to the mouth of the Amazon. After the long and insanely arduous trip, a publisher agreed to help him with a book about the journey, but only if he agreed to take on a professional writer to help him turn his scribbled field notes into a readable manuscript. The book turned out very well, and a few years later, I approached Starkell with the idea of turning it into a film. He was agreeable, but not if his co-writer was going to make any money from it. Since their original contract said he should, the project was kiboshed. Like Hall 130 years earlier, the nose was cut off to spite the face. Starkell later attempted to be the first to cross the Northwest Passage by kayak, coming within 48 kilometers of his goal, losing parts of his fingers and toes to frostbite along the way.

"It is our bounden duty, as it is an impetuous instinct, to rescue them, if possible, even though we may feel shocked at the sight of skeletons rising in their winding sheets from the tombs." Whether she financed him or not is uncertain, but, somehow, he scraped up the money to head back north, arriving in 1864.

For the next five years, Hall based himself in the tiny Inuit outpost of Repulse Bay, making numerous long, overland trips on his quest to find Franklin or his remains. In 1868, he headed out to the Boothia Peninsula, this time not with his usual Inuit pals but instead with a small group of seamen. Again, we see evidence of the short fuse and angry temperament so typical of nineteenth-century explorers. Once out on the land, they fell in with a group of natives from the Boothia Peninsula who seemed to have interesting information about what might be the Franklin story. Hall, at one point, discovered one of the seamen, Patrick Coleman, interviewing the natives about the subject. He flew into a rage, succumbing to the batshittery so common among nineteenth-century explorers. It was up to *him* to do the interrogating, not common seamen! One thing led to another. Hall pulled a pistol from his belt and shot Coleman in the stomach. He immediately regretted his impetuous action, handed his gun to the cowed and frightened group of Inuit, and attempted to save Coleman's life. To no avail. The seaman suffered for two weeks, then died. Hall was never brought to account for the killing. Justice was even rougher in the Arctic of the 1860s than in the wild west of Texas and Arizona.

Hall returned to Repulse Bay and spent another dark winter living with the Inuit. In the spring, he lit out again, determined to make it to King William Island, this time with Taqulittuq and Ipirvik. Finally, he hit paydirt: a ragged tent containing relics of the infamous expedition, including a silver spoon with Franklin's crest on it and a piece of a mahogany writing desk. Hall was able to confirm Rae's findings about the last days of the men, writing that "the tent was filled with frozen corpses—some entire and others mutilated by some of the starving companions, who had cut off much of the flesh with their knives and hatchets and eaten it."

Hall also finally faced up to the sad but obvious truth that no-one wanted to recognize: twenty-four years after the last sighting of the Franklin sailors, they were all dead and gone. It was a sad end to his long-held dream of finding survivors, but within days of admitting defeat, the resilient Hall had bounced back and found a new windmill to tilt at. "I cannot, if I would, contain my zeal for making Arctic discoveries," he declared. "How my soul longs for the time to come when I can be on my North Pole Expedition!" On August 13, 1869, he returned to New York with his two faithful Inuit companions, intent on raising money for his next adventure.

Lady Jane Franklin was against Hall's shift in focus. While he had been trudging through the Arctic snow looking for her dead husband, she had been traveling the world, proving once again that she was a far more adventurous and interesting traveler than Sir John. Her itinerary is exhausting just to read—from London to New York to Toronto to Niagara Falls to Brazil, Patagonia, and Chile. From there to California and British Columbia, then to Hawaii to meet the island's queen. From there to Japan, China, Singapore, Penang, and Calcutta. On to Spain, then back to India, then the Canary Islands and Northwest Africa, where she learned of Hall's discoveries. Immediately, she headed for Cincinnati, where she interrogated the explorer and tried to convince him to return yet again to look for more clues to the whereabouts of her husband. Hall demurred. He would go back to King William Island, he told her, but only after he had attained the North Pole.

Hall's change of heart did not prevent Lady Franklin from continuing her searches. Altogether, she spent 35,000 pounds looking for her husband and convinced other private parties to kick in still more. She wrote to Nicholas I, the Czar of Russia, pleading with him to send a mission north to search for the Franklin ships along the Siberian coast and Bering Strait. She appealed to US President Zachary Taylor for help. She visited a clairvoyant and received a visit from a man who claimed that his children had received nocturnal visits from their dead four-year-old sibling, "Little Weasy," who told them precisely where in the vast Arctic the Franklin ships could be found.

With all this ongoing, Lady Jane hedged her bets on finding her missing husband by formalizing his beatification. By now, she had managed to convince Britain not only that Rae was utterly wrong about the final days of the explorers but also, and just as importantly, that Franklin had completed the discovery of the Northwest Passage. She had a bust of Franklin made for Westminster Abbey, complete with an inscription by the poet laureate Alfred Lord Tennyson. The dean of the abbey objected to the front and center position in it she wanted for it, but in the end, as usual, she prevailed. She had two massive statues made of the explorer and sent the first to be prominently displayed in Hobart, Tasmania. After forcing the sculptor to make a variety of tweaks to further glorify her husband, she had the government mount the second in London. She lobbied to have it placed in Trafalgar Square, within sight of the monument to the greatest of British heroes, Admiral Lord Nelson. The powers of the day compelled her to settle for Waterloo Place, a more modest but still prestigious venue. The inscription reads, "FRANKLIN—To the great Navigator and his brave companions who sacrificed their lives completing the discovery of the North-West Passage A.D. 1847–48."

It was all bullshit. How a man who died at the north end of a different, unnavigable ice-clogged channel (Victoria Strait) can be considered to have discovered the Northwest Passage is a mystery, although the claim is made to this day by various monuments around London and some ill-informed British historians. Thank Lady Franklin for using the rags of John Rae's reputation to burnish her husband's fame, transforming him from a failed explorer into a national icon.

Franklin's ships remained lost for over 160 years, until 2014, when a Parks Canada vessel, also named the *Investigator*, finally discovered the wreck of the *Erebus* in 13 meters of water west of Adelaide Peninsula. Coincidentally or not, this was very close to Little Weasy's prediction. The monumental find was front-page news across Canada and England. Lost in the hoopla was the location of the discovery:

it definitively proved that the *Erebus* had not completed the final link in the Northwest Passage. [15]

In the 1990s, Trent University anthropologist Anne Keenleyside and archeologist Margaret Bertulli investigated and analyzed the 200 objects and 400 bones retrieved from the Franklin expedition. With an electron microscope, they discovered cut marks made by steel knives on ninety-two bones, marks they described as being "in a pattern consistent with intentional disarticulation." In simpler language, their scientific report confirmed that the survivors dismembered the bodies and carved away the flesh, just as Rae had reported. There are no statues in London to John Rae, the explorer who reported the truth and really did discover the final link in the passage.

By the 1870s, the urge to find Franklin had substantially abated. His 129-member team had obviously perished in a horrible manner. In our time, Sir John's reputation has been vastly reduced, even if the monuments still stand. Margaret Atwood refers to him, not maliciously, as "Halfwit Franklin." But the fate of his expedition continues to fascinate and inspire investigation. The Canadian government continues to spend lavishly in search of more information about the doomed journey. It is bizarre, this ongoing obsession with

---

15 Stephen Harper, then Prime Minister of Canada, glommed onto the discovery, partially out of national pride that it was Canadians who had found it (and the *Terror* two years later), partially as a symbol of Canada's sovereignty over the north—Americans are always sniffing around up there, suggesting the Arctic Ocean is international water—and also to score political points for himself and his Conservative Party. The wreck is still there. Private exploration of the ship is verboten, for what that's worth. I once filmed with a group of rogue divers who found and explored two other nineteenth-century British naval shipwrecks, the *Hamilton* and the *Scourge*, that had also been declared off limits by the authorities. I also saw live underwater imagery of those ships myself, without breaking any laws, from the same Parks Canada dive vessel the *Investigator* that later found the *Erebus*. The exact location of the *Erebus* is a closely guarded state secret, but it is somewhere within the parameters of 68°14′44 N/98°52′22″ W, to 68° 17′ 44′2″ N/98° 40′ 17.9″ W, to 68° 13′ 15′ N/98° 32′ 16.2″ W, to 68°10′16.5″ N/98° 44′ 19.3″ W. If you should go searching, know that if you do find it and disturb it in any way, Canada will likely track you down, lock you up, and pitch the key into the Arctic Ocean.

a portly, second-tier British traveler, but little in the history of Arctic exploration has been entirely rational.

*

Roald Amundsen

The first person to actually cross the Northwest Passage would not be a Brit but a Norwegian. Roald Amundsen is arguably the most accomplished polar explorer of all time. He was an expert seaman and a skilled skier, also a meticulous and smart planner and a good leader. He had no interest in having heroic adventures of the sort popularized in British books for boys. To him, what passed in those stories for heroism was bungling and cruel sacrifice.

While skilled at exploration, Amundsen had little talent for financing and spent much of his career either trying to rustle up funds for the next expedition or running from debts incurred on previous ones. At close to midnight one summer night in Oslo in 1903, he was on the deck of his vessel, a thirty-year-old herring fishery sloop named *Gjöa*, when his first mate bolted down the dock with news that a creditor was on the way, with a bailiff in tow. They were prepared to seize the boat and arrest him for fraud. Amundsen grabbed a fire axe, cut his mooring lines, and sailed away from the dock, or so the story goes. The yarn seems a bit apocryphal—few sailors would cut their lines when they could simply untie them. Regardless, Amundsen did immediately set out from Oslo harbor, leaving in this ignominious manner on his voyage to immortality.

With the assistance of a 13-horsepower engine (even smaller than Franklin's), he sailed into Lancaster Sound, where, as planned and predicted, the ship was trapped in ice for two winters. Amundsen and his men used the time to learn the Arctic survival and traveling skills of the Inuit. In 1905, the *Gjöa* broke free. Following the route he had learned from the journals of John Rae, Amundsen traveled down Rae Strait, under King William Island and across the top of mainland Canada to Alaska, where he became icebound for yet a third winter. There, rather than wait another year to tell the world of his accomplishment, he sledged 800 kilometers to the nearest telegraph office and made a $700 reverse-charge call to Fridtjof Nansen to announce his monumental achievement to the world.

Although Amundsen had now proved it could be done, the much-searched-for passage was not attempted again until 1940, when the Royal Canadian Mounted Police mounted a wartime expedition to sail it west to east. Again, they made use of Rae's route. In 1977, when Belgian solo sailor Willy de Roos became the first to sail a yacht through the passage, he again used the Rae Strait, as did Canadian adventurer Jeff MacInnis and Mike Beedell when they sailed through on a Hobie catamaran in 1986.[16]

*

Once Amundsen had conquered the passage, explorers had to come up with new northern adventures. One daffy idea was to increase the huge territory of northern Canada by snatching land from Russia. The harebrained invasion and attempted occupation of a Russian island by Canadian-led adventurers was a monumental clusterfuck. The instigator of the misguided attempt was Vilhjalmur Stefansson. The hero and only survivor of the expedition was a twenty-three-year-old Inuit woman, Ada Blackjack. The strange drama ended with four dead and the guns of the freaking Soviet warship *Red October* aimed at the island.

---

16 The MacInnis–Beedell voyage might be the most audacious attempt ever at the Northwest Passage. I have sailed and raced extensively in Hobie Cats and won Canadian championships in Hobie 16s in the 1970s. I know this tippy, over-powered beach cat well. Most sensible people would not try to cross a large lake on one, let alone challenge the epic Northwest Passage. But MacInnis and Beedell made it, helped by the intelligence given years earlier by John Rae.

Ada Blackjack

The early expeditions of Canada's Vilhjalmur Stefansson suggested he might become the most interesting, original, and successful of Arctic explorers, although even as an anthropology student at Harvard University, he dropped hints of the humbug that would dog his later life. Born William Stevenson in Arnes, Manitoba, he changed his name at the university to the almost unspellable Vilhjalmur Stefansson in order to give himself faux-Viking street cred.

From 1906 to 1912 Stefansson traveled extensively through the largely uncharted wilderness of the eastern Arctic. Like Charles Hall, Roald Amundsen, and John Rae, but unlike most of the British and American explorers who had preceded him, Stefansson adopted the customs of the Inuit. He learned from them, dressed like them, ate like them, and hunted and traveled as they did. He learned Inuktitut, respected Inuit customs, and wrote about the people in glowing terms when he returned to the south. His main message was that the north was "the friendly Arctic," a place, he claimed nonsensically, where "a family could live at the North Pole as comfortably as they could in Hawaii."

The public, the press, other explorers, and the Canadian government all responded enthusiastically to Stefansson, but he did himself no good when he began advancing theories and hypotheses for which he had little evidence. Most suspicious was his bold claim that he had found a new race of people in the high Arctic that he called the "Blond Eskimos." He further declared his belief that these people were descendants either of Leif Ericsson's Vikings or of survivors of—who would have guessed it—the infamous John Franklin expedition. The subsequent controversy led to mockery. Amundsen derisively dismissed Stefansson's claims, calling him "the greatest humbug alive."

The disastrous Canadian Arctic Expedition of 1913–1916 truly queered Stefansson's reputation. The excursion was a major event involving three ships, a large crew, and funding by the Canadian government. Stefansson, its leader, abandoned the main ship, the *Karluk*, when it became stuck in ice and marooned in the Arctic. He simply buggered off, claiming that he was going to hunt for food. He was absent for weeks. By the time he returned, the ship had drifted far to the west and been crushed by the ice.

The survivors of the disaster eventually made it to Wrangel Island, a large uninhabited Russian territory north of Siberia and the last known home of woolly mammoths some 4,000 years ago. The captain of the *Karluk*, famed Newfoundland seaman Bob Bartlett, crossed over both the island and the frozen ocean to seek help in Siberia. He eventually returned by ship to pick up the few survivors of the wreck.

Considering how badly the expedition had turned out, it was remarkable that Stefansson even considered sending another group of adventurers to the north, let alone that he succeeded in doing so. After several years of highly successful lecturing on the Chautauqua circuit about the "friendly Arctic" and becoming president of The Explorers Club, he came up with a bold new scheme to buff the reputations of both the Dominion of Canada and Vilhjalmur Stefansson. His plan was to send a group of young explorers back to Wrangel Island to plant the flag and claim it for Canada. He recruited three enthusiastic volunteers, two of whom were veterans of the *Karluk* debacle, who wanted to come back for more Arctic punishment. Unfortunately, all three were of the wrong nationality—all were American. Stefansson needed a bona fide Canadian to lead the expedition. He appealed to the president of the University of Toronto to ask if there were any likely candidates with good health, strong dispositions, and some scientific training. The president, Sir Robert Falconer, proposed a recent graduate, Allan Crawford, the son of one of the university's professors.

Allan Crawford

With his small team mostly assembled, Stefansson appealed to the Canadian government for support and financing. His argument was that making Wrangel Island Canadian would be a feather in the cap of the young country and be a practical addition to the Dominion as a potential site for a weather station, as an airstrip for trans-Arctic aviation, and as a site for reindeer breeding, walrus hunting, and fur trapping—as if Canada did not already have enough icy barrens in its possession.

The Canadian government turned Stefansson down. He went ahead anyway, certain he could eventually get the government on board and, if not, perhaps sell the idea to either Washington or London. Instead of paying the young adventurers, he persuaded them to buy stock in the new company he set up for the expedition. Combining that with some private investment and a little of his own money, he sent the four men to Nome, Alaska, with enough cash to purchase 5,000 pounds of food, guns, tents, equipment, and clothing, enough to last them a year in the Arctic. He recommended against taking much meat, convinced they would be able to hunt for all they needed. He also suggested they needn't buy much winter clothing. Instead, he wanted them to take some Inuit with them, especially Inuit women, who could sew winter pants and parkas from the sealskins and bearskins they would harvest. He instructed them to put the word out for suitable interested parties.

Some Inuit were interested, but as they sized up the inexperienced crew of young explorers and considered the nasty reputation of inhospitable Wrangel Island, they all dropped out. There was only one Inuk willing to join, and even she was very reluctant. Ada Blackjack was twenty-three. She had been abandoned by an abusive husband, and she needed the money. The $50-a-month being offered was more than she had ever seen in her life. On the other hand, she would be away from her young son who was suffering from tuberculosis, she was nervous about traveling with four strange men, and she was deathly afraid of polar bears. If not for her reputation in Nome, quite possibly undeserved, as a drinker and a prostitute, she might have begged off. In the end the local police chief, wanting her out of town, basically shanghaied her into the expedition as its seamstress (at which she excelled) and cook. Before leaving, she consulted with a shaman, who told her that he felt the expedition was doomed.

On September 9, the five left, sailing north. The next day they landed briefly in Russia, and without telling the Russian authorities the true nature of their mission, they stated they were headed for Wrangel Island. *Nyet*, comrades. The Russians made it clear that in their mind Wrangel was Russian territory and laughed at the intention of the travelers to go ashore, which they felt was physically impossible.

Five days later, with considerable difficulty, the group made it to Wrangel and landed on the beach. Virtually the first thing they did was raise the Union Jack, claiming the island for King George, the British Empire, and the Dominion of Canada. The American ship that had taken them to Wrangel returned to Nome, and soon news got out, infuriating not one but two of Canada's neighbors—the United States and the Soviet Union.

The team of land-claiming explorers began to settle in on Wrangle Island. The bitter Arctic winter would soon be upon them, and they had much to do. None had any real experience in wilderness homesteading, but they did their best. Ada began to exhibit a very pronounced crush on Allan Crawford. The Toronto grad student was both the leader and the best looking of the four men. He was mortified by the attention, but it was clear to all that Ada was utterly infatuated. "Oh, Crawford," she purred. "Oh, your beautiful green eyes."

The group began to fall apart. Ada, homesick and perhaps suffering from *piblokto* or Arctic hysteria, drove the men crazy, and, in turn, they treated her horribly—refusing to feed her, forcing her to sleep outside on the ground, threatening to dog-whip her.

While the explorers fought among themselves, the diplomatic controversy they had ignited burned through London, Washington, and Ottawa. Stefansson added fuel to the flames by promoting grand plans to colonize the island. The US State Department pronounced that "Wrangel Island, claimed by the explorer Stefansson for Canada, is in reality the property of Russia" and further stated that in its opinion the remote no-man's land was of no real value to any country. The British wanted nothing to do with the idiotic scheme and for once left the decision-making to the colonials in Ottawa.

Stefansson had his best luck in his homeland. He appealed by letter to the new prime minister, Mackenzie King, who introduced the subject in the House of Commons, declaring, "The Government certainly maintains the position that Wrangel Island is part of the property of this country." Stefansson took this as a win. He was convinced that Canada would soon financially support his schemes, and he was glad, knowing that the costs of extricating his explorers from Wrangel Island would be significant.

The five survived their first winter on the island. They endured temperatures as low as minus 40° (C and F, this being the point where the two systems collide and jointly tell you not to venture outside). They had a very close call with an attacking polar bear, and their food supplies began to dwindle. Ada's unrequited love affair with Crawford had at least subsided. She worked hard at sewing sealskin parkas, and relations among them began to improve. The five looked forward to the summer, when they expected a relief ship to bring Stefansson, more colonists, and supplies for their new piece of Canada.

It would not be that simple. Stefansson could not find the money to finance a relief ship, let alone a continued occupation of Wrangel Island. Eventually, he received $3,000 from his friend, the famous aviator Orville Wright, and another $3,000 from the parsimonious Canadian government, who finally made their modest commitment to the grand expedition. It was not enough, but it would have to do.

The team on Wrangel peered out to sea, searching in vain for a rescue ship. It wasn't until the short Arctic summer was nearly over that Stefansson finally hired Captain Joe Bernard, a skipper with a schooner in Nome, to try to make it to the island. The *Teddy Bear* left Alaska on August 20, 1922, but quickly ran into pack ice in the Russian Arctic. Skipper Bernard repeatedly tried ramming through the ice but, by late September, was forced to turn back for Nome, bitterly disappointed that he couldn't provide help to the young occupiers.

Stefansson blithely told the press, public, and parents of the Wrangel team that there was nothing to worry about. He was sure that his protégés would make it through a second winter, and he would send another mission to retrieve them the following summer. On Wrangel, the five were not so optimistic. Once it became obvious that help was not going to arrive, they began to consider an overland escape to Siberia. There was not enough food to last them all through another winter.

They waited through the long autumn for the sea ice to harden and thicken enough to take the weight of their heavy sledge. Crawford and one companion, Lorne Knight, would try to make the dangerous journey. Knowing there was a considerable risk he might die, Crawford prepared a will, creating a trust to give an annual award at the University of Toronto Schools—the private prep school he had attended. The Allan Crawford Prize in Chemistry and Physics is still awarded there today.

On January 7, 1923, he and Knight set out with five dogs. The mission quickly turned ugly. They were undernourished at the start, and neither they nor the dogs had the energy needed to pull their 700-pound sled across the Arctic through the darkest days of winter. After thirteen days they gave up and returned to camp, suffering from frostbite and scurvy.

With Knight now virtually an invalid, Crawford decided he and the two other men would make a second attempt to cross to Siberia. As the temperature fell to a staggering minus 56° C, Ada prepared what food she could for the men to take on the second sledding mission. She would stay behind to take care of Knight. Far away in

New York, Stefansson announced his retirement from exploration. And in Moscow, the Kremlin fired off an international complaint about the trespassers on Soviet soil.

The party of three headed south toward Siberia. They were never seen again. They may have gone through the ice into the Arctic Sea; they may have frozen to death; they may have been eaten by polar bears. No trace of them has ever been found.

That left Ada and Knight. If they were to survive, it was now all up to her. Knight was not just ill. He was dying. Unable to rise from his bed, he could not trap or hunt, he could not aim a gun to protect them, and he could not even think straight. Ada became a nursemaid to the increasingly abusive and incontinent Knight. Terrified of guns, she willed herself to learn how to use a rifle to shoot birds, a fox, seal or *nanook* to keep herself and her sick companion alive. Try as she might, Ada was not able to keep Lorne Knight from sinking into lethargy and despair. On June 23, she was unable to wake him. He was dead.

Ada was now the sole survivor of the ill-fated expedition. Her whole life, until that moment, she had been somewhat dependent on others to make decisions for her. Now, she was totally on her own—probably the only living person for hundreds of miles in any direction. She built a lookout tower and scanned the horizon for rescue.

Back in Ottawa, Stefansson was having a difficult time raising money to retrieve the party. He scraped up just enough to send another young adventurer, Harold Noice, to Nome to prepare another rescue run. Stefansson was supposed to find Noice the money to charter a ship but came up short. The tight summer sailing window began to close again.

Fortunately for Ada, diplomatic relations between Moscow and London were deteriorating. Lenin's government announced that it would be sending a warship from Vladivostok to regain possession of the Wrangle Island in the name of Russia. It promised to arrest and jail all those on it. The British government responded by saying that the capture of Allan Crawford and his companions would be looked upon as the "equivalent to an act of war." The saber-rattling helped

Stefansson's cause, and at the eleventh hour he managed to raise the money Noice needed. Some came from donations from private British citizens, including the granddaughter of Sir John Franklin, some from selling the newspaper rights to the story to the *Toronto Star*.

On August 2, Noice was finally able to depart from Nome, taking with him a dozen Inuit and a single white adventurer whom he had convinced to take over the occupation of Wrangel Island. The party had the usual problems with engine failure, ice, fog, and ship damage. Noice was philosophical; at least, he would have lots to write about in the articles for the *Star*.

Eighteen days later, on August 20, Ada heard a noise she at first took to be a herd of walruses, but then realized was the rumble of a ship's engine. She ran to her lookout tower, then to the beach, where she saw through the fog the masts of an anchored ship. She was met by Harold Noice, wading ashore. Overcome with gratitude, Ada was nevertheless mystified that Crawford wasn't with the man. Noice, for his part, was confused that Crawford and the others weren't with her. Together they came to the realization that Crawford and his companions must have died and that she was the sole survivor of Stefansson's grand expedition.

Noice left the new party of thirteen and supplies for another winter on the desolate island and took Ada back to Nome. There, shamefully, she was cross-examined by Alaskan authorities, who accused her of killing Knight, or at least not doing what she could to prevent his death. Noice stole her diary of her time on Wrangel and took off with Knight's journal. He and Stefansson spent much of the next few years fighting over the publication rights to the story, with Stefansson at one point threatening to have his lieutenant blackballed from The Explorers Club over the matter.

To pay off the many bills accrued from the ill-fated expedition, Stefansson offered to sell Wrangel Island, first to Canada for $30,000, then, after they ignored the offer, for the bargain price of $27,000 to the United States. It was absurd. Stefansson no more owned Wrangel Island than he owned the Rideau Canal or the Brooklyn Bridge.

Regardless, he found two suckers—the brothers Carl and Ralph Lomen, who purchased the "title" to Wrangel, in return for an agreement to pick up the new colonists Noice had left on the island. The Lomens attempted to do this the following summer but were again thwarted by the icepack. It was left to the Soviet warship *Red October* to smash through the ice, arrest the North American intruders, tear down the Canadian Red Ensign, and replace it with the hammer and sickle of the USSR. The ship returned to Vladivostok, and the would-be colonists were jailed first in Siberia and then in China. The sole American died in custody; the Inuit were eventually shipped home by the Red Cross.

There are no winners in this cockamamie tale. After being widely condemned for what *Saturday Night* magazine called "the tragic folly of the whole enterprise," Stefansson patched his reputation back together and in 1937 was once again elected president of The Explorers Club. Ada was acclaimed as "the female Robinson Crusoe" and by the Toronto *Mail & Empire* as "the first Eskimo heroine in history," but she was always very uncomfortable about being at the center of the media circus. She drifted through a long life, mostly in the Pacific Northwest and Alaska. Stefansson promised her a share of the royalties from his book *The Adventure of Wrangel Island,* but it was not a big seller, and he never paid her. She did outlive him. Stefansson died in 1962. Ada Blackjack died, aged 85, in Palmer, Alaska, in 1983.

The Wrangell Island debacle has not been totally forgotten. On August 16, 2022, a special election was held for an Alaska seat in the US House of Representatives. Democrat Mary Peltola defeated the infamous Republican Sarah Palin, with Peltola receiving 70,295 votes to Palin's 57,693. (Unsurprisingly, Palin claimed the vote count was "rigged.") Also on the ballot was Dr. Robert Ornelas, of the American Independent Party. Ornelas positioned himself as Native American, pro-life, an electoral college elector for the Trump-Pence ticket, and a supporter of the second amendment to bear arms. The main plank of his platform was that he wanted to have sovereignty over Wrangell Island returned to the state of Alaska. He and his supporters believe that the goofy sale of the island by Stefansson to the Loman brothers in 1925 was legitimate. Ornelas garnered an underwhelming 248 votes. The idea that the United States government would go to war with Russia over Wrangell Island seems about as remote today as the possibility of finding descendants of the Franklin expedition still living in the icebound Arctic.

CHAPTER 3
THE SEARCH FOR THE SOURCE OF THE NILE

The strange passion to discover the exact source of the Nile River began, believe it or not, with Ptolemy. The über-wise Egyptian mathematician/astronomer/geographer/astrologer/music theorist, even though he lived half a continent away, postulated that the great river began in a lake somewhere near the equator that was fed by streams coming down from what he called the "Mountains of the Moon." It took 2,000 years, buckets of nineteenth-century blood, sweat, tears, and much acrimonious debate, before it was agreed that the long-dead smart guy was basically correct. Notwithstanding the many conflicting and mistaken ideas from various explorers, it was finally determined that yes, the source of the damned river is indeed giant Lake Victoria, the second-largest lake in the world after Superior. And yes, Victoria is in fact fed by streams flowing from the nearby Ruwenzori Mountains.

So the real mystery of the Nile was not where it started but why so many people would go to such a heaping dose of ridiculousness to find its exact starting point. European explorers wandered around the dark continent on this quixotic quest long enough that the Africans began calling them *mzungu*—"men who walk in circles."

The man most central to the debate over the source of the Nile was Sir Richard Burton, likely the most colorful explorer of all time. He was born in England but spent few of his early years there. Indeed, he would later say that "England is the only place I never feel at home." His childhood was wild and rambunctious, almost as unruly as his adult years. He and his brother and sister were hellions, terrorizing

Sir Richard Francis Burton: aka, Ruffian Dick, fluent in twenty-nine languages and innumerable sexual positions, he earned a wicked scar by catching a javelin with his jaw and never got over losing a race to the source of the Nile to his puritanical partner John Speke.

governesses, teachers, parents, and whole neighborhoods as the family moved from one home to another in Italy, France, and, occasionally, England. He became an explorer at the age of twelve, descending into the crater of Vesuvius in search of Satan, who, according to Neapolitan legend, lived there. On another occasion, he and his brother orchestrated an orgy at a Naples whorehouse. His father threatened to horsewhip them for the transgression, and so, according to one of Burton's many memoirs, "we climbed to the tops of the chimneys, where the seniors could not follow us, and refused to come down till the crime was forgiven."

If he didn't like doing something, he didn't do it. He detested music lessons and smashed his instrument over his master's head. His inability to buckle under authority lasted his whole life. At Oxford, he and the other students were told that they were forbidden to attend the then-new sport of steeplechasing, which for some reason was considered "disgraceful." Naturally, Burton led a group to see the races. They were caught and hauled in front of the university's discipline committee. Burton, as ringleader, was expelled. He was expected to quietly leave. Instead, he departed dramatically and ostentatiously, blowing a trumpet and driving a carriage through several flower beds while "waving adieu to my friends and kissing my hands to the pretty shop girls."

Burton then determined that he was "fit for nothing but to be shot at for sixpence a day," so he joined the private army of the British East India Company and shipped off to India. There he studied both Sikhism and Islam, received a Muslim circumcision, and got himself the nickname Ruffian Dick. He also learned Hindustani, Gujarati, Punjabi, Saraiki, Marathi, Persian, and Arabic. Eventually, he would be fluent in an astounding twenty-nine languages. He acquired a large menagerie of monkeys and claimed to be able to recognize sixty monkey "words." He also studied the Quran so intently that he was entitled to call himself a *hafiz*—one who could recite it from memory.

He rejected the insular, snobbish life of his fellow officers and consorted with all manner of Indians, including hemp-drinkers, opium-eaters, and the gaudy harlots of the Bhendi Bazaar. He even managed to fall in love with a beautiful Persian princess. When she tragically died, he first fell to writing melancholy poems about her and then decided to totally devote himself to a life of adventure. He adopted the name, skills, and character of a Muslim doctor, calling himself "Mirza Abdullah" and taking long baths in a spectrum of dyes to darken his pale British skin to a more appropriate color.

In disguise, he took on various challenges, including trying unsuccessfully to liberate a young nun from a convent. By far his most famous/infamous journey was his undercover *Haj* pilgrimage to Mecca. It was not only wildly dangerous, with attacks from bandits commonplace, but forbidden for a non-Muslim to enter this most holy site of Islam under penalty of death. Burton's language skills and disguise protected him, but he was living on the edge.

His adventures, wildly inappropriate when viewed through the contemporary lens, were seen as an outrageous prank in his day, although then, as now, some saluted the courage, chutzpah, and work required to achieve the perhaps questionable goal. He not only succeeded but made a similarly dangerous journey to another of Islam's forbidden holy spots, the Ethiopian city of Harar.

Burton's next expedition was less successful. In February 1855 he set out for Africa with John Hanning Speke, the man whose name his would forever be connected with in the story of the search for the source of the Nile. Aiming to explore Somalialand, the pair were still near the coast of the Indian Ocean when their party was raided by 200 attackers. Speke was captured, bound, and threatened with castration and death if he would not renounce Christianity. He received eleven spear wounds, but eventually managed to

John Hanning Speke

escape, gnawing through his bonds with his teeth. He reconnected with his companion, Burton, who had received a blow from a javelin that went in one side of his jaw and out the other. They managed to evade their African attackers but had to abandon the expedition and return to England.

Having lost four of his back teeth, Burton could barely eat or speak. A skilled dentist and surgeon repaired him, although he healed with a wicked facial scar he would wear the rest of his life. Within a year, he and Speke were funded for a new expedition back to Africa, this time to search for the source of the Nile.

Like so many of the explorer teams chronicled here, Burton and Speke were an ill-matched pair. Burton was an unrepentant hedonist who loved alcohol, drugs, and sex. He was bisexual, and his diaries are packed with observations on native sexual practices. He regarded the techniques of Asia and Africa as superior to those in the West, as did many of the women with whom he had liaisons. His mistresses in India mocked his quick ejaculations (Indian women were said to believe this shortcoming afflicted all European men). That did nothing to discourage Burton, undoubtedly the horniest explorer in history.

If one believes the reports from Burton, who is not always reliable on the subject of the partner he often sparred with, the boyishly handsome Speke was a repressed homosexual with a mother fixation. He not only had an extremely unhealthy relationship with his mother but while in Africa (albeit frequently delusional from his many bouts of malaria) he confused her in his addled mind with another mother figure—Queen Victoria. Indeed, it was he who named the giant lake after her.

Speke also had a death drive, telling Burton he came to Africa to be killed. He was the most notorious killer of African animals, at least until the arrival of Theodore Roosevelt and Ernest Hemingway. On one day, Speke killed six hippos and mortally wounded a dozen more. His African bearers could not believe that he liked to eat the embryos of pregnant animals he had shot (psychoanalyze that one, if you will). Burton, hardly an environmentalist himself, could not stomach his partner's lust for slaughter.

One thing the men had in common, apart from their interest in African travel, was politics. Both were political and social reactionaries. Living in the era of revolutionary, egalitarian movements in Europe, of Simon Bolivar in South America and Karl Marx in England, of Abraham Lincoln fighting for the abolition of slavery in America, Burton was a backward political conservative, as was Speke. They shared these right-wing reactionary beliefs with many of the explorers of the nineteenth century—even the female explorers, who one might think would have had more progressive views. Lady Franklin was a high Tory, opposed to attempts to democratize England, abolish slavery in the colonies, separate church and state, and reform prisons. Gertrude Bell, the British explorer and archeologist of the Middle East, was also a founding member of the Women's National Anti-Suffrage League, very much on the wrong side of the fight for women's rights.

Once Burton and Speke had recovered from the wounds of their last debacle, they were all steamed to return to Africa for a go at the source of the Nile. Sponsored by the Royal Geographical Society, they left Zanzibar on June 5, 1857, heading for the then unmapped Great Lakes region of central Africa. Burton felt they needed 170 porters, but in the end could only find 36, and 30 pack animals, all of whom would be dead within six months.[17]

Dying porters and pack animals were not the only issues that beleaguered the rugged expedition. "As soon as we reached Dut'humi,

---

17 Porters are little known in the Americas, but they are a common feature of expeditions in Africa and Asia. On my trek to Everest Basecamp, our one porter, a diminutive Nepali, somehow carried the large backpacks of three of us in a wicker basket on his back. He was not a Sherpa. Sherpas guide and climb mountains. They do not lug packs. On my climb of Mt. Nyiragongo in the Congo, I counted (and paid for) forty-two porters hauling our stuff up the steep volcano. I had to pay *hongo* (unexpected extortion), as did Burton and Speke. While the use of porters is more ritualized and organized today than it was in Victorian times, it is still a complicated business.

where we were detained nearly a week," wrote Burton, "the malaria brought on attacks of marsh fever. In my case it lasted 20 days. Jack [Speke] suffered still more; he had a fainting fit which strongly resembled sunstroke, and it seemed to affect him more or less throughout our journey. Our sufferings were increased by the loss of our animals, and we had to walk often for many miles through sun, rain, mud, and miasmatic putridities." "Miasmatic putridities" is a semi-polite nineteenth-century term for a godforsaken shitstorm.

After many of his original porters died off, Burton tried to hire more. The Africans were reluctant to join his apparently suicidal mission into the land of crocodiles and cannibals, so he secretly bribed a witch doctor to foretell prosperity for the expedition. The soothsayer practiced his whackadoodlery, rattling gourds, and spinning goat horns. Wide-eyed African rubes were duly impressed. Burton asked, "Lil' help?" And perhaps against their better judgment, they responded, "K." They began by carrying the tents, food, and equipment of the explorers. Soon they would be carrying the gruesomely gastro-diseased explorers themselves.

Burton realized the dangers he was facing: "I was entering the 'unknown land' at the fatal season when the shrinking of the waters after the wet monsoon would render it a hotbed of malaria, but I was tied by scanty means and a limited 'leave'. It was neck or nothing, and I determined to risk it."

He admitted to being a man obsessed, living by maxims such as "man wants to journey and he must do so or he shall die," and "voyaging is victory," and "discovery is mostly my mania."

Burton and Speke wore on each other as their journey progressed. Even at death's door with malaria or other fevers, Burton's mind was active. He was a devoted chronicler of Africa, utterly fascinated with its people, their customs and their languages. Around the fire, feeling better, he acted out scenes from the often-ribald *Arabian Nights* he had translated into English. He reveled in the charms of African women. The dull, unimaginative, unintellectual Speke, on the other hand, found much of the long passage dreary. He could not converse with the Africans or Arabs, as he spoke nothing but English. He fell victim to another of the dangers of exploration—boredom. "There is literally nothing to write about in this uninteresting country," he haughtily declared. "Nothing could surpass these tracks, jungles, plains for same dullness . . . the country is one senseless map of sameness."

Tropical pests plagued the expedition. If the men weren't being bitten by mosquitoes, they were being bitten by red ants, which drove not just the two explorers but all their African assistants crazy with itches. The horrible tropical diseases went from bad to worse. Burton had to be supported by a porter, Speke by three. The fever affected Speke's brain, making him morose, suspicious, and jaundiced toward his friend and leader. He became dangerously delirious and so violent that Burton had to remove his firearms lest he injure or kill himself, or others.

Burton became partially paralyzed from malaria. Speke suffered from ophthalmia, which brought on almost total blindness. He was barely able to see their prize when after a nine-month march they finally spotted it.

"What is that streak of light that lies below?" asked Burton.

"I am of the opinion that that is the water you are in search of," replied Sidi Bombay, their main man and, IMHO, the hardworking hero of the troubled journey.

It was indeed Lake Tanganyika, the world's longest freshwater lake. Both men were so sick they could not really explore it, but Burton became convinced he had found the source of the Nile. He was wrong. The lake feeds the Congo River, not the Nile. His blind commitment to his mistaken belief would lead to one of the deadliest feuds in exploration history, and the trashing of much of his reputation.

His reputation was the least of his problems at that moment in his life. He lay in his sickbed in camp. The Africans were convinced he would die any day. Speke wasn't much better, but he revived enough to come up with a new idea. He heard there was another lake, even larger, further north. The Africans referred to it as *nyansa*, so he began referring to it as Lake Nyansa. It was a typical explorer's mistake.

Jacques Cartier asked the Iroquois what they called the place they were in, and they replied *kanata*, meaning "our village." Cartier proceeded to name the entire enormous territory Canada. When Speke began referring to his new goal as Lake Nyansa, he was actually saying "Lake Lake."

Speke proposed that Burton should try to recuperate on the shores of Lake Tanganyika while he pushed north to try to find the other lake. In possibly the worst mistake of his life, Burton agreed to the plan. His companion, still suffering from malaria, marched north for two weeks until suddenly "the vast expanse of the pale blue waters of Nyanza burst upon my gaze." Speke promptly decided to re-name the lake "Victoria" after his queen and, equally promptly, without proof, decided he had found the source of the Nile. "I no longer felt any doubt that the lake at my feet gave birth to that interesting river, the source of which has been the subject of so much speculation, and the object of so many explorers."

He returned to the Tanganyika camp and passed on the good news to his boss. Burton was unconvinced and livid that he had been left out of the great find. "The fortunate discoverer's conviction was strong, his reasons were weak," he wrote. With Burton physically unable to explore Lake Victoria himself, the party slowly returned to Zanzibar. The pair's fractured relationship deteriorated further as they angrily agreed to disagree about their conflicting opinions about which lake was the source of the Nile.

At journey's end, Speke departed for England without his partner, promising, according to Burton, that he would wait until they were both home before revealing any of their findings. If this was a promise, it was not kept. As Speke sailed, Burton brooded in Zanzibar, deeply regretting his choice of traveling partner, wishing he had explored alone or with some Arab companions, "or at least with a less crooked-minded, cantankerous Englishman."

Aboard the appropriately named HMS *Furious*, on which he sailed back to England, Speke fell in with a malicious traveler, Lawrence Oliphant, who seems to have convinced him to go back on his word to Burton. Only two days after his arrival back in London, he spoke to the Royal Geographical Society, encouraged by its president Sir Roderick Murchison, who had always hated Burton. Speke's good looks and gentle demeanor made him attractive to men like Oliphant and Murchison. Burton's scowling countenance and fierce intelligence intimidated them.

On his return to England, Burton was informed by the RGS that Speke would be leading an expedition back to Africa to confirm his belief that Lake Victoria was the source of the Nile. This time, Speke would travel with another Scottish explorer, James Augustus Grant. Burton, infuriated, was left out in the cold.

Speke got on much better with Grant. He had always found Burton's assumption of superior knowledge insufferable, and with Grant, who enjoyed his rifles almost as much as Speke, he no longer had to fear the disdainful looks that he received from Burton every time he wanted to slaughter more of Africa's wildlife.

While a crack shot and amiable hunting companion, Grant proved himself no more able to withstand the disgusting diseases of central Africa than Burton or Speke. After a month of fever, one of his legs became deformed with inflammation. Sidi Bombay saved the expedition. He wrapped Grant's leg in a poultice of cow dung, mud, and salt. Whether or not this muck helped, the leg did begin to improve, although not enough to allow him to travel. Speke, who had no interest in sharing glory, took the opportunity to leave Grant behind and charge off on his own to seek further evidence for his theory that Lake Victoria fed the Nile.

Unfortunately for Speke, he needed the assistance of the local tribes, and, unlike Burton, he found it difficult to communicate with them. He had neither Burton's linguistic skills nor his ability to sort out local custom by getting involved with women. Speke found female relationships difficult but managed in the Kingdom of Karagwe to flirt with a sixteen-year-old princess in King Rumanika's entourage. "Her features were lovely," he wrote, "but her body was round as a ball." Obesity was a sign of status and wealth in the kingdom. Speke measured one royal wife with a bust of 52 inches.

Eventually, King Rumanika agreed to assist the explorer in his travels. On July 28, 1862, Speke discovered a waterfall leading out of Lake Victoria and heading north. Finally, absolute proof that the lake fed the Nile!

Maybe. Speke named it Ripon Falls, after the head of the RGS. He eventually returned to Grant, and the two explorers headed back to the coast to make their way to England, where Speke would resume his feud with Richard Burton.

Dick-waving contests are common in the past 200 years of exploration history: Peary versus Cook, Scott versus Amundsen, John F. Kennedy versus Nikita Khrushchev, Jeff Bezos versus Elon Musk. For acrimony, Speke versus Burton is hard to beat. In the wake of their joint expedition, Speke published two articles in *Blackwood's* magazine in which he assumed complete credit for the discoveries made, even claiming to have done all the astronomical work and to have taught Burton the geography of the areas they passed through. Burton responded in kind, saying of Speke, "I could not expect much from his assistance; he was not a linguist—French and Arabic being equally unknown to him—nor a man of science, nor an accurate astronomical observer.... During the exploration he acted in a subordinate capacity, and . . . was unfit for any other than a subordinate capacity."

Each man sought to destroy the other's reputation in this nasty battle, and each sought to convince the Royal Geographical Society, the press, and the public of his theory on the source of the Nile. Burton claimed that a sunstroke Speke had endured in Africa had "permanently affected his brain" and complained that "everything had been done . . . against me. My companion stood forth in his true colours as an angry rival."

Speke responded, "It only rests between Burton and myself whether we fight it out with the quill or the fist," claiming that "I think I have been very mild, considering the amount of injustice he has done me."

Burton was not the only person Speke took issue with. He also wrote disparagingly about the armchair critics who had questioned his findings in Africa, calling them "geographers who sip port, sit in carpet slippers and criticize those who labour in the field."

While Speke was on his return trip to Lake Victoria, Burton had fallen on hard times. Tired of his "insubordination," the East India Company had dismissed him. He lost most of his very modest fortune while touring the United States and then took an ignominious diplomatic position in one of the most distant outposts of the British Empire, the godforsaken island of Fernando Po off the coast of Equatorial Guinea, explored by the blind traveler James Holman forty years earlier.

With both men back in England in 1864, the Speke-Burton feud hit new levels of derangement. They excoriated each other in the press and books. Burton at one point described in unnecessarily lurid detail and with tasteless humor Speke's inspections of the fat women of Rumanika's court and his supposed obsession with the tiny triangular bark-cloth *mbugus* that covered the courtiers' genitals. Lawrence Oliphant reported to Burton that Speke had said, "if Burton appears on a platform with me, I will kick him!"

"Well, that settles it," proclaimed Burton. "By God, he shall kick me!"

In an effort to settle the disagreement about the source of the Nile, the British Association for the Advancement of Science invited both men to do combat at its annual meeting in the city of Bath on September 16, 1864. The formal debate would be moderated by an even more esteemed explorer, David Livingstone. It was breathlessly anticipated by the *Times* as a "gladiatorial exhibition."[18]

---

18 The event is grandly re-enacted in the 1990 feature film *Mountains of the Moon*. The Irish movie star Patrick Bergin plays Richard Burton. Bergin has made a career out of playing historical desperados. He took from the rich and gave to the poor as Robin Hood in the 1991 feature film and he played the pirate Billy Bones in my version of *Treasure Island*.

Speke was extremely uncomfortable with the prospect of debating the erudite and witty Burton, whom he knew would likely run roughshod over him. A few hours before the debate, he jumped from his seat in the hall, exclaiming "I cannot stand this any longer."

A neighbor asked, "Shall you be wanting your chair again, sir?"

"I hope not," replied Speke, rushing from the room.

He located one of his guns and went off into the fields, hoping to calm his nerves by killing some grouse. At one point, he leaned his gun, muzzle up, against a stone wall which he then tried to climb over. Accidently or intentionally, he managed to pull the trigger, killing himself. Was it a suicide or a shooting accident? There's no proof either way. Burton thought he knew. "By God, he's killed himself," he exclaimed, before staggering off the stage. A coroner's jury judged it an accidental death. Whatever it was, the deadly game of exploration had claimed yet another victim.

*

Before departing the scene, Speke had inadvertently advanced the careers of our next explorers, the husband-and-wife team of Samuel and Florence Baker. They had launched their own effort to find the source of the Nile in 1861 and hoped to meet up with Speke and Grant somewhere along the way. After spending a year near the Sudan–Ethiopian border where Samuel learned Arabic and explored some of the Nile's tributaries, the couple headed to Khartoum and in December 1862 advanced southward up the river.

Baker was born into great wealth accrued from his family's colonial exploitation of Jamaica and Mauritius. Along with his first wife, Henrietta, he ran one of the family plantations for a short while. Finding it boring and not needing to work for a living, he decided instead to travel, first as a gentleman tourist, then as a very legitimate, audacious, and daring explorer. He produced two books about his time in Ceylon. After his wife Henrietta died of typhoid in 1855, Baker left their four daughters to an unmarried sister and hit the road again.

Unlike most explorers, he had no need to beg for assistance or sponsorship to get out into the wild. He had lots of money and paid for everything himself.

One of the first things he paid for was a new wife. While wandering around Bulgaria in 1859, he spied a beautiful Hungarian refugee named Florence Ninian von Sass, who was being held in the Widden Slave Market. When he learned she was about to be sold to the Ottoman Pasha of Vidin, he out-bid the Turkish buyer and took her for himself. They soon married and enjoyed one of the closest partnerships and greatest love stories in the history of exploration. Whether it was really a marriage is debatable. There is no record of any formal nuptials, and although they very much saw each other as man and wife, few in Victorian society would have approved of their unique pairing.

Little is known of Florence. She was born in Transylvania or Hungary in 1841 and was orphaned when her parents were killed in the Hungarian revolution of 1848. She was an equal to her husband in her commitment to wilderness exploration and traveled side-by-side with him in Africa, dressed in trousers and remaining cool when confronted by wild animals or unfriendly locals. She even allowed her fair skin to turn as brown as a berry in an era when most European women hid behind screens to protect their delicate pallor.

Heading south down the Nile from Khartoum, the Bakers eventually bogged down in the Sudd, a vast, tangled swamp infested with mosquitoes and crocodiles. At this point, Florence perhaps asked herself if she wouldn't have been better off living in that luxurious Turkish harem. They finally made it through to the raucous frontier town of Gondokoro. Three days after they arrived, they were amazed to see Speke and Grant walk into the village. "Speke," wrote Baker, "appeared the more worn of the two; he was excessively lean, but, in reality, he was in good tough condition; he had walked the whole way from Zanzibar, never having once ridden during that wearying march. Grant was in honourable rags; his bare knees projecting though the remnants of trousers that were an exhibition of rough industry tailor's work." Speke revealed that he had discovered Ripon Falls and thus confirmed Lake Victoria as the source of the Nile.

Baker was devastated. "Does not one leaf of the laurel remain for me?" he whined. Speke threw his countryman a bone, showing him the map of the eastern side of the lake he had explored. He suggested Baker explore the western side and also look for yet another lake rumored to lie to the west of Victoria. Baker jumped at this, especially on hearing there might be lots of animals to kill in that area. He delighted in what he referred to as "whole hectacombs of slaughter," frequently executed in as gruesome a manner as possible. Back in Scotland he had developed a method for killing a stag by plunging a 12-inch double-bladed knife into its heart. When the pleasure of shooting abated, he tried out this technique on African wildlife.

Baker also relished the opportunity to shoot lead into any African warriors that he felt were in his way. He is described in some histories as a "great Victorian swashbuckling explorer," but you don't have to dive deep into his misadventures to conclude that he was one of the most despicable cocknockers in the long sordid history of African exploration. He was a deeply racist negrophobe who had constant difficulties dealing with the guides and porters he and Florence needed for their travels. "The treachery of the Negro is beyond belief," he fulminated. "He has not a moral human instinct and is below the brute. How is it possible to improve such abject animals? They are not worth the trouble, and they are only fit for slaves, to which their race appears to have been condemned."

Even Baker's friendly relations with Africans frequently turned ugly. While negotiating for guides and porters with a man he mistakenly thought was King Kamurasi of the powerful Bari tribe (it was really the king's brother), Baker was offered a pretty virgin as company for the trip. The man then asked if Baker would leave his wife Florence behind in exchange. This sent Baker into a violent rage. "Drawing my revolver quietly, I held it within two inches of his chest . . .

I explained to him that in my country such insolence would entail bloodshed."

The Bari royalty were highly suspicious of Baker and thought he was lying about his intentions. They could not believe that a man would ever leave his own people and own country just to search for a body of water.

The Bakers continued west of Lake Victoria but soon ran out of food and were reduced to eating grass. Florence, like virtually every European explorer in central Africa, came close to dying of fever but survived and after much tribulation laid eyes on the lake that Baker named Albert Nyanza—Lake Albert.[19] Her husband definitively proclaimed that "The Victoria and Albert lakes are the two sources of the Nile." Okay, Sam. They are not, strictly speaking, since both are fed by upstream creeks that are themselves created by rainwater, but have it your way.

As well as finding Lake Albert, the Bakers were also the very first of the vanilla-hued crowd to lay eyes on the Nile's dramatic waterfall in the river flowing north from Lake Victoria. Samuel named it after the president of the RGS, Sir Roderick Murchison.

On their return to England, Samuel Baker and, to a much lesser degree, naturally, his wife Florence were acclaimed for their "discoveries." Of course, these were discoveries only if you forgot

---

19 I have only laid eyes on one of the smaller (but still substantial) African Great Lakes, Lake Kivu, which lies between Rwanda and the Democratic Republic of the Congo. Along with all the other usual dangers of African lakes—bilharzia, crocodiles, hippos, malaria, violent thunderstorms—Kivu has the potential for limnic eruptions of vast quantities of methane and carbon dioxide trapped under its waters. If this happens, it will kill by asphyxiation every living creature on the shores of the lake, including inhabitants of the city of Goma. A limnic eruption at Lake Monoun in Cameroon killed 1,700 people and 3,000 livestock in 1986. The inhabitants of Goma did not seem concerned about this when I visited. They have other things to worry about. The lawless, crime-ridden town is one of the poorest and most dangerous on earth. It also sits on the flank of a giant volcano, which twice this century sent red hot lava flowing through its streets.

what Ptolemy had already put on record and discount the fact that African peoples were familiar with them from time immemorial. As Dr. Hastings Banda, the first President of Malawi, said of European discoveries: "There was nothing to discover. We were here all the time." The celebration of these supposed firsts makes even less sense when you remember that humanity began in Africa, likely in the Olduvai Gorge in what is now Kenya. Over thousands of years, it was adventurous Africans who did the exploring—moving north and east to discover and populate Europe, Asia, Oceania, and the Americas.

But these sentiments and statements like President Banda's were not part of the culture of the 1860s. Baker was feted, published, knighted, and began to be referred to as "Baker of the Nile." Of course, not everyone was pleased, and he too had his share of detractors. When he heard of the knighthood, James Grant was enraged, reacting much the same way that both Keith Richards and King Charles did when they heard Mick Jagger was to be knighted.. "By God!" said Grant. "I never heard of anything more disgusting to us! The information about his woman too is not fair, for you know very well from poor Speke and myself the position she was in." The English public could care less what the grumpy Scot thought. They had already acclaimed Baker as their favorite African explorer. Well, their second favorite.

*

A decade after Baker's triumph, Britain's favorite explorer, David Livingstone was buried in Westminster Abbey. On April 18, 1874, the streets of Pall Mall and Whitehall were filled with people, many of them weeping, in the manner of the Princess Diana funeral 123 years later. The Prince of Wales and the Prime Minister, Benjamin Disraeli, attended the ceremony. It was the biggest funeral in England since Lord Palmerston's in 1865. Florence Nightingale called Livingstone "the greatest man of his generation."

David Livingstone

The near canonization of Livingstone is today a bit hard to understand. He was a missionary/explorer and unsuccessful at both. He started as a preacher, but realizing he was not a very good one, he gave up the racket to explore. He was considered the greatest geographer of his age, but miscalculations with his sextant deceived him into believing he had found the source of the Nile (that old bugaboo) when in fact he was on the upper Congo River. He succeeded in what he claimed was the first coast-to-coast crossing of Africa, but in the process, he discovered it had been done by Portuguese and Arab traders years earlier. His wife felt he was a terrible husband. His porters and assistants largely (although not universally) felt he was a poor leader. Sunday-school biographies elevated his character toward saintliness but had to remove his journal references to violently flogging disobedient or insolent porters to do so. As one analyst said, "he was unconcerned for their interests and lacked insight into their problems. He viewed their illnesses as malingering, disagreement as subordination, and failure as culpable negligence."

There is no doubt, however, that Livingstone had a fierce will to succeed. He pulled himself up from a dreadful, poverty-stricken childhood and dire circumstances in the slums of Scotland. His family tenement had no running water, no light, no heat. From the age of ten, he worked in a Scottish cotton mill, toiling from six in the morning until eight at night for six days a week, then suffering through Greek and Latin lessons for two hours more. Young Livingstone was a "piecer," clambering under the spinning looms, retrieving broken spools of thread, and recycling the remains of a giant mill.[20]

Very few of Livingstone's fellow child laborers were able to learn to read or write, or to ever graduate from the smoky mill. They were lifers. Not Livingstone. He determined to find a way to get out, by somehow getting enough medical training that he could qualify as a medical missionary.

Livingstone began his new career in South Africa at twenty-seven. He was soon at odds with other more experienced missionaries, presumptuously accusing them of not putting enough effort into saving souls. Not that he was having much luck himself. In thirty years of trying, he managed to make only one convert, and once Livingstone left his village, the man quickly recanted his love of Jesus.

Livingstone kept moving north to what he thought might be greener pastures for soul-saving, dragging his long-suffering wife, Mary, with him, keeping her pregnant most of the time. When the pair returned to England for a short stay, she and her mother tried to convince him to let her stay home. He wanted her with him, however, so the pair and their brood of six returned to Africa. While on the long voyage south, she discovered she was pregnant yet again. Livingstone was mortified, for he felt it proved to the world he could not control his lusts.

---

20 Coincidentally, I have done exactly the same job myself. On my first journey of exploration (if I may call it that) I hitchhiked around the United States, mostly in the deep south but also up into New England. While in Providence, Rhode Island, my traveling partner and I took jobs in a fibreglass mill to replenish our meager funds. My job was precisely the same as Livingstone's—when spools of thread broke, they were tossed in a basket and sent to me. I was taught to spin off these short-ends onto a huge rotating machine. The ancient Providence mill probably looked a lot like the one young Livingstone toiled in—a single giant motor (a steam engine in his day) powering all the machines on the floor; spinning axles overhead, well-worn leather belts all over coming down off them to run the machines; men and women sitting or standing at machines they expected to be at their entire working lives. But that's where the similarities end. I was nineteen, Livingstone was ten; I worked for eight-hour days, he worked fourteen. I was reasonably well paid, he wasn't. I quit after five days. He lasted eight years.

He was simultaneously fascinated and horrified by sexuality, a typical Victorian neurosis that was aggravated in his case by cyclothymia —hereditary manic depression.

Livingstone and family were attacked by the usual scourges —mosquitoes, malaria, fever—once back on the Dark Continent. "I could not touch a square half-inch on the bodies of the children unbitten after a single night's exposure," he once reported. He attempted his own solution to the scourge of malaria—a mixture he cooked up of quinine, rhubarb, opium, and calomel, the nineteenth-century wonder drug made of mercury chloride that was ultimately dismissed as a poison. The concoction, which became known as "Livingstone's Pills" or the "Zambezi Rouser," did seem to have positive effects, although ultimately it did not save either Livingstone or his wife from malaria.

It is easy to criticize from comfort and with hindsight, but Livingstone was a careless, sloppy explorer. He was the first European to see the Mosi-oa-Tunya ("The Smoke That Thunders") and the person who abandoned that name in favor of the boring moniker Victoria Falls. He then mapped the Zambezi River to the coast, convinced it was a passageway into the continent, but he took a shortcut that meant he missed seeing a vast stretch of rocks and impenetrable rapids that made it unnavigable. He then returned to England and convinced the British Foreign Office to finance a huge expedition and build a large river boat that would allow him to ascend the Zambezi, in the style of the *African Queen*.

The expedition was an abject failure. After an extended absence from her husband's travels, Mary Livingstone was aboard for part of it. She was angry and bitter about what she felt was his abandonment of their family and she told him so. He was shocked that she had taken to drink to ease her pain. They spent an unhappy three weeks together, then she died. After burying her, Livingstone pushed on in his river steamer, eventually running into the rocks and rapids he had missed on his previous trip. Reluctantly, he turned the boat around. He was now piloting it, as the professional captain had by now abandoned the voyage, sick of Livingstone's meddling. One of the physicians onboard wrote: "I can come to no other conclusion than that Dr. Livingstone is out of his mind and a most unsafe leader."

On the return voyage, Livingstone detoured to ascend the Shire River to Lake Nyasa (now Lake Malawi), which struck him as a good new possible base for missionary work. It turned out Arabs already laid claim to the lake. It was a staging point for their slave-trading operations and thus a very unpromising spot for Christian proselytizing.

The British Foreign Office recalled Livingston's ill-fated expedition, and the explorer returned to England in some disgrace. "We were promised cotton, sugar, and indigo and got none," thundered the *Times*. "We were promised trade, and there is no trade. We were promised converts to the Gospel, and not one has been made."

The Zambezi debacle cost the formerly "saintly and truly apostolic preacher of Christian truth" the support of the London Missionary Society. The British Foreign Office, too, was through with Livingston. He turned for help to the RGS, knowing it still had an obsession with the identification of the source of the Nile. Since the Burton–Speke debate had ended so abruptly and inconclusively, many within the august organization felt the issue was unresolved. Still, Livingstone was making a big ask. The affluent members were largely a snobbish group who considered Scottish missionaries infra dig. Livingstone was lucky to have the support of the president, Sir Roderick Murchison, who ignored the snippy comments of his members and sent him off on what would be his final journey to Africa—another quixotic search for the mostly pointless goal of finding the source of the Nile. He left England in 1865, arrived in Zanzibar in 1866, and lit out for a long trek inland toward Lake Tanganyika. For four years he trudged around the lake with a small band of helpers and a rapidly dwindling cache of food and supplies.

Throughout this long period of time, the British public, still fascinated by the great man, heard nothing from him, except for rumors that he was dead. He might well have been. Malaria and fever had laid him in a sick bed for weeks and sometimes months at a time.

Finally, in 1871, something happened that would change his life and reputation forever.

James Gordon Bennett Jr. was the high-flying, big-spending publisher of the *New York Herald*. One reliable chronicler described him as a "swaggering, precociously dissolute lout who rarely stifled an impulse. He drank, wenched, yachted, and played polo with spectacular gusto, and when, late at night, he took it into his pickled brain to bound into the nearest Bennett coach and drive the team through the dark at a frothing pace, careening wildly around corners, thundering over bridges, bowling aside anything in his way, stripping off his clothing as the wayward vehicle flew along and caterwauling at the moon, no one afterward told him how to behave."

Bennett liked to throw money around, usually at big stories. He once even tossed a wad into a burning fireplace because he didn't like how it was sitting in his pocket. He decided to send his ace reporter, Henry Morton Stanley, to Africa on the hunt to find the missing explorer. It is perhaps ironic that the reputation of one of the most ascetic figures of the nineteenth century was saved by one of the most outrageous and self-indulgent ones.

Bennett promised Stanley an unlimited pool of money to find Livingstone, but when Stanley arrived in Zanzibar to prepare for the overland trek, he discovered that Bennett had carelessly not sent the funds. Aghast, he was obliged to ask the US Consul to lend him the money he needed to pay for the arduous trip. Stanley, a man of modest means, worried that if he did not find Livingstone, Bennett would not re-pay his expenses and leave him bankrupt.

Stanley's background was even more deprived than Livingstone's. Born in Wales in 1841, his birth certificate was adorned with the word "Bastard." He was the illegitimate son of an eighteen-year-old barmaid and a father who died a few weeks after his birth. His teen mother turned him over as a baby to some neighbors. At about five, he was sent to the St. Asaph Workhouse for the Poor. There, according to historian Robert Aldrich, he was repeatedly raped and molested both by the headmaster and by older boys in the workhouse.

Like Oliver Twist, he escaped, and at eighteen managed to emigrate to the United States, landing penniless in New Orleans. He soon became caught up in the Civil War, fighting first for the Confederate Army, then, after being captured, for the Union Army, then, after being discharged, for the United States Navy. He is thought to have been the only person in history to have fought for all three services. After the war he became a journalist, reporting on other wars, battles, and revolutions in the American West, Abyssinia, Spain, and the Ottoman Empire.

Stanley's search for Livingstone was quite as challenging as the other explorations we have chronicled. It is clearly more difficult to find a single man lost somewhere in the vast reaches of Africa than it is to search for the source of a river, but Stanley, just as clearly, was not one to be daunted by obstacles. He suffered many bouts of fever. His horse and donkeys died. The rainy season made travel a nightmare. His two European companions, John Shaw and William Farquhar, proved to be difficult. One was a drunk, the other addicted to whores, a sin in Stanley's eyes due to his hang-ups over his mother's promiscuity. Both Shaw and Farquhar died on the long journey, and a huge number of his 100 porters either died or deserted.

It was yet another exploration shitshow, until it wasn't. Against all odds, on November 10, Henry Morton Stanley got what is widely considered the journalistic scoop of the nineteenth century. The village of Ujiji sits on Lake Tanganyika, in what is present-day Tanzania. There Stanley found the weakened, woebegone explorer. He greeted him with what have become probably the most famous four words in the history of exploration: "Dr. Livingstone, I presume?" Stanley managed to nurse Livingstone back to health and sent back excited journalistic missives to the coast, which saved him from bankruptcy and greatly improved the circulation numbers of newspapers in New York and London. He then helped Livingstone continue his explorations in search of the source of the bloody Nile. Eventually he left, returned to civilization, and wrote a bestseller with the tabloid-style title *How I Found Livingstone*.

Stanley begged Livingstone to return with him, but the old explorer, headstrong and confused, insisted he needed to continue his source-of-the-Nile explorations. Livingstone was no longer in the same postal code as reality. He carried on until May 1, 1873, when he died of malaria and dysentery in the village of Chipundu in present-day Zambia. His loyal followers, James Chuma and Abdullah Susi, removed his heart and buried it under a baobab tree and then dried his body in the hot African sun, wrapped it in calico, carried it 1,600 kilometers to the coast, and accompanied it back to England, where, as we've seen, it was buried with full national honors.

How was it that Livingstone, a failure at most of his endeavors, became elevated to near-sainthood? His religiosity and his bravery certainly helped. Livingstone was once famously attacked by a lion. He and his group were trying to kill it when it turned and attacked him. The illustration of the event was featured in many of the hagiographic Sunday-school biographies of the great man published during his life and after. The story was recounted in pseudo-Biblical terms, like Daniel in the lion's den, or Jonah swallowed by the whale. That Livingstone was spared was seen as a sign of God's favor, attributable to the explorer's inherent virtue and goodness. Livingstone helped convince the British of their own moral superiority and national virtue.

The journalistic skills of Henry Stanley also played a role, turning this most strange and unusual man—the unlikeable and irascible failure of the Zambezi expedition—into the Christ-like apostle of the dark continent. And it must be admitted that Livingstone had a certain amount of goodness in him. He probably did more than any other explorer to end the slave trade. He also treated the many Africans he encountered better than most of the other explorers we have been considering.

But let's not get carried away. More than any other explorer, Livingstone's advocacy of "Christianity, Commerce, and Civilization" meant he did more than most to inspire colonial imperialism in Africa. It's mindboggling that a man who experienced first-hand the most pernicious and cruel aspects of nineteenth-century capitalism in his childhood would actively want to import that smoky industrial model to Africa. His legacy, at best, is complicated.

*

Alexandrine Tinne

If David Livingstone got more acclaim than he deserved, Alexandrine Tinne got much less. The reasons are obvious: She was Dutch, not English. Her expeditions were independently financed, and she was not beholden to or supported by any geographic societies, armies, or government agencies. Mostly, of course, it was because she was female.

She was born to Philip Tinne, a wealthy slave ship and sugar plantation owner who when slavery was abolished was awarded a massive government compensation for the loss of his trade (funny how capitalism makes sure that happens). When he died, Alexandrine inherited a large portion of his great wealth and used it to finance her elaborate travels.

She began at sixteen with a crossing of Scandinavia by horseback. At nineteen, to compensate for the heartbreak of a broken engagement, she took off with her mother, first for Venice, then Cairo, then Luxor, then by camel to the Red Sea, then—here we go again—on the familiar mission of identifying the source of the Nile. She taught herself the new art of photography and outfitted two ships with a photographic studio, plant-collecting paraphernalia, books, porcelain, and silverware, and set off up the Nile with her mother, aunt, and various maids and servants.

As they pushed deep into Sudan, their expedition was stalled by the near-impenetrable Sudd swamp. She was also dissed, in extremis, by the usual dicks. "There are Dutch ladies travelling without any gentlemen," moaned Samuel Baker. "They are very rich and have hired the only steamer here for 1,000 pounds. They must be demented! A young lady alone with the Dinka tribe . . . they really must be mad. All the natives are naked as the day they were born."

The British satiric magazine *Punch* created its own put-down in rhyme, claiming that the notion of a female explorer was "just a trifle too seraphic" and that women "mustn't, can't, and shan't be geographic."

Alexandrine ignored the nay-sayers and carried on. She began buying slaves in order to free them, a simple solution that never seemed to have occurred to David Livingstone. With her boat mired in the muck, she returned to Khartoum and re-stocked for a second attempt, this time partially overland through the territory of the Nyam-Nyam of northern Congo, widely believed to be cannibals. Her report on this part of her explorations made its way back to London, where it was read to the RGS. Both John Speke and James Grant imperiously dismissed it, creating yet another explorer feud. Their sexist douchery, surprisingly, was over-ruled by the society's president, who declared "the ladies were really on the right road" to what he felt could be "a most important geographic result."

Not this time. The party succumbed to the usual scourge of African travel. Alexandrine's mother, aunt, and two Dutch maids all died of blackwater fever. Alexandrine returned to Cairo but did not give up her explorations. Instead, she purchased a yacht and sailed to Algiers. The impressive ship arrived with what the locals thought was an Oriental princess onboard, a beautiful "female Odysseus" attended by "Negroes and stately Nubians." Putting aside her interest in the Nile, she now took up the old racket of traveling to Timbuktu.

She learned the Tamachak language in order to converse with the desert nomads, the Tuareg, and set off from Algiers by camel.

She made it as far as the oasis village of Murzuch, where she unwittingly became involved in a local internecine dispute and was violently murdered.

Tinne didn't get any knighthoods or Westminster Abbey funerals, but her extensive collection of African photographs and ethnographic and botanical items were saved. Some were housed in the Liverpool Museum, others in a church built in her honor in Holland. However, both the museum and church were bombed by the Luftwaffe in WWII, and most of her two collections were destroyed.

Toward the end of the nineteenth century the obsession with finding the source of the Nile River finally began to fade. Roads, railways, and the industrial-strength colonial imperialism of men like Cecil Rhodes (in what became Rhodesia) and the loathsome Belgian King Leopold II (in the Congo) pushed the role of the African explorers toward obsolescence. New, younger explorers, no less mad and intrepid, moved on to new frontiers. Some headed for the jungles of South and Central America and to the remote mountains of Asia. Others, deciding the heat, bugs, and wild animals of central Africa weren't challenging enough, charged off for the frigid climes at the top and bottom of the globe.

CHAPTER 4

THE PERILOUS RACE FOR THE POLES

While Burton, Speke, Stanley, and Livingstone were slogging through tropical Africa, many North American, Scandinavian, and British explorers were donning parkas (thin crappy ones, mostly) to attack the North and South Poles. The passion for icy wastelands may be hard for the twenty-first-century mind to understand, but it was real back then. Said one British explorer, "It seems to us certain that the Arctic world has a romance and an attraction to it, far more powerful over the minds of men than the rich glowing lands of the tropics."

As the nineteenth century wore on, the search for the Northwest Passage (and Franklin) wound down and was replaced with a race to be the first to the very top and bottom of the earth—the North and South Poles. There is certainly romance in these polar regions, but there is also hard reality. Norwegian Fridtjof Nansen, who had tried to get to the North Pole, called the Arctic winter "an affliction, a punishment, and a plague; during which the air becomes condensed and the ground petrified. It makes faces to fade, eyes to weep, noses to run. It causes the skin to crack and change color. Its earth is like flashing bottles, its air like stinging wasps; its night rids the dog of his whimpering, the lion of its roar, the birds of their twittering and the water of its murmur, and the biting cold makes people long for the fires of Hell." The winter sucked, yet people kept coming. More than 1,000 people tried to reach the North Pole before it was successfully conquered. According to one reckoning, 751 died trying.

Like the race to the headwaters of the Nile, the contest to be the first to the North Pole was marred by bad geography and false claims. In 1909, two arch-rivals, both Americans—Dr. Frederick Cook and Robert Peary, would almost simultaneously announce they had achieved the objective. Both claims received massive attention from the press and public. Both are now considered fraudulent. There were few rules in the race and fewer scruples. Competitors thought little of slagging each other's reputations, sacrificing their teammates, and taking enormous risks with their own lives.

Also like the Nile quest, most of the participants in the race to the North Pole could not explain why they believed it to be so important to be first. "The attaining of this mythical spot did not then, and does not now, seem to mean anything," acknowledged Dr. Cook years later. "I didn't then, and do not now, consider it the treasure house of any great scientific secrets." Many of them had scientific pretensions, but as British mountaineer George Mallory accurately observed, "sometimes science is the excuse for exploration. I think it is rarely the reason." A race is a race, and nothing more, whether a marathon, a 100-meter dash, or the Monaco Grand Prix. The race to the North Pole had no intrinsic meaning. The winner got bragging rights and the glory of being able to say that they were first to stand on an indistinct, bleak spot of snow on the roof or in the basement of the planet.

The North Pole was first attacked by Captain William Edward Parry in 1827. His team reached 82° 45′ N, the highest latitude to be attained for the next forty-nine years. A legacy of his expedition, perhaps more useful to humanity than his geographic accomplishment, was canned food, first created to feed the crew on his long voyage. Unfortunately, no-one had thought yet to invent the can-opener; somehow, they made do without one.

The man who made the race to the North Pole into a race was American explorer Charles Hall, whom we met earlier on his earnest attempts to find remnants of the Franklin expedition. It is a sign of how highly regarded explorers were in the nineteenth century that even an oddball like Hall was able to get himself into the halls of government and personally petition both President Ulysses Grant and the US House of Representatives to fund his latest venture. Imagine the odds today of an explorer getting an audience with the US president to beg for cash. Hall asked for $100,000, a fortune at the time, to finance two ships north on an expedition to "claim the pole for America." In the end, Congress grudgingly said yes but gave him just $50,000, which meant he could only take one ship. Somehow Hall still ended up with two captains, a mistake that possibly cost him his life.

Hall's expedition was highly publicized and received hordes of applications from would-be adventurers wanting to join—many of them saying they would "accept any position" on the voyage—a sure sign, then as now, that they were likely qualified for none. Hall had to employ the services of a *New York Times* reporter to dissuade the applicants with an article describing the "damp blankets, fetid woolens, odoriferous furs, filthy Eskimaux, and myriads of unpleasant insects" they would have to endure, ending his piece with what the journalist considered the ultimate horror: "Outside, he will be met by the repulsive features of the Eskimaux, their still more disgusting modes of life, and the never ending line of ice and snow." What Taqulittuq and Ebierbing, the two Inuit he had brought south to help with his pitch and preparations, thought of this charming piece was not recorded.

The *Polaris* set sail on June 29, 1871. By the time they were in the cold waters of Davis Strait it was clear that the expedition was cursed. The two captains, Sidney Budington and George Tyson, were at each other's throats. Hall caught Budington stealing liquor and food from the ship's stores. The team of German scientists that had been forced on the expedition was in open defiance of the leader, Hall. There was marked disagreement about how, or even whether, they should make a bid for the pole, with Budington and the Germans ridiculing Hall as a novice and Hall and Tyson convinced that Budington was not only a drunk but a coward for not pushing further north. Hall's faithful companion Ipirvik described the anarchic situation as follows: "No cap'n; nobody cap'n. Cap'n Budington, he cap'n. Captain Tyson, he cap'n. Doctor, he cap'n too. Mr. Chester, cap'n. Mr. Meyer, cap'n; me cap'n; everybody cap'n—no good."

Finally on September 10, 1871, the ship anchored in a semi-protected cove that Hall named Thank God Harbor, and they settled in for the winter. A month later Hall headed north over the ice with two Inuit companions and the ship's first mate to scout out a route that they might take to the North Pole in the spring. On their return, two weeks later, Hall asked for a cup of coffee and after drinking it immediately fell ill. He was convinced he had been poisoned. He rapidly fell into a delirious state. Ten days later he was dead.

To this day, people talk of the supposed mystery of what happened to John Franklin. The death of Charles Hall is a far more tantalizing puzzle. As we have seen, the Arctic leads people to do nutty things. Living cooped up on ships can make people crazy, even in pleasant southern climes. The effect is multiplied when ships are locked in the ice through the long, dark Arctic winter.

There were many aboard the *Polaris* with motives to kill their leader, especially the creepy Captain Budington and the equally scummy chief German scientist Dr. Emil Bessels. Hearing that Hall had died, Budington remarked, "There's a stone off my heart." Bessels, laughing, declared it was the best thing that could have happened to the expedition. Bessels had another possible motive for getting rid of Hall. Both men were apparently romantically involved with the same young woman, prominent American sculptor Vinnie Ream, the creator of the statue of Abraham Lincoln in the rotunda of the US Capitol.

At the conclusion of the failed expedition, an investigation cleared the possible suspects and declared that Hall's death was due to what they called apoplexy and what we today would call a stroke. However, in 1968, Hall's biographer, Chauncey C. Loomis, received permission to exhume Hall's body. Samples of Hall's hair, skin, and fingernails were sent to the Centre of Forensic Sciences in Toronto. The results were explosive. In the last week of his life, they announced, Hall had ingested a large quantity of arsenic. It might have been accidental poisoning or suicide. More likely, it was murder.

The ship's crew buried Hall and spent the rest of the winter drinking, gambling on card games, bickering, and arguing about whether or not to still try for the Pole. Captain Tyson overheard what he called an "astounding" and "monstrous" proposal. Although he never revealed what this was, it has been suggested that the concocted plan was to return to America with a bogus claim that the expedition had made it to the Pole.[21]

---

21 If acted upon, it would have been a forerunner to a series of elaborately faked records by adventurers through the twentieth century, including Dr. Frederick Cook's claims to have climbed Mt. McKinley (now Denali) and to have made it to the North Pole, and sailor Donald Crowhurst's elaborately staged false claim that he had successfully sailed alone around the world.

It wasn't until August 12, 1872, that the *Polaris* broke free of the ice. Within three days, however, the incompetent and drunken skipper Budington had rammed the ship into an ice floe, and for the next two months it was caught in the pack ice in the channel between Greenland and Ellesmere Island, slowly drifting south. In a fierce November gale, Budington became convinced the ship was going to sink, and he ordered the crew to hurl the stores overboard onto the ice. Most of the goods were swept away. The demented captain next demanded the crew jump down onto the floe to retrieve what they could.

In the mayhem of the storm, the ice shattered, and the ship broke free. It became apparent that the *Polaris* was not sinking and that Budington's ridiculous orders had been for nothing. Now, however, twenty men, women, and children were stranded on an ice floe, with the wind blowing the ship away from them.

It was the beginning of a frigid six-month, 2,000-mile ordeal that slowly swept the castaways from the very high Arctic to the coast of Labrador, one of the most awful stories in the annals of Arctic exploration. Were they abandoned? George Tyson thought so, but at the inquiry months later, his ex-companions convinced the jurors that they had searched but failed to find the lost twenty.

The abandoned party consisted of Captain Tyson, nine other white men (almost all of them Germans), a black American cook, four adult Inuit, and five children, the youngest of whom was eight weeks old. They almost certainly would have perished were it not for Taqulittuq, Ebierbing, and the two other adult Inuit. The four built igloos on the ice for all. Ebierbing hunted for seals, and Taqulittuq cooked two meals a day for the party. The Germans acted like assholes, defying and abusing Tyson, frightening off the seals with random gunshots, refusing to work, and stealing from the natives. Even worse, as the food supplies dwindled and hunger set in, Tyson became convinced they were going to kill and eat the Inuit children. The Germans were also frequently sick, since they refused to take the advice of the Inuit not to eat the often-poisonous livers of the seals, bears, and narwhals that Ebierbing captured.

The ice floe was large, about a mile across, but had almost no life to sustain the large party. The group was entirely dependent on the hunting skills of Ebierbing and his hunting partner, Ipirvik. Day after day, in the winter darkness, with the temperature sometimes hovering at fifty below, the hunters would be out lying on the ice, patiently waiting for the possibility that a seal might imprudently stick his head above the ice in search of a breath of air. Seal hunting is difficult even for the Inuit today, but they are a tough, hardy people.[22]

It is remarkable that the party survived in its semi-starved, frozen state. The far north is probably the harshest climate on earth. George Tyson, to his utter chagrin, was trapped on the ice floe with minimal clothing because most of his kit had been swept away on the first night of the disaster. It took months on the ice before Taqulittuq was able to sew him a fur jacket from one of the seals that her husband had caught.

Everything seemed to be working against the group on their long, icy, nightmarish voyage, even the dogs. Although they were often starving, the humans could not eat the dogs since they might need

22 I traveled north of Igloolik by snowmobile on a seal hunt with a small group of Inuit. It was insanely cold, and the speed of the snowmobile added a wind chill that would produce frostbite in minutes. The lead hunter, the Inuit filmmaker Zacharias Kunuk, scanned the ice as he roared along. Every hour or so, he spotted a tiny blow hole in the ice (utterly invisible to me), brought the skidoo to a halt, pulled out his rifle, lay on the ice, and waited. Ten, twenty, thirty minutes would pass. On one occasion he glanced over at his *kabloona* companion, shivering on the komatik sled. He realized he might soon have an emergency on his hands. He abandoned the seal hunt, inspected my face and hands, demanded that I start running around in a circle to warm up while he and his fellow hunters pulled out snow knives and quickly built an igloo. He pulled out a rusty Coleman stove and began to melt ice to boil water and make tea for me. I was wearing a heavy parka, an Icelandic sweater, snow pants, and boots, but all were designed for a cold day in southern Canada. If your clothing can be worn in the south, it isn't anywhere near warm enough to wear in the Arctic. Kunuk was wearing seal and caribou skins. Although he has been feted on the Croisette by the Cannes Film Festival and offered membership in the Hollywood Academy, he continues to live and hunt in the Arctic largely in traditional Inuit fashion.

them for transportation were the ice floe ever to run ashore. Huskies are wildly ill-mannered dogs who love few things more than eating human excrement. These starving dogs would not only eat human shit but would ravenously attack the bare bottoms of the party as it was being produced. As one person squatted, another had to stand guard with a whip to prevent the teeth of the dogs from ripping into the other's backside.

Finally, in April, after five months on the ice, the sorry souls had drifted far enough south that they were in the hunting grounds of Newfoundland whalers. They saw and tried to signal to several ships, to no avail. By this time the group hadn't had anything to drink or eat for days, and again there were whispers of possible infanticide and cannibalism by the Germans. Finally, Ipirvik was able to shoot a polar bear, the meat of which tided them over until the end of the month, when they spotted another ship. Again, it was up to Ipirvik to save them. He paddled his kayak far out into the Davis Strait, chasing down the ship. He shouted from the water to convince the sealer to stop and persuaded him that he was with a group of white men (as the ship was unlikely to stop to solve a purely Inuit problem, whatever it might be). The sealer picked up all twenty from the ice floe and took them to Newfoundland.

Their incredible story was at first not believed. Arctic experts deemed it "impossible" and "ridiculous." Eventually, however, the American government sent a ship to St. John's to claim the survivors. Once they arrived in New York, their amazing tale was told by all the newspapers of the day. Tyson somehow became the hero of the ordeal, even though he had lain incapacitated in Taqulittuq's igloo for most of it. Neither her nor Ebierbing's role in keeping the party alive were mentioned in press accounts. Indeed, readers were basically led to believe that the un-named pair (simply listed as "natives") were nothing more than a burden on the group.

The two Inuit settled for a while in Groton, Connecticut (today the submarine capital of America), where, tragically, their daughter died in 1875. In December 1876, an ill and heartbroken Taqulittuq whispered, "Come, Lord Jesus, and take thy poor creature home." Before the New Year dawned, he did. She was dead at age thirty-nine.

*

In 1879, the ubiquitous New York newspaper magnate James Gordon Bennett Jr., underwriter of Stanley's explorations of Africa, purchased an old Royal Navy gunboat, re-named her the *Jeannette*, and sent her on an expedition to the Arctic. The route was through the Bering Strait between Russia and Alaska to search for the mythical but widely thought-to-exist Open Polar Sea, on which the ship would merrily sail to the North Pole.

Instead of a jaunt on this illusory body of water, the *Jeanette* was trapped in the Arctic ice for two years, drifting vaguely and slowly eastward. The captain, George De Long, wrote, "We are drifting about like a modern Flying Dutchman . . . thirty-three people are wearing out their lives and souls." On June 13, 1881, the ship was crushed and sunk. The crew escaped the sinking ship and began hauling its boats south across the ice, with dogs trying to pull their sledges and supplies. Unfortunately, after two years of inactivity cooped up on the ship, the dogs proved useless. Most were shot for food.

Their trip across the ice and then through northern Siberia involved the usual panoply of arctic exploration disasters—starvation, freezing, exhaustion, death. Of the expedition party of thirty-three, only thirteen made it back to the United States. Of course, their stories sold a lot of copies of the *New York Herald*. The survivors were acclaimed as heroes, given a civic reception and a lavish banquet at the famed Delmonico's Restaurant. Many succumbed to polar madness—some out on the ice, some after they returned to civilization. James Bartlett, a fireman on the expedition, was still gripped by arctic fever even though he was back in the U. S. and attempted unsuccessfully to kill his wife and did succeed in killing his niece and himself.

The expedition may have failed to achieve its goal, but it only increased the world's fascination with the icy Arctic and inspired travelers and scientists to look north. In the early 1880s, one of the world's first truly international scientific projects, the International Polar Year, was proclaimed. Participating were the Austro-Hungarian Empire (where it was conceived), nine other European nations, Canada, and the United States. The American contribution to the study was to send an expedition led by frontiersman Adolphus Greeley to a spot high on Canada's Ellesmere Island. It was not the pole, but it was closer to it than any other had ever been.

Greeley had lived a typically adventurous nineteenth-century life. He had led a Black regiment called the Corps d'Afrique in the Civil War and followed that by working for the US Army Signal Corps stringing the newly invented telegraph lines through bandit and Indian territory in west Texas.

With nineteen soldiers, two Inuit, and a civilian doctor named Octave Pavy, Greeley was dropped off near the northern tip of Ellesmere with supplies to last two years. Within weeks of building a shelter, which they dubbed Fort Conger, members of the crew were fighting like dogs with each other and their commander. Greeley told the team that he "was not a man to be trifled with and in case of mutiny he would not stop at the loss of human lives to restore order."

The Greeley expedition had some successes. One member of the team headed north by dogsled, traveling for 1,000 miles and reaching 83° 25′ North—further north than anyone had ever been. Scientific readings were taken through the long, dark winters. But generally, the expedition was a disaster. Greeley ended up arresting Dr. Pavy over a common issue that plagued exploration in this contentious period—an argument over the publication rights to the doctor's expedition diary.

Two ships that had been sent north to pick up the men were both defeated by the Arctic. The first was turned back by pack ice; the second sank. After two long years in the north and two winters in total darkness, Greeley and his men abandoned Fort Conger and headed south on their own. Packing their scientific instruments, what remained of their food, and their belongings, including Greeley's sword and dress uniform into their small boats, they headed south. Caught in storms and giant waves and disputes over navigation, they were soon bickering and questioning Greeley's leadership. The boss was accused of "frequent outbursts of passion-evinced insanity." Even his closest ally said that "all that his ignorance, stupidity, and an egotistical mind without judgement can do in the injury of our cause is being done."

By September the ice was forming yet again, and the men were forced back to land to somehow weather yet another winter in the Arctic. As their food diminished and the cold increased, the men began dying. The feet of one of them, Joseph Elison, turned black, then his eyelids and his lips froze shut. He couldn't eat, but he somehow found it possible to speak. "Please kill me, will you?" he asked his tentmates. His frostbitten fingers fell off, then Dr. Pavy amputated one of his feet. The other fell off on its own.

Another of the men died from consuming tainted alcohol. Insane with polar madness, it was said that he "would drink anything that had a suspicion of alcohol about it, even paint." The still-living hauled his body up a hill to bury him. The procession was described as "a ghostly procession of emaciated men moving slowly and silently away from their wretched ice prison in the uncertain light."

What little food they had began to go missing. One of the accused suspects, in what is one of the most haunting admissions in the annals of exploration, declared that "although I am a dying man, I deny the assertion. I ate only my own boots and part of an old pair of pants. I feel myself going fast but I wish it would go faster."

Another suspect was a private named Charles Henry, who had been jailed in years past for theft and forgery. After Greeley became convinced he was the thief, he ordered two remaining sergeants to shoot him, which they reluctantly did, neither ever disclosing whose bullet had killed the man. Henry was gone, but by then, so was almost all the food. Greeley and the others spent hours concocting imaginary meals they wished they could consume.

Finally, they were rescued. The leader of the search party that found them could not believe the sight of the emaciated men. "Greeley, is this you?" he asked.

"Yes, seven of us left," croaked the commander. "Here we are, dying like men. Did what we came to do. Beat the best record." He was nearly dead, but even in that condition he was still able to fixate on the Arctic grail and boast of his progress toward the pole.

Investigation of the bodies later showed that some had been subjected to cannibalism. The survivors became obsessed with food for the rest of their lives. Adolphus Greely, hailed as somewhat of a hero, became the first president of The Explorers Club. Every year, on the anniversary of their rescue, Greeley and other survivors would meet at the club for one of the meals they had dreamed of in the Arctic. Perhaps that is the origin of The Explorers Club's unusual dining habits.[23]

*

The disastrous Greeley expedition did not dissuade others from heading north. Of all the obsessed and driven characters that were drawn toward polar exploration, Robert Peary was perhaps the least likeable. He was a ruthless, self-serving egomaniac, interested in exploration not out of any scientific or geographic curiosity but simply because he felt it would bring him fame and fortune. "I must have fame," he told his mother. He also confided to her, "I must be the peer or superior to those about me to be comfortable." He certainly lived his life by these dicta. He and he alone got sole credit for his expeditions. He ran roughshod over his companions, many of whom ended their time with him with murder in their hearts. And he became the most celebrated Arctic explorer ever.

---

23 At the club's New York headquarters, the biggest event is the annual dinner, held for many years in the ballroom of the Waldorf Astoria Hotel. It features crazily exotic foods—lionfish, snake, roasted cockroaches, and once, at least according to club legend, bite-sized cubes of a 20,000-year-old mastodon that had been discovered frozen in the Arctic permafrost. The Ontario/Nunavut wing of the Canadian Chapter of the club, which I led for several years, meets monthly around a peregrine meal themed by the caterer to match the evening's speech.

With $500 from his mother and six months leave from the US Navy, Peary made his first Arctic journey in the summer of 1886, attempting to reach the top of Greenland on a dog sled with a single Danish companion. Running out of food, the two men turned back after 160 kilometers, having made no real discoveries. That didn't stop him from claiming to have found a new, supposedly important geographic feature that he named after himself. The so-called Peary Channel north of Greenland was duly added to all maps of the north until 1912, when Danish explorers Peter Freuchen and Knud Rasmussen, along with Inuks Inukitsork and Uvdloriark, made a 1,000 kilometer journey across Greenland to attempt to determine whether the Peary Channel really existed. They found that it did not.[24]†

Five years later, Peary was able to mount a new expedition to the north. This time, he had two important wingmen with him, Matthew Henson and Dr. Frederick Cook. Both are towering figures in Arctic exploration, used by Peary until they threatened his own fame, at which point he discarded them. The team traveled in June 1891 aboard the *S.S. Kite*, a sealing ship. The expedition covered more than 2,000 kilometers and guessed correctly that Greenland was an island and therefore not a land route to the pole. Peary suffered a terrible accident on this voyage. While the ship was ramming through surface ice, its tiller smashed into his leg, breaking both bones beneath his knee. Fortunately, Dr. Cook was with him. Like almost everyone who met him, Peary was impressed by the amiable and energetic surgeon and was extremely grateful to have him onboard to expertly set the bones and supervise his long recovery in a camp on northern Greenland. Although the two men worked well together

---

24 On their return trip, Freuchen was involved in one of the craziest events ever in the long wild saga of polar exploration. He was trapped by an avalanche under a heavy blanket of ice and snow. To extricate himself, he claimed, he molded a primitive knife out of his own feces, and once it was frozen solid used it to cut his way out of the cave. But trust armchair academics to spoil this great yarn by publishing a paper in the *Journal of Archaeological Science* titled "Experimental Replication Shows Knives Manufactured from Frozen Human Feces Do Not Work."

while in the Arctic, their friendship broke up on the return South, for the usual reason. Cook wanted to publish a book about his experiences with the Inuit. Peary demanded all the limelight for himself.

Peary made four more trips to the high Arctic in the 1890s with the goal of preparing for the attack on the pole. On one of them, the paranoid explorer, fearful that a Norwegian expedition led by Otto Sverdrup might beat him to his ultimate destination, headed out in wildly frigid conditions, so cold that his toes were frostbitten and had to be amputated. Matthew Henson had warned his boss that the conditions were too frightful to risk travel, but Peary would hear nothing of delay. While dealing with the crippled Peary, Henson exclaimed, "My god, Lieutenant, why didn't you tell me your feet were frozen?" The monomaniacal Peary replied, "the loss of a few toes isn't much to achieve the Pole." His missing toes were an impediment he lived with for the rest of his life. He never visited Antarctica, but he ended up walking with an odd, penguin-like gait both in the Arctic and on the streets of New York and Washington.

Peary was certainly brave and tenacious enough to take on everything the Arctic could throw at him. "The true explorer," he told the National Geographic Society, at their annual white tie banquet, "does his work not for the hope of rewards or honor [totally untrue, in his case] but because the thing he has set himself to do is a part of his very being, and must be accomplished for the sake of accomplishment, and he counts lightly hardships, risk, obstacles, only if they do not bar him from his goal. To me, the final and complete solution of the polar mystery, which has engaged the best thought and interest of the best men of the most vigorous and enlightened nations of the world for more than three centuries, and today quickens the pulse of every man or woman whose veins hold red blood, is the thing which should be done for the honor and credit of this country, the thing which it is intended that I should do, and the thing that I *must* do."

Much is swept away in that statement by Peary's insistence on "me." For instance, that he utterly depended on his traveling partner Matthew Henson, who could drive dog sleds and speak Inuktitut—two skills Peary did not have. Nonetheless, even in the high Arctic, Peary upbraided Henson, who was Black, for failing to call him "Sir." He also paid Henson less than what the other (white) expedition members were paid—$40 a month in contrast to $80 or $100.

As for the Inuit Peary traveled with in the Arctic, they were little more than tools, on a par with the dogs that pulled his sledges. He wrote:

> I have often been asked 'Of what use are the Eskimos to the world?' They are too far removed to be of any value for commercial enterprises; and furthermore, they lack ambition. They have no literature, nor, properly speaking, any art. They value life only as does a fox, or a bear, purely by instinct. But let us not forget that these people, trustworthy and hardy, will yet prove their value to mankind. With their help, the world will discover the Pole.

Consistent with his sub-human view of the Inuit, Peary blithely violated things they held sacred, including three meteorites that for hundreds of years they had mined for iron to create knives and spearheads. On his 1895 trip, Peary stole them, putting the massive stones aboard his ship to take them back to New York where his wife sold them to the American Museum of Natural History for $40,000.

Inspired by the meteorites, the museum's assistant curator, famed anthropologist Franz Boas, encouraged Peary to bring back Eskimo bones. The explorer dug up the graves of some recently deceased Inuit and sold these, too, to the museum. Boas then thought having some actual live Eskimos at the institution would be an even better idea, so on his next trip Peary obliged by bringing six south to New York: two of his best sled drivers, Nuktaq and Qisuk; Nuktaq's wife Atanga and their daughter Aviak; Qisuk's son Minnik; and another youngster Usaakassak. Sweet museum exhibit!

"They promised us nice warm houses in the sunshine land, and guns and knives and needles and many other things," said Minik.

The promises were never kept. Instead, the six were housed in the basement of the museum where they contracted colds that turned into pneumonia. Four died and their bodies were turned over to the museum for examination and study. To prevent Minik from learning about this gruesome research, the museum's scientists held a bizarre funeral in which a log replaced the body of his dead father. In the words of Boas, this was done "to appease the boy, and keep him from discovering that his father's body had been chopped up and the bones placed in the collection of the museum."

Peary ignored the tragedy. In his book about his expeditions to the Arctic he does not mention it and indeed refers to "his" two sled drivers as if they were still alive in the north. At least he did not feel, as many others did, that the Inuit should be Christianized or civilized —quite the opposite. He did not begrudge them their culture or their morality. In fact, he took an Inuit mistress, Aleqasina, and published a nude photograph of her in one of his books, shocking some of his strait-laced benefactors. When Aleqasina (or Ally, as he called her) became pregnant from Peary, she took up residence aboard his ship as it was frozen in the Arctic ice. This added a certain amount of drama to the expedition when Peary's wife, Josephine, made a surprise visit the following spring, only to find Aleqasina onboard, proudly showing off Peary's offspring. Matthew Henson also found himself an Inuit girlfriend and fathered a child. Descendants of both men's children still live in northern Greenland. Peary and Henson weren't the only southerners contributing to the arctic gene pool in the nineteenth century. It is believed that Captain George Washington Cleveland fathered children with eight different Inuit women and is related to as many as 3 percent of the Inuit population living in Nunavut today.

*

In 1893, Norwegian explorer Fridtjof Nansen set out with a new and (many said) crazy plan to reach the North Pole. Adolphus Greeley described it as "Dr. Nansen's illogical scheme of self-destruction."

Both Americans and the longbeards of the RGS in England severely underestimated Nansen and his mentee, Roald Amundsen, the new Vikings from Sweden and Norway.

There is no doubt that Nansen's plan was audacious, maybe to the point of nutty. He proposed to intentionally sail a custom-built re-enforced ship, the Fram, into the ice pack in the Eastern Arctic Ocean and then let the westerly currents pull the ice-locked ship through the Arctic and hopefully right across the North Pole. "Most people considered it madness," wrote Nansen, "and were convinced that I was either not right in the head or was simply tired of life."

Unlike the British, who usually put together huge cumbersome expeditions, Nansen handpicked a small team of thirteen, without any rank or hierarchy. All were Norwegians for, as he said, "only Norwegians and Eskimos can sit face to face on a cake of ice for three years without hating each other." To explain his long monotonous trip, he liked to tell the story of the Eskimos who had traveled to a fjord seeking grass for hay. When they arrived and found the grass too short, they simply sat down and waited for it to grow long enough for their needs.

In case the team had to abandon the ship and travel by sledges, they brought with them huskies, but like so many polar explorers they found the dogs to be almost unmanageable and savage toward each other. "There is not a trace of chivalry about these curs," wrote Nansen. "When there is a fight, the whole pack rush like wild beasts on the loser."

After two years aboard the icebound ship, Nansen finally had had enough of the tedium and decided to make a dash for the pole by sledge. Taking only one companion with him (and some of the dogs that were still alive), he headed north on March 14, 1895. Like so many others caught up in the Arctic, with the glittering vault of stars and the flaming Northern Lights above him, he was gutted by his own insignificance. "Toiling ant," he wrote, "what matters it whether you reach your goal or not."

Three weeks later he realized he was not going to reach his goal, so at 86° 13' N, he and his companion, Hjalmar Johansen, turned back. With the ice beginning to melt under them and their food running low, their return was disastrous. They began to kill the dogs, one by one, for food for themselves and for the remaining dogs. They couldn't do it simply, as they needed to preserve their bullets for protection against polar bears, so they dispatched them by hand, sometimes with a knife, other times by strangling them to death.

In July, they finally spotted land. Unbelievably, it took them another month to get to it, strapping their sleds on top of their two kayaks to create a makeshift catamaran. By then, another winter was coming on. The pair dug a miserable hovel on the rocky shore of an out-island in Russia's remote Franz Josef Land and proceeded to wait out another eleven months in the Arctic, living in the darkness and consuming polar bear and walrus meat. Finally, in June 1896, they were accidentally discovered by a British explorer named Frederick Jackson.

After sailing back to Norway, Nansen was received with a huge hero's welcome by his king and some of the largest crowds the young country had ever seen. Accolades came in from around the world. British mountaineer Edward Whymper wrote that Nansen had made "almost as great an advance as has been accomplished by all other voyages of the nineteenth century put together."

Nansen became one of the best-known and most respected citizens of Norway. After retiring from exploration following his harrowing Arctic journey, he developed a variety of other interests. Many explorers are glory-seeking egomaniacs, with little interest beyond their own success. Not Nansen. He became a diplomat, working first to help win worldwide acceptance of Norway as a distinct country, independent of Sweden and Denmark, then devoting himself to the League of Nations (predecessor to the United Nations), primarily working on behalf of displaced persons and refugees from WWI and other conflicts. In 1922, he was awarded the Nobel Peace Prize for his humanitarian work with refugees.

And what of his ship, the *Fram*? After Nansen and Johansen left it for their dash for the pole, it continued its agonizingly slow march across the Arctic. It managed to prove Nansen's theory of polar drift by making it all the way to Spitsbergen Island in the Svalbard archipelago in the Greenland Sea north of Norway.

*

While in Spitsbergen, the crew of the *Fram* met a fellow-Scandinavian explorer, preparing an even madder attack on the North Pole, this time by balloon. Salomon Andrée was an odd duck. He never married and seemed to many to be fixated on his mother, with whom he lived for much of his life. He stated that he could never marry because he would "risk having [his wife] ask me with tears in her eyes to abstain from my flights, and at that instant, my affection for her, no matter how strong, would be so dead that nothing could ever bring it back." For most of his life he was unattached, but in the year before he set off on his fateful flight, he did conduct a long indiscreet affair with a Swedish professor's wife.

His real mistress was his passion for ballooning. From 1893 to 1896, he tested himself and his theories by making nine balloon flights. The last quarter of the nineteenth century was a period of wonderful new innovations and inventions. The telephone, the refrigerator, the matchbook, the typewriter, the escalator, the skyscraper, the movie projector and movie camera, the gasoline engine, Coca-Cola, the light bulb, and synthetic cloth (rayon), were all first created in this period. The hydrogen balloon fitted right into the new era.

The public was fascinated with all this new technology and lionized the men willing to risk their lives playing with it. In spring 1896, when Andrée displayed his balloon in Paris, 30,000 people came to see it, including the president of France, who sent "to the three courageous men of this daring enterprise the warmest wishes for a successful outcome, which will be followed with the greatest and most intense attention in France as well as everywhere else in the civilized world."

With his French presidential seal of approval, Andrée packed up his balloon and took it to Spitsbergen, along with the tons of machinery required to produce the vast amount of hydrogen necessary to keep it aloft. Unfortunately, he could never solve the two basic problems of balloons—temperature and wind. Temperature, which can be affected simply by a cloud passing overhead, has a huge effect on a balloonist's altitude. And unlike, say, a sailboat, which can be accurately steered in practically any direction, even almost into the wind, the balloon is virtually uncontrollable.[25]

Shiploads of reporters arrived on Andrée's remote Arctic island with plans to see him off and file stories. One Philadelphia newspaper wrote that "the daring of the aeronauts and the extremely novel enterprise in which they risk their lives give to Andrée's departure something of the interest which attended the sailing of Columbus' ships upon their immortal voyage." There was never a shortage of hyperbole in the exploration racket in this era.

Meeting up with the *Fram* in Spitsbergen, Andrée was pleased to hear he had not been beaten to the pole by Nansen. But the summer of 1896 was one of frustrating winds. Andrée waited and waited and then admitted defeat, packing up his balloon and returning to Sweden.

Over the following year, Andrée began to lose interest in his madcap expedition, not least because his main sponsor, Alfred Nobel, and his muse—his mother—both died in the winter. While in mourning for "the thought of someone [his mother] in whose arms they wish to rest," he began to question his scheme. By then, however, he was trapped in the momentum of his own publicity. Andrée, his massive balloon, and his complicated hydrogen manufacturing equipment returned to Spitsbergen in the summer of 1897. The winds were not much better but Andrée, along with two companions and thirty-two

---

25 Like most who have tried it, I love exploring by balloon and have done it over the Cappadocia region of Turkey and the Valley of the Kings in Egypt. Those are areas with very predictable prevailing winds. The Arctic, in contrast, has winds from all directions, which is why so many thought Andrée's mission was suicidal.

carrier pigeons that would be released to report their positions, finally flew on July 11. He took sufficient provisions for four months, a boat, a sled, and a cookstove that could be lowered below the gondola so as not to ignite the highly explosive hydrogen-filled canopy. Andrée hoped that if he did come down, it would be on ice. When asked by the reporters what he would do if the balloon came down on open water, he simply answered, "drown."

Three days later, the balloon crashed, not in the ocean but on an ice floe. It had been blown 200 miles north and then east. Andrée and his team were in a disastrous situation, trapped on a wilderness of ice. The carrier pigeons were of little help. No-one knew where they were arriving from. The balloonists had disappeared, swallowed up by the Arctic. For the rest of the summer, Andrée and friends attempted to walk south to a barren uninhabited spot called White Island pulling sledges of 300 and 400 pounds. Nansen had briefly tried pulling 250-pound sledges and called it almost an impossibility.[26]

For thirty-three years, the fate of Andrée and his compatriots was a mystery. Finally, in 1930, a whaling ship discovered three skeletons and a saved diary of their final, awful weeks. "We think we can well face death, having done what we've done," wrote Andrée. "How soon, I wonder shall we have successors? Shall we be thought mad, or will our example be followed?"

The answer to Andrée's question is "both." Of course, they were mad. And, of course, people followed them. The world, as the nineteenth century ended, was still in the grip of northern madness.

*

The next assault on the far north was not undertaken by small groups, but by hundreds, thousands, tens of thousands of

---

26 I crossed part of frozen Frobisher Bay in Nunavut with our team pulling sledges (or "pulks" as they are now called) made of aluminum, each carrying around 100 pounds of supplies. Any more than that is masochism.

individuals heading bravely into the frigid wilderness. This time the ostensible reason for their journeys was not scientific or geographic discovery, but gold. As one might expect, gold was usually an excuse. The real reason was personal achievement, excitement, and adventure.

In August 1896, local miners discovered gold in the Yukon's Klondike Creek in the far northwest of Canada. It took almost a year for word to get out, but when it did, it sparked perhaps the most colorful migration of all time and one of the wildest events in Canadian history. Over 100,000 adventurers headed north to the Yukon. Such was the geographic ignorance of the time (little changed today) that many thought they were actually heading for the North Pole.

Some followed Andrée's example. A character styling himself Don Carlos Stevens planned to build the world's largest balloon to fly adventurers to the gold fields. In Kalamazoo, another entrepreneur organized what he claimed would be a regular service to the Yukon, flying every two weeks. In Dublin, someone idiotically claimed his balloon would take fifty passengers to the gold fields (over 6,000 kilometers against the westerly winds and the Jet Stream).

In the end, nothing came of these cockamamie schemes. Instead, the usual routes to the Yukon were overland from Edmonton, or, more commonly, by steamer from San Francisco or Seattle to Skagway, Alaska, then a climb over the Chilcott Pass to Lake Bennett, then, after building a makeshift boat, down the Yukon River to Dawson City, a village of 500 that ballooned to 30,000 in the summer of 1898. For a year it was the largest city in Canada west of Toronto, a boom town with dance hall girls, casinos, and bars everywhere. The gold seekers did not think of themselves as explorers, but they really were—forging new trails into the Canadian wilderness. Most had even less idea of what they were getting themselves into than the dimwitted British explorers of the past. The Yukon's winters are much colder than the North Pole's. The coldest temperature ever recorded in North America was in Snag, Yukon: −81° F.[27] The Royal Canadian Mounted Police, aware that many of the gold seekers had no clue what they were in for, demanded that each of them carry a ton of supplies up the Chilcott Pass, enough to get them through the winter.

The Yukon sourdoughs had the time of their lives, but only a very few got rich from panning gold in the territory's cold creeks. Most of the money was made by those who supplied the prospectors rather than by the prospectors themselves. Donald Trump's real estate empire was begun on the Trail of '98, where his grandfather built and ran a brothel. The huge Pantages theatre chain was started in Dawson City by Alexander Pantages and Klondike Kate. It later expanded across North America.

Apart from adding a little to the world's understanding of the geography of Alaska and the Yukon, the gold rush contributed enormously to the public fascination with northern adventure. One of the films that played in the Pantages chain was Charlie Chaplin's *The Gold Rush*. The most famous scene in the film involves Chaplin eating his boot for dinner, an image likely inspired not by any incidents in the Yukon, but rather by the stories of the Franklin expedition of years past. As a young boy growing up in England, Chaplin undoubtedly would have read about Franklin's boot diet in one of the many books glorifying Arctic explorers for ten-year-olds.

*

With the north suddenly crowded, other even more adventurous explorers turned their eyes to the South Pole. Antarctica, only discovered in 1820, was the last great mystery in land geography.

---

27 Don't think that once you get to a certain temperature it all feels the same. I once spent some time with a character named "Caveman Bill," who lived in a cave on the Yukon River, summer and winter. I asked Bill about temperatures, and he laughed: "Oh, gawd. If you've been living at −45, once it gets back up to −25, it feels positively balmy!"

Lieutenant Adrien Victor Joseph de Gerlache had a very impressive name, but a rather short exploration resume. Nonetheless, when he presented his proposal to the Royal Belgian Geographical Society, the small country's scientific establishment responded enthusiastically. De Gerlache planned all manner of scientific discovery, including, most importantly, searching for the South Magnetic Pole. He never came near it, but then, like so many of these expeditions, science was just the excuse. The real goal, as usual, was personal glory for de Gerlache and national glory for the oft-ignored country of Belgium.

The scientists applauded but did not pull out their check books. The expedition was budgeted at 300,000 francs. De Gerlache appealed to King Leopold, but the king's focus was on raping the Congo with the help of explorer/journalist Henry Stanley, not Antarctica. The explorer next appealed directly to the public with a kind of nineteenth century GoFundMe campaign. He successfully raised most of the money in tiny one- and two-franc contributions. Some rich benefactors and the Belgian government put up the rest and De Gerlache was set. He purchased a ship, an eleven-year-old Norwegian Arctic whaling vessel and re-named her the *Belgica*. He then began searching for scientists, explorers, and crew.

As there was a very heavy nationalistic bent to the expedition, de Gerlache tried hard to find men with Belgian citizenship. They were few and far between. The two most interesting volunteers were, respectively, Norwegian and American. Both used the *Belgica* expedition as training for their own more famous later expeditions. Twenty-four-year-old Roald Amundsen, in my opinion the most accomplished of all polar explorers, volunteered without pay for the adventure and was hired as first mate.

De Gerlache knew he should have a doctor aboard his potentially harrowing and dangerous expedition, but he could not find one in Belgium willing to work for the miniscule wages he was offering. This proved to be blessing in disguise, for he ended up with one of the few people on earth—perhaps the only one—who qualified as both a surgeon and an experienced polar explorer.

Dr. Frederick Cook, who had proved himself to be a great asset in Robert Peary's Arctic expedition of 1891, had a great desire to return to the cold. In summer 1893, he had gained more northern experience by chartering a seventy-eight-foot schooner called the *Zeta* and leading a group of well-heeled paying clients on a cruise to Greenland and Labrador. He returned with a dozen or so huskies and two Inuit teenagers, Kahlahkatak and Mikok. Amusingly and somewhat amazingly, Cook set the pair up in a tent pitched on East 55th Street in Manhattan and entertained the locals by taking his dog team and the two teenagers in their Eskimo furs on sightseeing trips through downtown. He also got the beautiful sixteen-year-old Kahlahkatak a vaudeville gig doing an entrancing Inuit dance at a New York curiosities museum.

Recognizing that the North Pole had become crowded, Cook set his sights on Antarctica. His expedition, meagerly financed by his vaudeville act, consisted of little more than his enthusiasm and a box of letterhead of the "American Antarctic Expedition." He tried to tap the robber-barons of the era such as Andrew Carnegie but to no avail, so in 1894 he organized another tourist expedition north. This one proved to be somewhat of a nautical disaster, with one major collision with an iceberg off Nova Scotia and a second with a submerged rock that stove in the ship's hull in Labrador. Cook got his passengers off the sinking ship and home more-or-less in one piece and, always the self-promoter, tried to spin the voyage as a success. "A delightful trip," he called it, "replete with adventures, abounding in situations, not free from danger, and taken all in all, I have not heard one member of the party that had a complaint to make." This was a bald-faced lie. He had received a barrage of complaints about the cruise. But Cook was an ever-optimistic con-man of the sort that would be satirized by L. Frank Baum a few years later in *The Wonderful Wizard of Oz* (1900).

Cook returned to the task of pitching his proposed Antarctic trip, amping up the sell to Barnumesque levels. "We cannot say Antarctica has not gold and diamonds as well as Africa," was one claim he made to the *New York Times*. "Nor do I deem it by any means improbable to find there an isolated tribe of men, feeding and dressing from the liberal sea farms." Potential backers looked behind the curtain and did not like what they saw. Cook seemed doomed to life as a Brooklyn doctor dealing with bunions and distemper, until he chanced upon a small article in the *New York Sun* about the imminent departure of an Antarctic expedition from, of all places, Belgium. Cook fired off a telegram to de Gerlache, who at first rejected him, but then, desperate to have a doctor on board, even an American one, agreed. Cook boarded a steamer and headed south to meet up with the *Belgica* in Rio.

The largely disastrous *Belgica* expedition got off to a bad start. The ship was caught in a gale in the notorious Bay of Biscay. The crew tried to fight through it with the controversial, but then-common technique of pouring oil on the ocean to calm the waves (from which we get the expression "oil on troubled waters.") Everyone was seasick. "The captain stands on bridge, steering and vomiting," wrote young sailor Carl Wiencke. "The scientists lie on the hatch and vomit. The engineers sit in the engine room and vomit and the deckhands vomit down from the top deck." The hotheaded captain, slipping on some vomit on the deck, angrily picked up the ship's cat and threw it overboard. The action did not endear him to his crew.

The multi-national ship split into factions. Amundsen at one point had to wrestle a revolver from an unruly, mentally unbalanced deckhand, uncertain whether he was going to try to kill himself or others. After they picked up Cook in Rio, the cursed voyage continued to have difficulties. Four crew had to be fired in Punta Arenas. Delays meant they were likely to arrive very late for the short Antarctic summer. Then, in Tierra del Fuego they crashed into a rock, and were stuck and in mortal danger. After twenty-two hours, they were able to kedge themselves off. It had been a most unpleasant close call, but Cook was later able to quip about it that the rock they struck had been "the *Belgica*'s first geographic discovery."

The grounding was followed by an even worse disaster. Crossing the infamous Drake Passage (named for yet another explorer), crewman Carl Wiencke fell overboard and drowned. Finally, on January 23, two months too late for a sensible exploration of Antarctica, they spotted the icy continent. They steered the ship into the channel still used as an entry into the Antarctic peninsula and now named after the leader of the Belgian expedition the Gerlache Strait.[28]

Keen to get his feet on the southern continent, Amundsen took his gear ashore on January 26 to ski across the snow through flocks of bemused penguins. It was, he felt, the first time anyone had skied on Antarctica—his first *first*, the initial entry in what he hoped would be a long list of polar records achieved in his life. Cook also went for a first—becoming the first person to photograph the new land. He took dozens of pictures of the icebergs, mountains, and wildlife. De Gerlache, Cook, and Amundsen made an eight-day exploratory investigation of the Antarctica coast, in which Amundsen noted he chalked up several more polar firsts: first sledge journey in Antarctica; first overnight stay; and after a complex bit of mountaineering, highest altitude reached on the continent. The Norwegian recorded all these firsts and noted everything he was learning from Cook. Planning to become the most skilled polar traveler in the world, Amundsen would suck up knowledge from whoever had it—Canadian Inuit, German scientists, his mentor Nansen, and now, Cook, whose surgical approach to polar trekking and whose upbeat demeanor he greatly admired. The bond between the two men was for life, with Amundsen not abandoning Cook even after the doctor was disgraced and an inmate in Leavenworth Prison.

---

28 I was able to sail through the Gerlache Strait myself on a Russian icebreaker a few years back. It is unchanged—a dramatic and breathtaking channel surrounded by high mountains, dotted with blue icebergs that have calved off the glaciers. The ship anchored in the strait, and I was allowed to get ashore and camp overnight in a tent on snow-covered Wiencke Island, named after the drowned Norwegian sailor from the *Belgica* expedition.

De Gerlache pushed his captain Georges Lecointe to sail deeper down the long channel, but it was now February. The short Antarctic summer was over and the ice was starting to freeze. The delays they had endured on the ocean and in South America meant they were not going to make it to their intended destination of Cape Crozier and McMurdo Sound. Instead, they were likely to get caught in the ever-thickening ice pack. Many of both the crew and scientists aboard were anxious to get out of the ice and head back, at least to Argentina. De Gerlache was of two minds. He knew getting frozen in for a winter could be extremely dangerous to the ship and the men. But he also felt if he turned back without having made any substantial discoveries, he risked being portrayed in the Belgian press and to his financial backers as a failure. He dithered until it was too late. On March 5, the ship ground to a halt, frozen in place for the winter. Amundsen and Cook were delighted. This is what they had come for. Little did they know how long they would be trapped. Little did they know the expedition would become a disaster.

The grumblings from the crew and scientists on board began to increase. Like many of the explorers of this era, de Gerlache was a poor leader of men. With his old-school European ways, he felt himself superior to his crew and let them know it. It was up to Dr. Cook, the egalitarian American, to try to improve morale and prevent mutiny. He canvassed the entire ship for input. The first complaint was that there were no women aboard. The second was the food. De Gerlache had scrimped. The canned goods onboard were inferior, and the ship's cook was unskilled. Cook couldn't do much about the lack of females, but he did find a solution to the food issue. He had learned in his time with Peary and the Inuit in the Arctic how important it was to eat fresh meat to prevent the dreaded disease of scurvy. He determined to provide it here.

Cook encouraged the men to eat penguin and when available seal, but none were at all keen on the fishy, smelly foods. De Gerlache, in fact, refused to eat them, and this failure contributed to his rapidly declining health. Many began to deteriorate. "We became pale, with a kind of greenish hue," wrote Cook. "The stomach and all the organs were sluggish and refused to work." Even worse, an awful ennui and irritability took over.

> If we could only get away from each other for a few hours at a time, we might learn to see a new side and take a fresh interest in our comrades, but this is not possible. The truth is, that we are at this moment as tired of each other's company as we are of the cold monotony of the black night.

The black night continued, accompanied by the frightful groaning of the ship as it was squeezed by the ice, the squeals of the many rats in the bilges, the howling wind, and mysterious screams that many heard but none could account for. "We are in a mad house," said one of the Belgian scientists. A penguin they had brought aboard as a pet died, then Nansen, the ship's cat, then one of the most-liked sailors. The crew mourned his death and continued to get sicker and weaker. Both de Gerlache and Captain Lecointe suffered from scurvy.

Cook not only attended to the ill but came up with elaborate games to try to take their minds off their misery. Convinced that the main cause of polar madness was the lack of sunlight, he forced the most afflicted men to stand naked in front of a blazing wood or coal fire as a substitute for the missing sun. Still, wrote Cook, "the men felt that they would surely die, and to combat this spirit of abject hopelessness was my most difficult task."

As their supply of fresh penguin meat depleted, the three strongest members of the expedition, Cook, Amundsen, and Lecointe set out on July 31, the dead of the southern winter, for a multi-day hunting expedition. Cook taught Amundsen some very useful techniques for polar travel he had learned from the Eskimos—most importantly, how to build an igloo. But like everything on this voyage of the damned, their long trek was a failure. They caught no penguins, they came very close to running out of food, the temperature dropped to −45°, and they were trapped on a drifting ice floe and almost died.

When Cook finally got back to the ship, he discovered that one of the crew had literally gone insane, and that not just his but all the sailors' heartbeats had risen to dangerous levels. Further, de Gerlache was overcome with guilt, believing that it was his lust for glory that had caused all these ills.

Cook began to feel that if the ship did not break free of the ice in the approaching summer and they had to withstand another winter in Antarctica, they were likely to become another tragedy of exploration—another *Terror*, another *Erebus*, another *Jeanette*. After he heard Cook's concerns, Captain Lecointe came up with a plan to use tonite, the ship's explosive, a mixture of nitrate and gun cotton, to blow a passage in the ice to free them. He inspected and tested the explosive and discovered that it had lost all its explosive power—ruined either by the long voyage, the tropical heat, or the Antarctic cold. The men were devastated, their escape plan was in tatters. Typically, the always-upbeat Cook was able to joke about the awful discovery. Noting that the packaging for the tonite explosive advertised it as "more powerful than dynamite and much safer," he quipped that indeed it was "decidedly safer."

Another of the sailors, the Norwegian boatswain Tollef Tollefsen, also went mad. The ship, even while locked in place, began sinking. As the summer solstice of December 21 came and went, with no sign of the ice letting them go, Cook, Lecointe and De Gerlache came up with a bold plan that most of the others thought impossible. They would attempt to cut their way out of the two-meter-thick ice, using ice-saws to fashion a canal. It would need to be 400 meters long, and they would have to work in shifts around the clock in order to prevent the channel from refreezing. No-one was convinced it would work and all were weak and ill, but what was the alternative? If they didn't cut their way out, they would spend another desperate winter iced in, and if that happened, they would all likely perish.

The task was not only insanely difficult, but also disgusting. Along with the ice, the men spent weeks cutting through a year's worth of human excrement that had been deposited around the ship.

They were buoyed by the discovery that if they carefully cleaned the tonite explosive they could make it work. In their desperate state they were wildly careless with it, warming the sticks up over an open fire to get them working. "Never has there been a conspiratorial gang of anarchists or nihilists as passionate as Lecointe, Amundsen, Cook, and me," wrote one of the ship's scientists.

Even with the tonite charges and the backbreaking sawing, they could not get free. Amundsen, convinced they never would, proposed an alternative plan—manhauling the ship's two heavy boats to the edge of the ice and trying to make some kind of escape (similar, presumably, to the one Shackleton would make in 1915) from the southern continent. This plan was almost as crazy as the canal. The men were in no shape to haul the heavy boats. They nonetheless prepared for it, and brought up the winter parkas from the hold, only to find that the rats had eaten and destroyed them. So much for that. Back to sawing.

In March, with the days getting shorter and the temperature falling, the expedition finally caught a break. A violent ocean storm helped smash up the ice and clear the canal for them. Their ship was pointed in the wrong direction, but with some carefully placed tonite they smashed enough ice around the ship to make a little harbor in which they could make a three-point turn, spin it around and head out the canal. They were by no means free, but after many more days of tricky and difficult navigation, they slammed their way through the ice floes and finally, on March 14, were released from the icy grip of Antarctica.

Their misadventure was not over. The southern tip of South America, of course, is one of the most treacherous nautical passages on earth. The *Belgica* had great difficulties getting past Cape Horn, through the Cockburn Channel and around the dangerous rocks known as the Furies. Finally, it dropped anchor in the Chilean town of Punta Arenas on March 28, 1898. In April, the expedition began to break up. Amundsen was commandeered to take the madman Tollefsen back to Norway. The sailor, definitely "out there," never recovered from the dreadful experience and spent the rest of his life in a mental institution, another victim of the deadly game of exploration.

After learning his fiancée had died while he was in Antarctica, Cook got on a steamer and returned to America. De Gerlache, with a skeleton crew, took his ship back to Belgium. Since he had by now spent all his funds, he could not buy coal for the steam engine and had to rely on wind for the long voyage. It took him two and a half months to get home.

De Gerlache was greeted as a hero in Belgium. The successes of the ill-fated expedition were played up; the failures ignored. He was not well, however. The trip had taken a terrible toll. He needed to spend a full year on the French Riviera recuperating before trying to make a return to polar exploring. This time, just before WWI, he built a new purpose-built expedition vessel he called the *Polaris*. He ran out of money before he could finish it, and had to sell it to Anglo-Irish explorer Ernest Shackleton, who renamed it the *Endurance*. It was destined to become the most famous ship in the history of Antarctica exploration.

*

Robert Falcon Scott

Shackleton was a key figure in the next Antarctic expedition, conceived only months after the completion of the abortive Belgian assault on the snowbound continent. He was an important lieutenant on this expedition under a man whose name has become synonymous, at least in Britain, with pluck and courage—Robert Falcon Scott.

The son of a brewer, born in Plymouth in 1868, Scott was a junior officer in the Royal Navy. As the new century dawned, he felt it unlikely that he would see further advancement in his career. He had a low sense of self-esteem and a reputation for being moody. Some now believe that his naval records were subsequently censored to conceal negative evaluations. Writer Roland Huntford posits that "the Navy regarded him as a dud" and thought the future British hero to be mentally unstable. "Under normal conditions he would never been allowed anywhere near a ship of the line."

Scott's future seemed grim until in 1899 he heard that the RGS was organizing an Antarctic expedition. He knew the RGS president, Sir Clement Markham, and presented himself as the possible leader, never mind that he had no experience or even interest in polar exploration. Markham warmed to the idea. Scott's youthful good looks and deep blue eyes did not hurt his chances. London gossips often noted that Markham seemed to prefer the company of handsome young men to women. Markham not only promoted Scott to the important position but spent much of his tenure at the RGS defending Scott against those who felt he was the wrong person for the task. This debate led to Markham being characterized by others in the society as "an old fool" and "a humbug."

Scott's first Antarctic expedition began in 1901 aboard a specially built ship, the *Discovery*. The fifty-member team was made up primarily of naval officers, men with training and experience for the ocean, but none for travel in the high altitudes and the bitter cold of the southern continent. The men spent the long dark winter of 1902 trapped inside their anchored ship. When the sun finally returned Scott set out with two men, Edward Wilson, a high-spirited artist and doctor, and Ernest Shackleton.

The trio used huskies in the Inuit fashion, but Scott in particular was hampered by sentimentality and lack of skill with them and the dogs began to get sick. Before turning back, the team did reach a new furthest point south, 400 miles from the pole. On the return, their last dog died and the men were forced to haul their heavy sledges. Shackleton then also fell sick. Unable to walk, he had to be pulled in the sledge. Scott resented this and made it clear that he saw Shackleton's physical condition as a kind of moral failure. They did eventually return safely to the ship and after spending yet another winter locked in Antarctica, sailed home to England.

Shackleton's illness and the ill-will between the two men meant that he and Scott would never work together again. The failure of the huskies meant Scott would never again trust using dogs, a decision that would lead to the disasters on his next and most famous expedition.

*

Robert Peary was meanwhile solidifying his plans to finally reach the opposite pole. He had managed to find a group of very wealthy benefactors to bankroll his passion. The modern age of marketing hype was just beginning and Peary made full use of it. His model was the British tea baron Sir Thomas Lipton, who used his own obsession (quite equal to Peary's) to win the America's Cup yacht racing trophy to promote his tea company. Peary convinced a variety of American capitalists that they could similarly promote their products and potentially gain a level of immortality by bankrolling his next expedition. With their help, he built a new ship that he named the *Roosevelt* after the adventurous new president of the United States. He hired the best skipper he could, the Newfoundlander, Bob Bartlett.

The *Roosevelt* headed north in September 1906 under Peary's command. After ramming deep into the Arctic ice, it was finally forced to stop and Peary forged on by sledge. It again proved a very difficult trip. With Matthew Henson leading, they had to find their way around dozens of pressure ridges and open water breaks in the ice.[29] Peary this time made it to within 180 miles of the pole, but again had to turn back without reaching his objective. "I have failed once more," he stated. "I shall never have the chance to win again."

29 I have traveled by ski in the Arctic with renowned Nunavut-based polar guide Matty McNair, a woman who has skied to both the North and South Poles, and I can confirm that in many ways traveling over frozen water in the North is much more difficult than over land in Antarctica. Antarctica has its own challenges (the altitude, for one), but at least the ice and snow are largely flat. The frozen Arctic Ocean is a messy, uneven jumble of huge, jagged chunks of ice, often very difficult to navigate. It is also somewhat unsettling, knowing that it is tidal water, so the ice is not always supported beneath by water. On Frobisher Bay, where we were, the difference between high and low tides can be as much as 11 meters.

The same year as Peary's expedition, Dr. Cook was attempting to gain for himself the credibility necessary to raise money for his own North Pole attempt. He set out to become the first person to climb the tallest mountain in North America, Mt. McKinley (now Denali). He announced that year that he had indeed summited the mountain and as proof released a dramatic photo of himself standing at its peak. The accomplishment was celebrated at the time, but it was eventually proved a fraud. Supposedly taken on top of Denali, the photo was in fact shot on a much smaller and less challenging mountain.

Before the deceit was revealed, both Peary and Cook were feted at the December 15, 1906 meeting of the National Geographic Society. No less a personage than Alexander Graham Bell described Dr. Cook as "one of the few Americans who has explored both extremes of the world and now he has been to the top of it."

Cook and Peary knew of one another's intent to go for the pole and each was determined to be first. In August 1908, Peary and the *Roosevelt* were back in the Arctic with eighty-nine men, including sixty-nine Inuit and 246 howling sled dogs. In February of the next year, the team set out across the broken pack ice. This time, Peary used an innovative technique, sending advance parties ahead to break the trail and leave caches of food for the men on the final push (and the return). Bob Bartlett led the way with three Inuit, Pooadloonah, Ooqueah, and Harrigan, breaking trail for Peary and Henson's group. As they closed in on their destination, Peary told Bartlett his job was done and sent him back toward the ship. This eleventh-hour rejection was contrary to Peary's earlier promise that Bartlett would accompany the explorer to the pole. In all probability, Peary simply did not want to have to share the glory with someone as accomplished as the famed Newfoundland navigator.

Peary was now manically determined to finish the job. If he did, he felt that he would be acclaimed as the greatest explorer in the world. Perhaps the greatest in all of history. If he didn't, he would be relegated to the dustheap of exploration history, and he'd also have to return much of the sponsorship money he'd been offered. With Henson,

Egingwah, Seeglo, Ootah and Ooqueah, Peary struggled forward against the Arctic cold, assured that if they made it he could claim, as he later did, that he was absolutely the first white man to get to the pole and knowing that he alone could accurately determine where they were.

On April 6, 1909, Peary's sextant told him he was there—or did it? His odd behavior both at the pole and on the trip home, together with his undisclosed calculations, led many to question his claim. By sending Bartlett back, Peary had left himself without a navigationally trained companion who could verify his achievement. He was certainly close, but was he ever really there?

Peary certainly convinced himself that he'd made it. Months later, reaching Newfoundland, he sent news of his victory to the world with a telegram reading "Stars and Stripes nailed to Pole." He also sent American President Taft a personal telegram saying "HAVE HONOR TO PLACE NORTH POLE AT YOUR DISPOSAL." Taft, not particularly known for his wit, nonetheless sent back a rather humorous response: "THANKS FOR YOUR GENEROUS OFFER. I DO NOT KNOW EXACTLY WHAT I COULD DO WITH IT." He followed this with some effusive congratulations.

While in St. John's, Peary discovered to his horror that five days earlier Dr. Cook had announced that he had made it to the pole, meaning that every newspaper in North America had already carried banner headlines attributing the heroic achievement to his rival.

In March, 1908, knowing that Peary was still making preparations in New York, Cook had set out for the pole with the support of only two Inuit hunters. He claimed to have reached the North Pole on April 21, 1908. "We are at the top of the world," he claimed. "The flag is flung to the frigid breezes of the North Pole."

Who was there to contradict him? Neither of his Inuit companions could have or would have questioned or been able to corroborate the mathematical correctness of Cook's celestial navigation. When questioned later about their journey, however, the two Inuit said they were never out of sight of the mountains of Axel Helberg

Island—shocking testimony, for it suggests that they and Cook were not only not at the North Pole but nowhere near it.

The small party had a terrible time getting back to land. With food and energy running low, the trio had to camp out for eight months, living like Neanderthals in a butt-ass Arctic cave in the side of a mountain, fighting off ravenous polar bears. When spring finally came, they trekked over 1,000 miles to finally reach a Danish settlement in Greenland. From there, Cook traveled by steamer to Copenhagen and en route announced his singular accomplishment to the world. He was greeted by a giant turnout of press and dignitaries, who showered him with accolades and acclaim.

While receiving raves and gold medals in Denmark, Cook received the news that Peary had also made it to the pole. He was surprisingly sanguine about it, saying "there's honor enough for both of us."

Peary did not share Cook's good nature. Not for a minute did he believe Cook's story. From Nova Scotia, he fired off a telegram to the *New York Times*. "I AM THE ONLY WHITE MAN WHO HAS EVER REACHED THE POLE. DO NOT TROUBLE ABOUT COOK'S STORY. HE HAS SIMPLY HANDED THE PUBLIC A GOLD BRICK. I HAVE HIM NAILED."

The gauntlet was thrown down. The *Times* took up Peary's cause. The *New York Herald* sided with Cook. In Paris, *Le Petit Journal* took no sides but reported the whole imbroglio with relish, illustrating its cover with an image of two fur-clad adventurers fist-fighting over the American flag dug into the North Pole, while bemused penguins looked on. Illustrators were always getting the poles confused, adding penguins to the north and polar bears to the south.

The battle played out in the world's newspapers for many weeks. At first, Cook seemed to be winning in the court of public opinion, even with Peary and his powerful friends continuing to belittle the doctor's claims. Ernest Shackleton weighed in, stating that he found Cook's reported speeds of fifteen nautical miles a day on the ice impossible to believe. He and others usually maxed at 4 miles a day. This issue became even more cloudy after Peary claimed that his team had averaged 25 miles a day.

When Danish explorers such as Peter Freuchen and the celebrated British investigative journalist Philip Gibbs began looking more skeptically into Cook's story, the explorer left by steamer for New York. He was greeted on arrival by either 50,000 (according to his enemies at the *New York Times*) or "hundreds of thousands" (according to his friends at the *Herald*). New York gave him the freedom of the city and 1,200 tuxedoed members and guests of The Explorers Club roared their approval at a dinner of the Waldorf Astoria. The public and most the world's press were still with him. The *Toledo Blade* polled its readers on the polar battle and found that 550 were with Cook, only ten with Peary. The city of St. Louis offered Cook $10,000 for a single speaking engagement.

But the pendulum began to swing against Cook. Peary arranged to have Cook's Inuit assistants cross-examined, gaining their admission that they had never been out of sight of land. Or at least that is what the interpreter claimed they said. Who knows who is telling the truth in this ignoble tale.

For its part, The Explorers Club began to question the veracity of Cook's Mt. McKinley climb. It backed off when Cook threatened to sue but others took up the cause. "Big Ed" Barrill, Cook's guide on the adventure, stated the pair had never climbed above 5,000 feet. He also said he had never been paid his promised fee for leading Cook. Cook countered with good proof that Peary's wealthy supporters had given Barrill money—a bribe, in effect—for these statements.

Peary sat for a very cursory and brief investigation by the National Geographic Society, after which it announced its faith that he and not Cook had been the first man at the pole. Cook and his new assistant, Walter Lonsdale, disappeared into seclusion in Toronto, where Cook appeared to suffer a nervous breakdown.

Cook's lawyer, a man with the colorfully imposing name of H. Wellington Wack, announced that he had evidence that "persons hostile to Cook" (Peary and his cronies, presumably), had laid "one of the most diabolical plots that had been hatched against an explorer or any other man." Wack claimed they tried to poison him in order to steal the records of the Cook expedition.

A desperate Cook attempted to restore his reputation by submitting the records of the expedition to various authorities in Denmark. Unfortunately for him, no one bought his shaky presentation. Explorer Knut Rasmussen, previously a Cook supporter, now called the matter "a scandal" and said the papers submitted were "most impudent . . . no schoolboy could make such calculations. It is a most childish attempt at cheating." Another Danish explorer of the day, Commander Horgaard, bluntly called Cook an imposter.

In New York, the big toys of the Christmas season, Dr. Cook dolls dressed in sealskin parkas driving miniature sleighs, were suddenly unsaleable. The Explorers Club, of which Cook had once been president, voted to kick him out. In just eight months, Cook had plunged from international hero to international pariah. He was vilely described as a "monster of duplicity" and a "monumental faker."

Matthew Henson

As Cook's reputation sank, Peary's grew. Of course, the others who had (or had not) stood on the pole with the leaders got virtually no recognition at all. Ahwelahtea and Etukishook, the two Inuit who had risked their lives for Cook each received a penknife and some matches for their months of labor. Matthew Henson didn't get much more, never mind that he was technically the most important man on his expedition since, unlike Peary, he could drive a dogsled and speak Inuktitut. Obsessed with keeping the glory for himself, Peary began distancing himself from his loyal servant almost from the moment the flag was planted on the "pole." After the pair returned to the United States, Peary virtually cut off all contact between them. "From the moment I declared to Commander Peary that I believed we stood on the Pole, he ceased to be my friend."

Henson, in fact, had a decent claim to have been the very first person to the pole. "I was in the lead that overshot the mark by a couple of miles. We went back then and I could see that my footprints were the first at the spot." It was Henson, not Peary, who unfurled the flag and planted it in the snow.[30] But in the racist climate of the United States in 1909, it was not hard to convince the press and public that a Black man could only have had a very secondary role to play in an expedition with a white leader. It was always Peary who had "discovered" the North Pole, not Peary and Henson, and certainly not Peary, Henson, Egingwah, Seeglo, Ootah and Ooqueah.

Henson was at least able to get a book published, *A Negro Explorer at the North Pole*, and in 1937 he was given membership into The Explorers Club. It took them twenty-eight years to admit him, but still, he was a Black man with full membership status. It was another forty-four years before they would admit the first woman.

*

While Peary and Cook fought over which of them—if either—was first to the North Pole, Amundsen and Scott basked for some time in the adulation given them for their achievements, then both began planning what to do next.

Scott slowly prepared for another assault on Antarctica, only to discover that someone else had stolen a march on him—Ernest Shackleton, his partner (until their falling out) in the last expedition. Over Scott's protests, Shackleton mounted his expedition in 1907. He found it difficult to raise money, but with the little support he did

---

30 Flags, actually. Peary was very keen on flags and had Henson plant the flags of the United States, the Navy League, the Daughters of the American Revolution, the Red Cross, and his Bowdoin College fraternity, Delta Kappa Epsilon, in the ice. Presumably, their tattered remains are still blowing around somewhere up there.

receive, he was able to purchase an old whaling ship with the unfortunate name of the *Nimrod*.[31]

Ernest Shackleton

Shackleton confronted the usual issues of ice navigation as he approached the continent and ended up anchoring the *Nimrod* not where he wanted but in McMurdo Sound. One of the best harbors in Antarctica, it was proprietarily claimed by Scott as his own, adding to his antipathy with Shackleton. McMurdo is now the site of both the United States and New Zealand bases in Antarctica and also the site of the most active volcano on the continent, Mt. Erebus, which some members of the team climbed.

Using Siberian ponies instead of dogs to haul supplies, "The Boss," as his team called Shackleton, headed for the pole along with three companions. They explored a route on the Beardmore Glacier that cut through the mountains. Shackleton used Peary's new technique of sending out advance teams with stores of food that would be left for the main party to pick up. Even these shorter journeys proved to be brutal. Raymond Priestley, a geologist who was on one led by Shackleton's Second-in-Command, Jameson Adams, later described the misery and cold and Adam's response to it. "For three days we marched to a monotonous repetition of blasphemy every few steps from Adams, his favourite being 'Jesus fucking God Almighty.'"

The cold was intense. The ice was dangerous. The ponies proved ineffective. After six weeks of difficult travel, their last pony fell down a deep glacier. From then on, the men were obliged to haul

---

31 Superstitious sailors in the nineteenth century placed a lot of import into the name of their ships. The name *Nimrod* was acceptable back then, as the classic etymology for the word is "great hunter," but after seventy-five years of Bugs Bunny sarcastically referring to weekend warrior Elmer Fudd as a "nimrod," the generally understood meaning of the word today is "doofus."

the sledges. In the usual manner of polar exploration, they began to get on each other's nerves. One wrote that following Shackleton was "like following an old woman. Always panicking." Another confided that he wished one of the team "would fall down a crevasse about 1,000 feet deep," and referred to his companions as "grubscoffing useless beggars." Yet another, cartographer and surgeon Dr. Eric Marshall, called Shackleton "a consummate liar and a practised hypocrite." "By God," wailed Marshall, "I have been a damned fool to trust him. He is incapable of a decent action or thought."

After sixty-nine days of very difficult travel, Shackleton realized they were not carrying enough food to make it to the pole and return safely. On January 9, 1909, at a spot less than 100 miles from their destination, they turned around and headed back. Asked later about his decision, he sensibly said that it was "better to be a live donkey than a dead lion."

One man very happy Shackleton's team didn't make it to pole was Robert Falcon Scott, although the failure of the attempt made it more difficult for him to raise money for his own expedition. It wasn't until news that not one but two explorers—both American—had made it to the North Pole that his opportunity emerged. A wave of British nationalism about the goal of planting the Union Jack at the other end of the earth enabled Scott to finance his expedition. He quickly chartered a ship, assembled a team (again, enthusiastic amateurs, all British), wrangled ponies, and in June 1910 left the docks of Cardiff for Antarctica.

As he sailed down the Atlantic, Scott worried that his rival Shackleton might make another attempt to beat him to the pole. What he did not know was that an even more formidable foe had entered the race.

Roald Amundsen, following his very successful crossing of the Northwest Passage, had been aiming to add another feather to his cap by being the first to the North Pole. He was preparing his new ship, the *Fram* (previously owned by Nansen), for a journey north when he received the shocking news, as Scott had, that both Cook and Peary claimed they had made it to what the latter referred to as the "DOP" (the Damned Old Pole). Amundsen didn't know how to respond to this devastating news, until he ran into his old friend Dr. Cook in Copenhagen. Cook suggested an audacious alternative adventure. "The North Pole is now out of the picture," he said. "Why not try for the South Pole?"

Amundsen was not sure about the ethics of heading south when his commitment both to Nansen and to the Norwegian public had been to go for the North Pole. He also knew that the British considered the South Pole the sole domain of Scott and Shackleton. Furthermore, Scott, already in the South Atlantic, had a good lead on him. Cook, ever the enthusiastic promoter, pooh-poohed these concerns. "Scott doesn't know how to travel with dogs," he told Amundsen. "Scott's overload will hang him. You know that the South Pole will never be reached except by dogs or wings."

On August 9, 1910, Amundsen left Norway and headed south. This raised no alarms as he claimed his intention was to attack the North Pole from the eastern or Alaskan side of the Arctic, which required him to sail around Cape Horn and up the Pacific. In retrospect, this looks more clearly like a ruse, as any attempt to reach the pole from Alaska would be three times further than from the usual set-off point at the northern tip of Ellesmere Island.

In Madeira, Amundsen assembled his team and shocked them all by announcing they were no longer going for the North Pole but were instead heading for the South. He knew he was upsetting his crew, his country, his King, his mentor Nansen, and certainly his fellow explorer Scott by announcing this radical new plan. If he came back having failed to reach his goal it would be in disgrace, so for him was a matter of life or death. Only by winning could he save his reputation. Before leaving Madeira, he sent Scott a courtesy telegram, informing him of his plans. The race was on.

Both the Scott and Amundsen ships battled gales while crossing the Drake Passage en route to the Southern Continent. Both ultimately anchored in McMurdo Sound, with the *Fram* in a spot 60 miles closer to the pole. Both parties overwintered, with Amundsen's team spending the time attending to minute details of the clothing, sledge construction, dog harnesses, and packing needed for fast polar travel, while Scott's team focused more on scientific observations of Antarctica.

Typical of the high-minded scientists in Scott's team, many of whom considered the race to the South Pole crass, was naval surgeon George Murray Levick, who just went off on his own to winter in an ice cave on Cape Adair where he studied the mating habits of Adélie penguins. He ended up writing two books, one for popular consumption, which left out all the juicy bits, and the other, written in Greek to hide its salacious content. The x-rated book described the habits of what Levick called the "hooligan cocks" of the penguin colony, who fucked everything in sight, female or male, injured or healthy, mature or just born, alive or dead. "There seems to be no crime too low for these penguins," he wrote. His report was too indecent for Sir Sidney Harmer, Keeper of Zoology at the British Museum of Natural History, and it went unpublished until 2012.

Undistracted by penguin necrophilia, Amundsen, with four men on skis and fifty-two dogs set off on October 19, 1911, in −46° F weather. Thirteen days later Scott embarked with a much larger, more cumbersome team. He was using ponies, dogs, and motorized sledges. All traveled at different speeds. The motorized sledges broke down in the cold, the ponies died, and the all-British team found it difficult to control the dog teams.

Amundsen's plan, worked out with Cook years ago during the cold nights of the *Belgica* expedition, was to travel with many dogs and light sledges, cold-bloodedly killing the slowest dogs as they traveled to use as food for both the remaining dogs and themselves. The Norwegians had deep affection for their dogs but an even stronger commitment to getting to the pole and back.

It was not easy. At one point the temperature fell to a bone-chilling −68° F. Nonetheless, on December 14, they arrived at their goal, in good health, well-rested, well-nourished, and scurvy-free. They spent a day, made a series of sextant observations to confirm the location, and then began the long trek back, knowing that whatever happened along the way, they had won the last great prize of polar exploration.

Meanwhile, with their motorized sledges broken down, their ponies dead, and their dogs sent back to the coast, Scott's team of five men, not the more conventional and appropriate four, man-hauled 700-pound sledges up the Beardmore Glacier and toward the pole. Unlike the Norwegians, who were wearing Arctic furs, the British were in canvas jackets, which were not warm and did not wick the sweat from their skin, so they were not only always cold, but also always damp.[32]

Scott's team covered 800 miles in seventy-eight days. As they closed in on the pole, they spotted from a distance what appeared to be a dark natural feature—perhaps a rock. As they drew closer, they discovered the awful truth—it was a tent, left by Amundsen, with a Norwegian flag flying above it.

The men were devastated. They had been beaten by thirty-four days. "The worst has happened," wrote Scott. "Great God, this is an awful place, and terrible enough for us to have labored to it, without the reward of priority."

Inside the tent they found a note from Amundsen reading:

Dear Captain Scott,

As you are probably the first to reach this area after us, I will ask you kindly to forward this letter to King Haakon VII. If you can use any of the articles left in the tent, please do not hesitate to do so. With kind regards I wish you a safe return.

Yours truly, Roald Amundsen

---

32 The British have a great fascination for cold climates, but historically they have not been successful at dealing with the challenges. I once worked on a project about an ultra-marathon race in the Yukon that began in −50° C weather. The most favored competitors in the event were a tough team from the famed British SAS Special Forces. They were the fittest, best equipped, and best trained, but the first to abandon the long frigid race. It was ultimately won by a fifty-year-old woman from Colorado.

Feeling patronized by Amundsen, buffeted by snowstorms, plagued by cold weather, frostbite, and bad luck, an utterly depressed Scott headed back with his four companions. It was a devastating journey. The story of Edgar Evans is one of the most unfortunate of this saga. He was the only common seaman of the five (his rank was petty non-commissioned officer; the others were all ranked as fully-commissioned officers and considered gentlemen). Norwegians and Americans had abandoned military hierarchy on exploration expeditions years earlier, but not the British. Evans had to address the others as "Sir" and knew that both Edward Wilson and Lawrence Oakes looked down their noses at him. Evans found sharing the confines of the small tent with his betters psychologically confusing and after being badly injured in a fall into a crevasse, he was the first of the five to die.

Some days later, the men were trapped in their tent by a raging blizzard. Oates, in excruciating pain from frostbite, told Scott, "I'm just going outside. I may be some time." He pushed his way out of the tent and was never seen again. A few days later, the remaining three, trapped in their tent without food or fuel, all died. It took nine months before a rescue party from the ship found their frozen bodies inside the snow-covered tent. One of the rescuers tried to describe the expedition but couldn't. "This journey has beggared our language," he said. "No words could express its horror."

England was devastated, most especially Scott's patron Sir Clements Markham of the RGS, who managed to damn the explorer's Irish and Norwegian rivals at the same time as he hero-worshiped Scott: "Even now I can hardly believe it. There has passed away, if it is really true, a very exceptionally noble Englishman. What struck me most was his chivalrous generosity in dealing with contemptible self-seekers such as Shackleton and Amundsen. Very rarely have so many qualities been combined in one man."

*

The poles had been conquered, but the penguins and polar bears had not yet seen their last visitors. Ernest Shackleton spent a few years collecting medals and basking in the glory from his near shot at the South Pole before heading coming up with a new plan that he grandly called his "Imperial Trans-Antarctica Expedition," a crossing from one side of the white continent to the pole and then down the other side. As an adventure, this one would outshine all the others, and is still widely remembered and celebrated today in IMAX films, television documentaries, commemorative Scotch whiskies, submarine search parties, and daring re-enactments.

To recruit a crew for this audacious new expedition, Shackleton placed a small ad in the *Times* as follows: "Men Wanted for hazardous journey, small wages, bitter cold, long months of complete darkness, constant danger, safe return doubtful, honor and recognition in case of success." At least, that is how the oft-told story goes. Legitimate-looking copies of the famous ad, printed on yellowed newsprint, sit in museums and archives and are printed in dozens of books. On the hundredth anniversary of the expedition in 2013, researchers looked closely at the provenance of the ad and declared it a fake. The American spelling of honor in the ad, without the "u" that Shackleton would have used, is one of several indicators of its phoniness.

Regardless of whether he publicized his plans by ad or some other way, Shackleton was besieged with some 5,000 applications. The explorer interviewed the potential candidates eccentrically, asking them, for instance, if they could sing. Sometimes, he made immediate hiring decisions just because he liked the look of the applicant. Through these methods he found Frank Worsley, an extremely good navigator and a man who, considering how things turned out proved to be a lifesaver. In the end Shackleton took all the glory, but New Zealand sailor Frank Worsley was the man who deserved much of it.

The team was set to depart in the fall of 1914, just as Britain entered the Great War. Shackleton and his men offered to abort the mission and volunteer themselves and their ship to the fight on the continent. At the last moment, the first lord of the Admiralty, Winston Churchill, magnanimously told them that their grand expedition was too important, that England could manage without them, and that they should proceed south.

Shackleton's ship, the *Endurance*, sailed on October 26, 1914. By late November it was deep in the South Atlantic at South Georgia Island. The Norwegian whalers told them the Antarctic ice was more extreme than they had ever seen it and highly recommended against heading further south. But since when have British polar explorers looked to Scandinavians for advice? Shackleton ignored their concerns and the advice of Captain Worsley and continued sailing into the icepack—a ludicrous decision, in the eyes of some historians. Pushing deeper south, the *Endurance* by January was caught in the ice of the Weddell Sea. By October, the ship was being crushed. The men removed everything they could and abandoned the vessel. On November 21, she sank, providing their official photographer, Frank Hurley, the opportunity to take some of the most dramatic photographs ever of a failed exploratory expedition.[33]

The story of the *Endurance* is another classic in the British genre of heroic, glorious failure. Sir John Franklin, the Charge of the Light Brigade, the Boer War, Robert Falcon Scott, the battle of the Somme, the Shackleton expedition, Mallory and Irvine's attempt to climb Mt. Everest, the defeat and evacuation at Dunkirk—all unmitigated disasters, yet all spun into stories of pluck, courage, and brave British manhood.

Regardless, it is a story of astounding perseverance. For two months, the men lived on an open ice floe. Finally, Shackleton determined they should attempt to drag their 1,000-pound lifeboats across the ice. Shackleton could be an egalitarian, inspiring leader. The men nicknamed him "The Boss" not because they hated him but because they loved him. Other times, however, he could become autocratic. When the ship's carpenter, Harry "Chippy" McNish, complained that they

---

33 Over a hundred years later, in March 2022, a complex expedition led to the discovery of the shipwreck 10,000 feet underwater in the Weddell Sea.

were destroying the lifeboats by dragging them across the ice, The Boss pulled out a revolver and angrily threatened to shoot him for mutiny.

The crew finally made it to the edge of the ice, then conducted a harrowing five-day voyage to Elephant Island, the first of the South Shetland Islands off the Antarctic Peninsula.[34]

Shackleton realized that if they stayed on Elephant Island waiting for possible rescue, they would all most certainly die, so he conceived of what is now considered the all-time most audacious feat in the annals of maritime exploration. He, along with Worsley, the mutinous carpenter McNish, and three others left the rest of the party and made an astounding voyage by sail in the lifeboat James Caird to get help on South Georgia Island, 720 nautical miles away. The men had almost no protection from the cold, rough seas and hurricane-force winds. They all knew that if they missed their tiny target, they would almost certainly be goners. Worsley had to steer by sextant, celestial navigation, and dead reckoning. Somehow, he did it. In wintery mid-May, after sixteen brutal days and nights at sea, they landed at South Georgia. But they were on the west side of the island. Help—a settlement and whaling station—was on the east side.

Although none of its members were mountaineers, the team determined its only salvation was for three of them to climb over the peaks of the island to the other side. Now starving, cold, and weakened from their months of deprivation and their grueling ocean voyage, the arduous climb through the steep mountains proved to be the most difficult leg of their disastrous expedition.

The crossing of South Georgia is also, from our armchair perspective, the most interesting. It is one of the most extreme examples of a widely experienced phenomenon of explorers, sailors, lost airmen and others who believe that in their worst moments of duress, they have a spirit or guardian angel traveling with them.

---

34 I have explored Elephant Island and its neighbor Deception Island. They are bleak, grim places. Deception does have the advantage of having a volcano, which slightly warms the sand and rock. Elephant has nothing but a large bay that is popular as a mating ground for southern right whales.

"Boss, I had a curious feeling on the march that there was another person with us," confessed Worsley. Tom Crean separately reported the same delusion. Shackleton was frightened by the weird feeling, but secretly concurred. "It seemed to me often that we were four, not three."

While Shackleton resisted discussion of the otherworldly subject a reporter for the *Daily Telegraph* described a conversation with the explorer:

"In your book you speak of a Fourth Presence."

He nodded his head.

"Do you care to speak about that?"

At once he was restless and ill at ease. "No," he said. "None of us cares to speak about that. There are some things that never should be spoken of. Almost to hint about them comes perilously close to sacrilege. This experience was eminently one of those things."

Other explorers have been equally reticent about reporting the strange phenomena, but it happens with uncanny regularity. Joshua Slocum, the extraordinary sailor who sailed alone around the world from 1895 to 1898, wrote of one of the most difficult moments of his voyage in his wonderful and very popular book. He was incapacitated after eating a gift given to him in the Azores of unripe plums and over-ripe cheese. As he was lying in agony on the cabin floor, his thirty-six-foot sloop was hit by a major North Atlantic squall.

"I became delirious," wrote Slocum. "When I came to from my swoon, I realized that the sloop was plunging into a heavy sea, and looking out the companionway, to my amazement I saw a tall man at the helm. His rigid hand, grasping the spokes of the wheel, held them as in a vise. 'I have come to aid you. Lie quiet . . . and I will guide your ship tonight.'"

Slocum was mystified by the phantom helmsman, but he felt "truly grateful to the strange sailor of the night," who apparently steered the boat all night through the storm.

Sandy Wollaston, a British explorer active in Shackleton's time, was as reluctant as his Antarctic counterpart to discuss the strange arrival of a mysterious spectral guide on his adventures deep in the mountains of New Guinea. Alone, and beset by rainstorms, high altitude, bugs, heat, and fog, Wollaston was in rough shape but reported the presence of "another white man" guiding him through the jungle. Every time he topped another ridge, he said, the man was going over a further one. Every time he rounded the bend of a path, the man was disappearing around the next. "Was he really a stranger?" asked Wollaston, who was unable to answer his question.

In 1933, mountaineers Eric Shipton and Frank Smythe were attempting the first ascent of Mt. Everest, when they both began to suffer from the effects of high altitude, lack of oxygen, sleep deprivation, and lack of food. Both became convinced that there was a "third man" climbing with them. Separated from Shipton, Smythe decided that he should have something to eat to build up some energy. He took a slab of Kendal mint cake from his pack and carefully divided it in half to feed the imaginary companion who was with him.

Shipton reported a similar sensation. "All the time I was climbing alone," he later wrote, "I had the strong feeling that I was accompanied by a second person. This feeling was so strong that it completely eliminated all loneliness I might otherwise have felt. It even sensed that I was tied to my 'companion' by a rope, and that if I slipped 'he' would hold me."

The Waste Land, probably the most famous poem of the twentieth century, was inspired by the story of Shackleton's phantom companion. T. S. Eliot wrote:

Who is the third who walks always beside you?

When I count, there are only you and I together

But when I look ahead up the white road

There is always another walking beside you.

Eliot stated that these lines in the poem were inspired from his reading of the Shackleton party's experiences. He used the word "third," which led to the phenomenon being called the "Third Man Factor," which is also the title of a book about the subject by John Geiger. The number is not necessarily three—it simply refers to an additional imaginary person perceived to exist in a period of stress. It happens in different kinds of circumstances. Children who have suffered trauma often create an "imaginary friend" to ease their troubles.

Some posit that these hallucinatory visions show the origins of a belief in God and angels. All the major monotheistic religions sprouted from the tough, hard deserts of the Middle East. In situations at least as difficult to those of the explorers of the 1800–1940 period, more than 5,000 religious hermits retreated to the wilderness in the first years of Christianity. Were these experiences the cauldron from which a belief in God, in Jesus, and in guardian angels was formed? Shackleton didn't want to explore these thoughts. As he told the reporter, "There are some things that should never be spoken of."

Ernest Shackleton and his two partners did make it to the whaling station. They were met by utterly incredulous whalers, who could barely believe their amazing story. An expedition was organized to pick up the men on the other side of the island, and another to pick up the rest still on Elephant Island. They all eventually returned to England, where Shackleton was wildly acclaimed, heralded as the latest champion in the so-called "heroic age of exploration."

On their return, many of his crew, even though they had just suffered through the most hellish of ordeals in Antarctica, immediately signed up to fight in the WWI trenches of the Western Front in France and Belgium. Many, within months, were dead.

*

For years after his claim of "discovery" of the North Pole, Robert Peary basked in the glow of hero worship. But always unsettled by the Cook affair (and perhaps by details of his dash to the pole that he never made public), Peary decided he needed more recognition. He had received the imprimatur of the National Geographic Society, which sounds more official than it is. The society was then (and largely remains) a magazine publishing company, its goal the same as all others—to sell magazines. Editor Gilbert Grosvenor was a close friend of Peary's and did everything he could to throw his weight behind the explorer and have him celebrated in articles in the famous, yellow-trimmed journal. Others were not so convinced. Congressman Robert Macon denounced Peary as "a fake, pure and simple." The US Navy, petitioned by Peary for a major promotion (and thus a pension), was highly suspicious of some aspects of the polar expedition, but eventually, weary of the kerfuffle, promoted him to the rank of Rear Admiral. Peary dumped the rear part and for the rest of his life styled himself as Admiral Peary.

In 1916, Congressman Henry Hegelsen of North Dakota uncovered the very damning secret report the Navy had made on Peary's expedition and he read much of it into the Congressional Record. Peary survived this new attack, but it became the basis for several revisionist books about the Peary legend. The controversy continued until 1973, when Dennis Rawlins, a noted American astronomer and professor of physics, seemed to settle the issue with a dispassionate, highly detailed, mathematical analysis of the trips of Cook and Peary. His conclusion? Both men were more-or-less charlatans. Neither of them made it to the North Pole.

Of course, both explorers were long dead by then. Peary died on February 20, 1920. He was buried with full military honors in Arlington cemetery. His gravestone still reads "Discoverer of North Pole."

Cook's later life was considerably less charmed. For several years he toured the vaudeville circuit, sharing the stage with magicians and exotic dancers. He spun his Arctic tale and encouraged the audience to hiss whenever he mentioned the name "Peary." After that act grew stale, he joined the Texas oil boom of the early 1920s, starting two questionable companies, the first called the Texas Eagle Oil Company and the second known as the Petroleum Producers Association.

In 1923, he was charged as a swindler in a stock fraud very similar to the kind of scheme Charles Ponzi had devised only two years earlier. His messy past did not help him when it came time for sentencing. The judge told him, "Now, Cook, you may stand up. This is one of those times when your peculiar and persuasive personality fails you, doesn't it?" The tough judge then sentenced the ex-explorer to fourteen years and nine months in Leavenworth Penitentiary.

Since the United States, under newly appointed drug czar Harry Anslinger, was embroiled in a war on marijuana, opiates, and cocaine that primarily targeted jazz musicians and the doctors who still prescribed the newly illegal drugs, Leavenworth had many doctors inside its grey walls. Since Dr. Cook was the only one there for something other than what was considered medical malpractice, he was appointed prison doctor. He spent much of his time dealing with the anemia he called "prison pallor" with the same regimen of diet and exercise he had developed in the Antarctic and Arctic.

Cook refused to let family or friends see him in prison. In 1926, however, he did agree to see a visitor from the past. Roald Amundsen, now on a speaking tour of North America, took a detour to Kansas to see his old partner from Antarctica.

"I want you to know," Amundsen told him, "Even if all the world goes against you, that I believe in you as a man."

Like Cook, Amundsen had been bruised by some of the response to his explorations—in his case, by the vicious sniping by the British press that claimed he had used deception to beat Scott to the South Pole. (He later called the British "a race of very bad losers.") He had also been hit by major personal financial difficulties following the trip.

"Our lot has been a hard one," he told Cook in French, so that the Kansas jailers could not eavesdrop. "From the depths of poverty to the heights of glory. From brief spells of hard-earned success to the scourge of condemnation. I have wondered for years how you stood it. I have had the same, with perhaps not so much of the knife in it, but with quite as much of the pain of envy."

Later, the press asked Amundsen about his jailhouse visit with Cook. "To me he was always a genius," said the Norwegian. "Cook was the finest traveler I ever saw."

Many, myself included, consider Amundsen to be the greatest explorer ever (or probably second-greatest—see the epilogue). In the spring of 1926, he and sixteen others (including American adventurer Lincoln Ellsworth, wearing, of all things, Wyatt Earp's wedding ring) took off on the dirigible *Norge*, again aimed at the North Pole. The designer and pilot of the airship was an Italian named Umberto Nobile, who steered it with a yapping little dog in his lap. Amundsen considered Nobile to be a pompous and reckless fop, but the *Norge* was expertly piloted to a spot where it could hover for long enough for the team to drop Italian, Norwegian and American flags on the pole.

Only three days earlier, American pilot Richard Byrd had returned to base from a flight in a trimotor monoplane in which he claimed to have flown directly over the pole. He, too, received a huge amount of adulatory press coverage for his trip. Sceptics, however, soon began to also question his claim. His log of the flight had strange erasures and changes of the sextant data, and an independent analysis of his fuel consumption seemed to show that he had missed the target by many miles. If neither Peary, Cook, nor Byrd had made it to the pole, notwithstanding their bold claims, then Amundsen was indeed the first not only to the South Pole, but also the North.

Amundsen got his share of acclaim, but as is the case with theatrical or literary reviews, the pleasure of receiving the good ones does not compensate for the sting of the bad. The British continued their anti-Amundsen drumbeat. Italian dictator Benito Mussolini excoriated him for having slagged Nobile's character (and, by association, Italy's). Perhaps, as well, Amundsen was succumbing to the polar madness that had afflicted so many others in the north. Even his hero, Fridtjof Nansen, thought something had gone wrong with him. "My impression is that he has entirely lost his balance," wrote Nansen to the president of the RGS. "I think there are various unmistakable signs of some kind of insanity."

The "Last Viking," now fifty-five, ignored the naysayers. He yearned to return to the north. "Oh, if you only knew how wonderful it is up there," he told an Italian journalist. "That is where I want to die, and I wish death would come to me in a chivalrous way."

He got his wish. In May 1928, he heard that Nobile, in another airship, had gone again for the North Pole and on its return had crashed on the ice north of the Svalbard archipelago. Amundsen impetuously jumped in a flying boat to head out over the North Atlantic to search for the Italians. He was never seen again. The Arctic again was proving itself to be, in Lincoln Ellsworth's words, "the Kingdom of Death."

CHAPTER 5

THE LOST CITIES OF
LATIN AMERICA

The northern Canadian barrens are mostly dull and monochrome. The Sahara Desert is a vast, never-ending sea of sand dunes. Britain is geographically bland and if you believe explorer John Speke, Africa is "one senseless map of sameness." Latin America, by contrast, is a delicious, crazy jambalaya. The southern end of Central America has more biodiversity than anywhere else on earth. Peru, alone, has just about everything. Geographers have determined there are thirty-four different climate zones on earth. Amazingly, twenty of them can be found within the borders of Peru, along with a fabulous geographic stew of 20,000-foot mountains, giant glaciers, the world's deepest canyon (twice as deep as the Grand Canyon), the world's biggest river, its driest desert, and a good chunk of the world's largest, most intense jungle—Amazonia. An explorer's paradise.

Latin America also has great mysteries. Sir Walter Raleigh, Queen Elizabeth's favorite explorer, went out on a huge, massively financed expedition to find the fabled city of El Dorado, which he thought he would find in Venezuela. He didn't find it and returned home to be executed (for unrelated reasons), but the legend and lure of lost cities bursting with golden treasure and dusty mummies, protected by ancient curses and dripping with the blood of ritually sacrificed virgins, continue to enthrall readers and explorers to the present day.

Early in the nineteenth century, a New Yorker named John Lloyd Stephens became obsessed with the idea of searching for the lost cities of Latin America. He managed to get himself an appointment as American ambassador to the short-lived Federal Republic of Central America and then used that opportunity to bugger off from his office in 1840–1841 to explore the wilderness rainforest that today straddles the border of Honduras and Guatemala.

Unlike Raleigh, Stephens found what he was looking for—a vast, sprawling city of pyramids and temples hidden in the jungle. The structures, covered in hieroglyphic writing, were clearly the creation of a civilization as advanced as any in Old World antiquity. His book about his explorations, one of the biggest nonfiction bestsellers of the entire nineteenth century, transformed public opinion regarding the indigenous people of the Americas. Even to prejudiced minds of that era, it was clear that the Mayans who had created the massive city of Copán were not savages, the word then most often used to slag the Americas' first inhabitants.

In the manner for which Americans are known around the world, Stephens convinced the owner of the land housing the lost city to sell it to him for a measly $50. He proposed that he would tear it apart, put all the stones and statues on barges and tow it back to the United States, where he would reassemble it as a tourist attraction. Perhaps, one imagines, in Orlando. His grand scheme came to naught, and the ancient city disappeared back into the jungle, hidden and overrun by trees, vines and creepers, populated only by monkeys, birds and snakes.

In a world filled with weird and wacky religions, the Church of Latter Day Saints, also known as The Mormons, is among the wackiest. The church is convinced that the ancient cities of Central America prove that the Mayans must be descended from the Lamanites, one of the lost tribes of Israel. They supposedly emigrated from the Middle East to Central America in around 600 BC, and were later visited by Jesus Christ, who converted them to Christianity. The Mormons sent several archeological and exploratory missions to Central America to prove this ridiculous theory. When the archeologists returned without proof and now expressed doubt about this dogma, they were excommunicated.

As the Honduran ruins were reclaimed by the jungle, a new legend was born. Another city, known as the *Ciudad Blanca*, or the "Lost City of the Monkey God," was said to exist even deeper in the wilderness. For over 100 years, it was thought to be mere fiction. Amazingly, in 2012, in a very remote region of La Mosquitia, completely hidden by one of the most impenetrable tropical forests on earth, an archeological team using Light Detection and Ranging technology (LIDAR) discovered the remains of the mythical city.

While the legend of *Ciudad Blanca* excited wannabe explorers throughout the late nineteenth and early twentieth century, it was massively eclipsed by an astounding discovery (or recovery) in 1911 by Hiram Bingham III, a man who personifies more than any other the popular perception of an explorer. Indeed, he was the model for the most famous fictional explorer of all time, Indiana Jones.

His grandfather, Hiram Bingham, was also an iconic model—in his case for the uptight, holier-than-thou missionary admired by some in the nineteenth century and loathed by others. The first Hiram's territory was Hawaii, where he built schools

Hiram Bingham

and churches and tried to convert the locals to his brand of fire-and-brimstone Christianity. Hiram made no bones about his revulsion toward the "almost naked savages" of Hawaii, with their "appalling, swarthy, sunburnt skins." He did everything he could to destroy Hawaiian traditions and culture—particularly surfing and hula-dancing. He made some converts, but he was mostly hated, not only by Hawaiians, but also by many of the American settlers to the islands. When he had to return to the United States for a period, the settlers were polled by the board of commissioners of the missionary service as to whether they would like to see him back. The answer was a resounding "No." Hiram became the model for the inflexible missionary played by Max Von Sydow in the movie *Hawaii* that was based on James Michener's best-selling book of the same name.

Hiram sired Hiram II, father of the man we are interested in, Hiram III. The odd attachment to the name Hiram would be continued for another generation. Hiram IV did more for humanity than all the previous three combined, spiriting many French Jews including painter Marc Chagall and philosopher Hannah Arendt out of Nazi-occupied Vichy France during WWII. Hiram IV ended the tradition, siring eleven children, none of whom, thankfully, were named Hiram.

Hiram II was another uptight missionary, his beat, worked much less successfully than his father's, being the Gilbert Islands (now Kiribati). Hiram III's mother was pregnant with him when she and Hiram II left the Gilberts in 1875, heading back for Hawaii. One of Hiram III's biographers, Mark Adams writes of his parents: "judging from their photograph, they rival his grandparents as the least fun couple ever to sail the South Seas."[35]

Hiram III's Calvinist father put great stock in these lovely words from Proverbs 23: 13–14: "Withhold not correction from thy child: for if thou beatest him with the rod, he shall not die. Thou shalt beat him with the rod, and shalt deliver his soul from hell." Not surprisingly, Hiram III was keen to get away from rod-bearing papa. He sailed from Hawaii to America when he was sixteen. Able to work his way into the posh prep school Phillips Academy, he advanced to Yale University, the institution that was central to both his later fame and infamy as a South American explorer.

In 1906, Bingham ran into a moderately renowned explorer, later denounced as a scoundrel, named Alexander Hamilton Rice. The two men determined to make an expedition together to trace the great revolutionary leader Simon Bolivar's footsteps across Venezuela and Colombia. Bingham decked himself like the caricature of an explorer one sees in *New Yorker* cartoons: pith helmet, safari suit, and riding boots, armed with both a Winchester and a revolver. Had he shown up at The Explorers Club in this get-up, there would be no need to show his membership card. The cowed receptionist would have let him right in.

---

35 Missionary work, in some ways the closest racket there is to exploring, is still a big thing in the South Pacific. In my travels in Micronesia, Tonga, and Vanuatu, I have encountered many missionaries, usually Seventh Day Adventists, recognizable in their standard uniform of black shoes and pants, short-sleeved white shirt, and skinny black tie, with Bible in hand. They even made a few spectacularly unsuccessful attempts to convert me in remote, grass-roofed island airport waiting areas, while they and I waited for our planes.

The South Americans they met were less impressed. Indeed, they were totally suspicious of the gun-toting, armed-to-the-teeth *Yanquis.* Bingham imperiously dismissed their concerns, but in truth they were well-founded. American military authorities had previously used archeologists as spies. The British Foreign Office used explorers such as Gertrude Bell, St. John Philby, and Percy Fawcett as spies in North Africa and the Middle East. In Latin America, it was the height of the United States' application of the Monroe Doctrine by gunboat diplomacy. President Theodore Roosevelt had recently denigrated Venezuela's President Cipriano Castro, who South Americans considered "The Lion of the Andes," as "an unspeakably villainous little monkey." It was hardly surprising the locals thought Bingham and Rice must be there to foment a revolution or coup.

When it came to relations with the Indigenous people and locals, the duo mostly acted like dipshits. At one point they abandoned two of their guides, leaving them without shelter, fire, or food. On several occasions at closed taverns Bingham whipped out his guns, demanding at gunpoint to be fed. Once, he even did a runner—charged out without paying the innkeeper over some imagined slight. Later in Colombia, Rice left Bingham behind, "owing to his conduct," and began describing him as "incompetent."

Abandoned by his exploration partner, Bingham was so out-of-sorts that he turned down an invitation to visit the hidden Lake Guativita, source of the original legend of El Dorado, where to honor the gods, the Incan king regularly was covered in gold dust and cleansed of it by plunging into the lake. Hundreds of conquistadors and explorers had gone looking for El Dorado, and now Bingham, offered a look, couldn't be bothered to check it out. Although he would later modify his views, at this point he was contemptuous of the original inhabitants of South America, calling them a "backward race" that made it easy to understand how the "brave, bigoted, courageous" conquistadors had overwhelmed them (an interesting trio of adjectives).

On his return to the good old USA, he turned his story into his first book. It was generally well received, although mocked by the *New York Times* for the author's tendency to exaggerate the dangers he had experienced in the wilds of South America. The book led to him receiving a fellowship in the RGS of which he was fiercely proud. For the rest of his life, he insisted that his name be accompanied by the letters FRGS.

He also, finally, received an offer from Yale to work as a lecturer on South America. The course he cooked up has been described as "one part history, one part geography, one part jingoism." Other professors at the Ivy League school began to question his academic gravitas when they saw exam questions he was coming up with such as, "What Spanish American countries offer 1) excellent, 2) fair, 3) poor opportunities for (a) a Mining Engineer, (b) a Soldier of Fortune, (c) a Capitalist, (d) an average Yale graduate with good health and a capital of $5,000?"

Bingham now had a measure of status and stability and also wealth, for he had married the heir to the Tiffany fortune. But he yearned for more. The world was still obsessed with exploration at the dawn of the twentieth century. Kipling had just penned "The Explorer," with the command:

> Something hidden. Go and find it
> Go and look behind the Ranges
> Something lost behind the Ranges.
> Lost and waiting for you. Go!

Sir Arthur Conan Doyle had set aside his Sherlock Holmes mysteries for a while to write *The Lost World*, a best-selling adventure about four explorers in deepest South America. Peary, Cook, Amundsen, Scott, and Shackleton were all making headlines with their forays to the poles. Bingham was convinced he could find equal fame for himself among the ancient Inca ruins of Peru. Ignoring his wife's plea, "do not form the habit of living your life without me," he left her and his five sons for a second trip to Peru.

This time, Bingham sailed to Argentina and headed north by train and eight-horse stagecoach. In Bolivia, he had a unique interlude, meeting up with "two rough-looking Anglo-Saxons," who he discovered were accomplices of the famed American desperados Butch Cassidy and the Sundance Kid. The outlaws had just been shot by Bolivian soldiers, and Bingham bought one of the dead men's mules. He was impressed with the animal, saying, "when his former owner had had the benefit of the mule's fleet legs and his splendid lungs, there was no question of his being caught by the Bolivian soldiery."

Bingham made it to Cusco, the once-magnificent, gold-plated Inca capital where 400 years earlier Indians had watched with tears streaming down their faces as Spanish explorers looted and destroyed their city. He then pushed further north into the mountains to begin his search for other lost cities, real or imagined. He climbed up trails so steep that at times he had to crawl "on all fours . . . hanging on almost by our eyelids." Bingham and a team of indentured Indian guides made it to the Incan ruin of Choquequirau, the "Cradle of Gold." Bingham thought he might still find gold there, but he was too late. By the 1800s, treasure hunters had ripped the site apart with pickaxes. The area's local prefect, J.J. Nuñez, had followed them to complete the looting of the site, using dynamite to smash down its walls. If there ever had been gold there, it was now gone.

Bingham settled for ancient bones. North American and European scientists were always interested in seeing native skeletal remains. Their idea was to compare them with those of whites to prove theories of racial superiority. Bingham considered himself an academic, but he was not an anthropologist and did not act like one. Hunting for bones to take back to Yale, he dug up skeletons and skulls willy-nilly, often breaking them in the process and storing them without documentation. His native helpers were shocked by his treatment of their ancestors' remains. An amused and supercilious Bingham wrote that "they had been in doubt as to the object of our expedition up to that point, but all doubts then vanished and they decided we had come there to commune with the spirits of the departed Incas."

Back at Yale, the bones did capture the attention of the university's antiquities department. Bingham's star was rising, but it was nowhere near what he felt might be its potential zenith. For two years he stayed home, taught at Yale, and raised his boys. Then the exploring bug bit again. He announced in 1911 a much more ambitious expedition back to the Andes, this one with a team of scientific assistants, financed not just from his wife's Tiffany fortune, but from sponsors including the Winchester Arms Company (for he again intended to take boomsticks to South America), the Eastman Kodak Company, the United Fruit Company, and *Harper's* magazine.

Bingham tantalized the press with the prospect of this time really finding the "lost cities" of the Incas. And what of Inca gold, mummies, and buried treasure, asked the reporters? "Oh no," said Bingham. "Should anything be found in that line, it would become the property of the Peruvian government." It was an accurate and noble sentiment, but when Bingham got to the ruins, he promptly broke it. He knew the law; he just didn't follow it.

While heading toward the high mountains in the search for Incan cities, Bingham stumbled on a discovery perhaps even more monumental than the one that would make him famous—a set of bones that he thought might be dated at over 40,000 years old—long before the Incas. It was potentially a very significant discovery but an academically dangerous one. Much of the "discovery" story of pre-Columbian America was based on the notion that the natives had only been around for at most a few thousand years. Therefore, it was argued, Europeans had every right to replace this transient, adolescent society with their own. If these bones suggested people had been living in the Americas for 40,000 years, it shook this belief to its core. As one anthropologist said, "the question of early man in America became virtually taboo, and no anthropologist, or for that matter geologist or paleontologist, desirous of a successful career would tempt the fate of ostracism by intimating that he had discovered indications of a respectable antiquity for the Indian."

Fortunately for Bingham's reputation, if not the advancement of science, he very quickly became distracted by an uncontroversial find that no-one could argue with, one that would set him up for life and make his reputation as one of the most celebrated explorers of his time. He left the 40,000-year-old bones behind.

He and his team headed up the jungle valleys, following white-water rivers roiling with meltwater from the snow-covered peaks. The big find was about to happen, but not before the explorers experienced a terrible accident. An Indian boy (his name was never recorded) who was carrying the expedition's surveying instrument, a heavy and awkwardly shaped alidade, slipped while crossing a log over a river and was swept away downstream. Two of Bingham's American associates went down the riverbank to search for him and, according to the story they told Bingham, didn't find him but did find his poncho and the alidade, lodged against a rock.

That was the story Bingham later repeated, briefly, in his journal. In it he blamed the boy for "disobeying" orders about crossing the log and grumbled that his associate "has been trying for two days to repair the damage to his alidade."

Other Indians on the trip would later report a much different story. They claimed that the North Americans had ordered the boy to go first across the log to test how slippery it was, and that they had found his drowned body, but not wanting to slow the expedition down, had removed the instrument and pushed his body back into the rushing water.

Bingham never mentioned the incident again. He did not report the death to the boy's family. One of Bingham's own sons, in his somewhat critical biography of his explorer-father, wrote that he perhaps "felt Indians were more expendable than surveying instruments, and the instruments, though damaged, were saved."

Only two days later, on July 24, a hungover tavern-owner named Melchior Arteaga offered to show Bingham some interesting ruins. Bringing along a young Peruvian soldier for protection, the trio began to clamber up a mountain slope. "A good part of the distance we went on all fours, sometimes holding on by our fingernails," wrote Bingham. His guide continually warned the explorer to be careful about where he put his hands. The vines he was clinging to, he kept reminding him, might hide deadly vipers.

The river, and perhaps the dead boy's corpse, were now 2,000 feet below them. Finally, to Bingham's great surprise, they arrived at a remote clearing where an equally surprised Indian family was farming. The family, the Richartes, were frightened by the six-foot four-inch gringo, worried that he was some sort of government tax collector or army recruiter. Once assured that he was not, they offered up a lunch of water and yams. Wanting to sleep off his hangover, Artega enlisted the Richartes' eight-year-old boy to lead Bingham up the rest of the way.

After another hour of intense climbing, Bingham's young barefoot guide turned a corner, threw his arm out and presented an extraordinary sight that took away what was left of the explorer's breath. It was the lost city of the Incas—Machu Picchu, a site described by everyone who sees it with adjectives like majestic, sublime, magnificent, and utterly impossibly magical. It was an incredible moment for Hiram Bingham III. Today, over 800,000 people a year visit Machu Picchu, but the thrill of discovery belongs particularly to Bingham.[36]

With night coming on, Bingham had little time to linger on his first visit to Machu Pichu. He made the difficult descent, possibly experiencing the counter-intuitive phenomenon that it is often more complicated climbing down a mountain than it is going up. It took him a while to grasp the magnitude of the find he had just made. He continued searching for other Incan ruins and even went off on a side trip to try to climb the "virgin peak" of Coropuna. He knew he had a rival to be first to its peak, the American alpinist Annie S. Peck. He dismissed Peck as "a hard-faced, sharp tongued old maid of the typical New England type" and felt it his duty while in Peru to beat her to the top of the 6,377-meter volcano, long considered sacred by the Incas.

Once he had Coropuna under his belt, Bingham went off on another historical detour, exploring the story of Tupac Amuru, one of the last

---

36 I have experienced something close to first discovery on a couple of occasions. It is a unique thrill. A few years ago, I was deep in Colombia on the remote Rio Caño Cristales, a rainbow-hued river—colored yellow, green, blue, black, and mostly bright red, only mapped in 1969. On the expedition, I learned of a possibly even more unique find. Our Colombian guide mentioned that some ancient petroglyphs had been found on a cliff some distance away in the jungle. Our guide had not seen them. No-one had, other than a local adventurer, Walther Ramos, and a couple of his pals. I was traveling with my then twenty-six-year-old daughter. Ramos agreed to take us the next morning. We met before dawn and climbed into a long dugout canoe with an outboard on the back. As we were about to leave a mutt came skittering down the bank, jumped in and took up a position at the very bow of the boat, staring intently ahead like Leo in *Titanic*. We roared down the Guayabera River for about an hour accompanied by macaws and spectacular Peruvian stinkbirds. As we slowed and nosed on to a tiny sandbank on the shore, a spot indistinguishable to me from anywhere else on the wilderness river, the dog leapt from the boat and tore into the jungle. We climbed the steep hill for a half hour, using the vines, like Bingham, to pull ourselves forward, until coming to the site, a small cliff covered with painted images of women, caimans, and birds. It was an inspirational sensation to be able to uncover something that few people had seen before, or at least not for many, many years.

of the Inca emperors, who fought against the invading conquistadors and was eventually brutally executed by the vicious Spaniards.

It was only when Bingham got his photographs of Machu Picchu developed that he began to realize the momentousness of his discovery. When he showed them to his Peruvian hosts, "they were struck dumb with wonder and astonishment. They could not understand how it was possible that they should have passed so close to Machu Picchu every year of their lives since the river road was opened without knowing what was there."

Bingham had been careful not to photograph a piece of graffiti he had seen on one of the walls of Machu Picchu. He did investigate it, however, and found that the painted inscription "Lizarraga 1902" had been put there by a local farmer who had apparently visited the site nine years earlier. Worried that the graffiti might suggest he was not the person who had "discovered" Machu Picchu, Bingham would have the name carefully scrubbed from the rock on his return to the site a year later.

Bingham's photographs generated even more excitement once he got them back to the United States. The *New York Sun's* headline was typical: "EXPLORERS FIND CITY THAT WAS: WHITE WALLED TOWN OF THE INCAS DISCOVERED IN PERU SNUGGLED UNDER CORNFIELDS. YALE PROFESSOR ASTOUNDED AT BEAUTY OF ARCHITECTURE."

The *New York Times Magazine* pulled out all stops:

> Just now, when we thought there was practically no portion of the Earth's surface still unknown, when the discovery of a single lake or mountain, or the charting of a remote strip of coast line was enough to give a man fame as an explorer, one member of the daredevil explorers' craft has "struck it rich," struck it so dazzling rich, indeed, that all his confreres may be pardoned if they gnash their teeth in chagrin and turn green with envy.

Even the *National Geographic*, which had turned up its nose when offered stories of Bingham's previous expeditions, was jazzed about this one. Editor Gilbert Grosvenor not only commissioned a story from him about his find, with photographs of course, but he offered to help finance a grander expedition the following year. The gang at *National Geographic* also asked Bingham to postulate the history behind Machu Picchu and both they and Yale wanted him to bring back Incan bones and relics that could be put on display in the United States. Their demands would prove the undoing of the explorer.

Not an archeologist or a trained historian, Bingham dreamed up some horseshit designed to make Machu Picchu to appear as important as possible. He theorized that the site was either "the birthplace of the Incas" or "the last home of the Incas." It was neither. His ideas did not seem far-fetched back in the day, but they have in recent years they have been completely dismissed by archeologists as balderdash. Today, the most prominent theory today as to why Machu Picchu was built where it is has to do with the most important, but often forgotten factor in relations between Spanish explorers and conquistadors and the natives of the Americas: disease.

In 1491, before Columbus made his fateful trip across the Atlantic, the population of the Americas was about 75 million. There were 37 million in Mexico and Central America, about 30 million in South America, 5 million in North America and 6 million in the Caribbean. Columbus' ships landed with virulent pathogens of measles, tuberculosis, yellow fever, and other diseases previously unknown in the New World. Most of the sailors on Columbus' ships were largely immune to the diseases (although many, including the famous captain himself, did fall ill on the Atlantic passage). The natives who met them in the New World were defenseless to the new germs.

Exactly how many Indians died across the Americas is hard to quantify, so let's just look at one island where the numbers were recorded. Hispaniola, containing today the countries of Haiti and Dominican Republic, was Columbus' favorite island. He raved that it was "the most beautiful land I have ever seen." In 1492, there were somewhere between half a million and a million people living on the island. By 1508, the Spanish diseases had reduced the number to 60,000. In 1518, the explorers added smallpox to the stew of pestilence served to the natives. By 1542, the number of native Taino Indians on Hispaniola was zero. They were all gone. The Spaniards had to begin importing African slaves to replace the now extinct race as a labor force for their plantations.

This story was repeated in one way or another throughout the Americas. In Peru, the story of Pizarro's brutal war against the Incas is considered the worst genocide in history. How did the relatively small number of conquistadors manage to defeat the Incas? Guns, horses, and armor had something to do with it, but the real answer was disease. "When the Christians were exhausted from war," wrote one of the friars accompanying and blessing the warrior/explorers, "God saw fit to send the Indians smallpox." In North America some British invaders did not wait for God to send smallpox. They took blankets infected with the disease and handed them to the natives as presents.

Smallpox was the worst but by no means the only disease the Incas had to contend with. One that the Incas were particularly paranoid about was leishmaniasis.[37] As the Incan royalty retreated into the Andes to escape from the rapacious Spaniards, they had to find a

---

37 I have come across leishmaniasis myself, fortunately without getting infected, while exploring a remote cave on Mt. Elgon on the border of Kenya and Uganda. There the disease is hosted by hyraxes, small mammals found across Africa. The explorers who discovered the Lost City of the Monkey God in Honduras in 2012 and the writers and photographers who were part of the expedition were also exposed to leishmaniasis and suffered badly from it. As famed immunologist Anthony Fauci told the team, by going into the remote jungle and getting leishmaniasis, "You got a jolt of what it's like for the bottom billion people on earth." With climate warming, the danger is rapidly growing. Increased heat is bringing leishmaniasis to more temperate climates. It has already expanded north into Texas and Oklahoma and is expected to be right across the United States and into southeastern Canada by 2080. It may, by then, also push up the warming slopes of the Andes to Machu Picchu.

location with an elevation high enough to prevent transmission of this devastating disease, but low enough where they could cultivate their crops—particularly coca, the stimulant plant then and now considered a sacrament. The site of Machu Picchu fit the bill exactly. The downside of the spot was that it was so insanely remote and difficult to access—which is the reason it lay empty and hidden for so long after it was abandoned.

Unlike most of the exploratory expeditions of this period, Bingham's were largely free of disease. They were not, however, free of controversy. In his grand expeditions of both 1912, and 1914–1915, Bingham transformed, at least in the eyes of the Peruvians, from being an explorer to being a *ladrón de tumbas*—a *huaqueando* grave robber. Bingham's team was no longer just there to take photos and measurements. It was there to crate up artifacts, pottery, skulls, and skeletons, and steal them away to fill the galleries of Yale's newly built Peabody Museum. The Americans enlisted hundreds of Peruvian Indian laborers to clear the Machu Picchu site of vines and brush, and then to dig for archeological treasures. The Indians were appalled that the *Yanquis* were digging up the bones of their ancestors, but there wasn't much they could do about it. They weren't slaves, as they were being paid (a pittance) for the work, but if they didn't do it, they could be thrown in jail by the Peruvian police.

Some Peruvian authorities were also upset by what was going on at the excavations at the old Inca city. The country's top newspaper, *El Comercio,* asked whether soon Peru would soon "become the only country in the world without Peruvian antiquities." Bingham's team was slagged as "conquistadors with trowels." When the Peruvians discovered that Bingham's team had made more than 200 excavations without a permit, they moved in and confiscated crates of artifacts Bingham had packed to send to Connecticut. Bingham is said to have "exploded with rage" over the actions of the host country. He called for the help of American diplomats and British businessmen to get around the embargo. No slouches when it came to imperialist grandstanding, the British responded appropriately. The president of the British-run Peruvian Corporation bloviated, "in the plainest kind of English, what happened was a disgrace to any country pretending to be at all civilised [sic]," and that if they did not wish to have the world look upon them as savages, they "should clear Yale of the charges and let the expedition continue its work."

The uncowed Peruvians responded by setting a trial date. An inquest was held at which soldiers dramatically pried open the crates, revealing the potshards and bones, and driving Bingham nuts. The subsequent legal battle came down to differing valuations of the value of the artifacts between the American explorers and Peruvian archeologists. Ultimately, Bingham's white skin, fancy titles, university degrees, and club affiliations won the day against the dark-skinned local Latin academics. Bingham had his crates nailed back up and prepared again to try to spirit them out of the country. As a final act of defiance, he bought a secret collection of relics from the mysterious Nazca site (also in Peru, but not Inca-related) and with the help of his British friends smuggled all this loot out of the country. Knowing that his name could be a red flag at the border, Bingham had the crates addressed to a J. P. Simmons. "It seems to me a strange thing to do, to consign the goods to a fictitious character like J. P. Simmons," he wrote, "but I suppose it was necessary under the circumstances." It isn't really that strange a thing to do. South American cocaine smugglers do it all the time.

Peru may have been mad at Bingham, but the United States was not. Yale loved the relics and filled its museum with them. The *National Geographic* devoted an entire issue of the magazine to Bingham and his Peruvian antiquities. He celebrated his new success by entering politics. In one crazy twenty-four-hour period he simultaneously held the offices of lieutenant-governor and governor of Connecticut while also representing the state in the US Senate (he resigned after one day as governor to become a senator). When the tall, slim, handsome, silver-haired ex-explorer decked out in Tiffany-bought finery arrived, the eyes of the ladies in the gallery were said to have popped. "Did you see the new Senator from Connecticut?" they whispered. "I tell you; he can put his clothes in my trunk."

The political honeymoon was short-lived. After hogging the Senate floor, snootily socializing only with Washington's wealthiest, imperiously correcting his colleagues' pronunciation of foreign words, and breaking the rules by putting a lobbyist on the congressional payroll, the Senate took the extreme step of censuring him, making him one of only nine Senators in history so distinguished. He was voted out in 1932, a victim of Franklin Roosevelt's Democratic landslide. In 1937, his wife divorced him for "cruelty, cold indifference, and an attitude of superiority." He did write another book about his South American adventures, and he returned to Machu Picchu during WWII, to help open the "Hiram Bingham Highway."

The highway brought new visitors to the lost city. One was the revolutionary Che Guevara, on his famous motorcycle trip around South America. To his eyes, the site was an expression of a powerful indigenous America untouched by the conquistadors. He described Machu Picchu as "an arm outstretched out to the future, a stony voice with continental reach that shouts, 'Citizens of Indo-America, reconquer the past!'"

> "Here's the tragedy," deplored Che. "All the ruins were cleaned of underbrush, perfectly studied and described and . . . totally robbed of every object that fell into the hands of the researchers, who triumphantly brought back to their country more than 200 boxes containing invaluable archeological treasures. . . . Bingham is not the culprit, objectively speaking, nor are the North Americans in general. . . . But where can we admire or study the treasures of the indigenous city? The answer is obvious: in the museums of North America."

Two years later, in 1954, Paramount Pictures shot a feature called *Secrets of the Incas*, starring Charlton Heston as an explorer based on Bingham. Heston is arguably Hollywood's all-time stiffest movie star (maybe second stiffest, after Ronald Reagan), and the film, shot on cheesy backlot sets as well as at Machu Picchu, is quite awful, but it was used by Steven Spielberg and George Lucas as inspiration for their parody/homage *Raiders of the Lost Ark*, in which Harrison Ford (a great improvement over Heston) plays the Bingham-inspired lead character, Indiana Jones.

After the death of Bingham in 1957, the legacy of both he and the Yale-Peabody Museum began to suffer. His claim to have "discovered" Machu Picchu came into question. Some Europeans appear to have visited the site before Bingham and the site appears on Peruvian maps dating to 1874. As Paolo Greer, an oddball Alaskan gold prospector and pipeline worker who is considered one of the world experts on the Incas says, "No gringo discovered Machu Picchu. Machu Picchu was never forgotten."

Peru first asked Yale to return the artifacts in 1920. The university refused. In 1960, Peru again began to lobby to have the artifacts Bingham took returned to their country, and again it got nowhere. Unfortunately, the last forty years of the twentieth century were tumultuous in Peru, with coups, revolutions, massive inflation, a war with Ecuador, the Shining Path revolutionary group, and the controversial presidency of the Japanese/Peruvian Alberto Fujimori, to mention a few highlights. Only in the new century did things settle down enough to permit Peru to work seriously at regaining the Bingham treasures. Fujimori went to jail. In 2001, a new and proudly indigenous president, Alejandro Toledo, the first native president, was elected. His wife, Eliane Karp, a French archeologist, took on the cause of getting Peru's cultural heritage sent home.

As far as Yale's lawyers were concerned, the artifacts did not belong to the people of Peru, but to Hiram Bingham and since he was now dead and had passed on the pieces to the museum, Peru had no case. In 2007, Yale and Peru appeared to reach a compromise agreement, with the university promising to send back 380 of the artifacts. But when Peruvian archeologists went to New Haven to look them over, they discovered that many of the prize pieces were moth-eaten, damaged, stolen, or missing, and that human bones from the collection were being used in undergraduate osteology classes. They also learned that the size of the collection was far greater than Yale had admitted, not 5,615 pieces but over 46,000.

Peru felt it had no other choice but to sue the university, which it did in December 2008. Yale, with its massive endowment fund, could afford to fight the lawsuit and it did. Coincidently, its lawyers were simultaneously defending another lawsuit brought by the descendants of the Apache chief Geronimo for the return of the chief's skull, which had been disinterred in 1917 and displayed at Yale's Skull & Bones Society, an exclusive student secret fraternity whose members include both Presidents Bush and many other American muckety-mucks.

By 2008, internet trolling had become a thing. One post by an American about the issue read, "Whatever happened to 'to the victor go the spoils?' If a Peruvian explorer had found a bunch of American artifacts before we were a country and now refused to give them back, that would be fine by me as well. Yale found them. Yale took them. Yale has them. End of story."

Opinions were just as strong in Peru. Mention Bingham's name there and you are likely to hear that "he would have been shot if had come back to Peru." Or that what he did was akin to someone visiting a friend's house and surreptitiously snatching a few souvenirs off the coffee table before leaving.

In 2010, events moved quickly. On October 23, with Yale refusing to budge, the Peruvian government threatened to press criminal charges against the university for "illicit appropriation" of the artifacts. It followed with a letter to President Obama asking him to intercede. On Friday, November 5, Peruvian president Alan Garcia led a demonstration through the streets of Lima. In Cusco, there were similar protests led by people dressed in traditional Inca garb. That same week, runners in the New York City Marathon wore shirts reading "Yale, Return Machu Picchu artifacts to Peru." By November 19, it was over. Yale suddenly and surprisingly capitulated, agreeing to return all the relics, bones, and skeletons Hiram Bingham had collected back to Peru.

*

Machu Picchu was by no means the only tantalizing lost city in Latin America. Another, even more remote and mysterious, was the Lost City of Z.

Percy Fawcett

Percy Fawcett and Theodore Morde, two of our final batshit adventurers, were among the very last of their kind, obsessed independents venturing into the unknown with little more than a machete, a compass, and utter bloody-minded tenacity.

Born in Torquay, Devon in 1867, Percy Fawcett was described as an explorer with "unrivaled powers of endurance." He was a fearless man "of indomitable will" and 'infinite resource" who could "out-walk and out-hike and out-explore anybody else." His ambition was not modest. Regardless of the cost, he planned to find what he called "the great discovery of the century," a lost civilization. The press and public were fascinated by his adventures in the first decades of the twentieth century. The *London Graphic* claimed that "not since the days when Ponce de León crossed unknown Florida to search for the Waters of Perpetual Youth . . . has a more alluring adventure been planned." The *Daily Mail* said his expeditions "captured the imagination of every child who ever dreamed of undiscovered lands." The *Atlanta Constitution* called them "perhaps the most hazardous and certainly the most spectacular adventures ever undertaken by a reputable scientist."

How the newspapers got the idea that he was a "reputable scientist" is a mystery. He was a soldier and, most definitely, an explorer, but he was hardly a scientist. He had what seems to have been the typically horrible childhood of many Victorian explorers, with a dissolute, drunken father, an uncaring mother, a hated British public school (Westminster) replete with canings from the masters and vicious fagging by the older boys. Memories of his youth would trouble him through his life. Although he had no particular interest in becoming a soldier, his mother forced him into it because she "liked the handsome uniforms." The Army sent him to Ceylon, then a British colony, now Sri Lanka, where he was sent on a mission to find a lost city reputed to be in the jungle. Unlike his later and much more difficult forays in South America, he found something: the ruins of Anuradhapura, a city built 2,000 years earlier. He also found what he called "his destiny." He would become a professional (though frequently unpaid, and penurious) explorer.

Fawcett returned to England to undertake a one-year course on exploring then given by the Royal Geographical Society. He treasured his membership in the RGS and carried the course textbook on all his future expeditions. *Hints to Travellers* offered first-aid tips (wounds from arrows or spears ought to have "boiling grease poured into the wound"), surveying skills, anthropological advice ("it is established that some races are inferior to others in volume and complexity of brain, Australians and Africans being in this respect below Europeans"), and guidance on everything from how to make pillows out of mud to how to physically subdue a cannibal. After hours of cramming with his wife Nina, Fawcett passed the exam with flying colors. Had she known what Fawcett's next twenty years of exploring would do to her life, Nina might not have worked so hard to help him.

The RGS was impressed with its new recruit and sent him off on a mission that involved more spying than exploring. This was not unusual at the time, as previously noted. Many explorers were enlisted in espionage. For instance, one of the presidents of the RGS, Francis Younghusband, was a legendary spy in India, Kashmir, and Tibet. Fawcett was sent to Morocco, either by the RGS, or the British

Foreign Office, or, probably, a combination of the two. His task was to infiltrate the Moroccan royal court and take notes. He seems to have adopted disguise to do this. He succeeded, telling his superiors the Sultan was "weak in character" and that "personal pleasure is the first consideration, and time is passed bicycle trick riding, at which he is a considerable adept, in playing with motorcars, mechanical toys, photography, billiards, pig sticking on bicycles, feeding his menagerie."

Pleased with Fawcett's work in Morocco, Sir George Taubman Goldie, president of the RGS, and an imperialist pooh-bah who had been largely responsible for adding Nigeria to Britain's holdings, offered him a new task. Fawcett accepted the assignment of surveying the unmapped frontier area of Bolivia and Brazil with the additional requirement that he provide intelligence that might resolve issues between rival groups engaged in the then-highly lucrative rubber trade along the border.

Fawcett also did a bang-up job at this complicated task, finishing it almost a year ahead of schedule. He proved himself to be amongst the toughest of explorers, able to handle all the difficulties of South America—heat, bugs, disease, hostile natives, and snakes. At one point his group came upon an anaconda that he later claimed was sixty feet long (almost certainly an exaggeration—the longest officially recorded is just under twenty-eight feet).[38] Unfortunately, he was also showing signs of the irritability and intolerance of what he saw as weaknesses in others that would dog all his later expeditions.

After the success of his first South American trip, Fawcett was keen for more. His next was an exploration of the Verde River, one of the many rivers running through Mato Grosso in Brazil in search of the Lost City of Z, a project that would consume the rest of his life. Fawcett

---

38. At whatever length, anacondas are extremely impressive animals. I was once part of a team that searched for an anaconda and found one that we pulled out of a thicket in the Venezuelan Llanos wilderness. Our snake was 17 feet long and was so heavy it took four of us to pick up. After we let it go, it slithered past my legs and my camera and swam back out into the wetlands.

based his belief on the existence of an ancient indigenous jungle city that he fancifully named the Lost City of Z on a document he found in the National Library of Brazil known as Manuscript 512. The aging, stained paper, originally found in 1839, purports to describe a huge, ruined city containing arches, temples and statues that had been seen by Portuguese *bandeirantes* (adventurers/explorers/slavers/treasure hunters) in 1753. Other explorers had gone hunting for the lost city, most notably Sir Richard Burton. Fawcett determined he was the man who was going to find it.

Fawcett adopted *Nec Aspera Terrent* (Difficulties be Damned) as a motto and had it engraved on a signet ring. Like many in the era, he was very big into aspirational, spiritualist quackadoodle. He was a follower of the infamous Ukrainian mystic Madame Blavatsky, whom her biographer describes as either "a genius, a consummate fraud, or simply a lunatic." Blavatsky founded the Theosophical movement which attracted a wide group of adherents, including, for a time, Fawcett. She was charged with producing fraudulent paranormal phenomena and fabricating tales of her own worldwide explorations and travels, but none of that seemed to bother Fawcett or her many other followers, who worshipped the transgressive pseudo-psychic.

Fawcett needed something to believe in, whether it be Theosophy or his motto *Nec Aspera Terrent*. He certainly had lots of damned difficulties on this expedition. For starters, he had the very basic problem that his team ran out of food and found it impossible to hunt animals to eat. People frequently assume that Amazonia must be full of edible wildlife ready to be picked off. Unfortunately, for explorers running low on supplies, that is not the case.[39]

---

39 On my visit to Amazonia, I set up an infrared trap camera to confirm that there are large mammals there like tapirs, wild pigs, deer, and jaguars that come out to feed and drink at night, but I never saw any in daylight, and it is no surprise that Fawcett's party didn't. It is a surprise that the Fawcett's party was unable to catch any fish. I have never had such good fishing as I experienced on the Amazon tributary I was on, but some South American rivers are poisoned by tannin from rotting trees, and apparently Fawcett was on one of them.

His men went for more than a month without eating, and he began to fear mutiny and cannibalism. Just in case, he confiscated everyone's guns. As he put it, "starvation blunts one's finer feelings."

None of them ate each other, but five of his team did die. Fawcett returned as a virtual skeleton. The ordeal only strengthened his determination to find the Lost City of Z, never mind that his wife and three children were now living in genteel poverty, "Deep down inside me a tiny voice was calling," he wrote. "At first scarcely audible, it persisted until I could no longer ignore it. It was the voice of the wild places, and I knew that it was now part of me forever. Inexplicably —amazingly—I knew I loved that hell. Its fiendish grasp has captured me, and I wanted to see it."

Brits in the Edwardian years were beginning to fear that traditional British values, the stuff that built the empire, were on the wane. People like Fawcett, who seemed a throwback to the supposedly heroic era of brave Livingstone and Burton, were lionized. Charles Darwin's son, Leonard, now president of the RGS, declared that Fawcett showed there was still a place "where the explorer can go forth and exhibit perseverance, energy, courage, forethought, and all those qualities which go to make up the qualities of an explorer of the times now passing by." Fawcett had fierce critics, but he also had enough supporters that he was able to raise the funds for another expedition into the Bolivian jungle and find new assistants to aid him in his quixotic quest. Single-minded, sociopathic manic obsession is not uncommon in the exploration racket and it wears on people. Many of Fawcett's assistants deserted him on this 1911 expedition. "Why would he not stop and let us sleep or eat?" bitched one. "We were working 24 hours a day and driven like bullocks before the lash."

The worst experience anyone had this time out with the crazed explorer was biologist James Murray. Yet another Scot, Murray was a biologist who had served with Shackleton's *Nimrod* expedition from 1907 to 1909. Had Fawcett looked closer at the story of Murray's time in Antarctica, he might have questioned whether he was the right person to take with him into the jungle. Even before heading off with Shackleton, the overweight Murray admitted that biological expeditions he had made in the lochs of Scotland had given him "rheumatism, inflamed eyes, and God knows what." He confessed that "I was just a little uneasy in my mind foisting upon Shackleton such a wreck of humanity." During the long winter at McMurdo Sound, the crew took to calling his cabin "the taproom," an indelicate reference to Murray's constant diarrhea.

Murray seemed to be able to hide his afflictions from Shackleton at first and was mostly in his good books of Shackleton. "You have never for one moment caused me the slightest anxiety in any way." Shackleton told him. "I am most deeply indebted to you for the good quick influence you have had on the Expedition; also for the good sound advice you have given me. I am not a good hand at saying things in praise, but I hope you will know that your high character has been an incentive to me keeping up my heart in downward times." Nice sentiments, Ernie, but The Boss' opinion would soon change.

As Shackleton set off toward the pole, he appointed Murray to run the basecamp. Once "The Boss" had left, Frederick Evans, one of the masters of the *Nimrod*, staged a revolt of sorts and attempted to take over as head of the camp, a typical explorers' wank-off. Murray's inability to deal with the rebellion tarnished his reputation. On their return to London, Shackleton wrote an unflattering portrayal of Murray in his book about the expedition. Murray was offended and asked that it be edited out of a subsequent edition, something Shackleton never did.

The problems of the Antarctica expedition paled beside those of the Amazon. Murray was not fit and could not keep up with the grueling pace set by Fawcett. Nor could Murray exist on the meager rations provided. He resorted to stealing extra food. Few crimes were considered graver. "On such an expedition the theft of food comes next to murder as a crime and should by rights be punished as such," said Theodore Roosevelt of his own journey into the green hell of Amazonia. Fawcett would certainly have agreed. He called Murray a "pink-eyed weakling" and barked at him, "You have no right to be tired."

Murray also lacked the constitution to accept Fawcett's manner of confronting the often-hostile Indian tribes they encountered in the jungle. After years of violent interactions with crudbucket rubber-tappers who had intruded into their land, enslaved them, and killed them, the natives had good reason to be wary of white interlopers. So while some of the native tribes Fawcett's party met were friendly toward Fawcett's party, others were extremely hostile. Fawcett's rule was that neither he nor his men were ever to return fire, even when they were being targeted by the Indians' poison-tipped arrows. "Die if you must," he told his men, "but never kill or shoot at the Indians." Murray resisted the rule. He couldn't believe his eyes when the team was pelted with arrows by a large group of angry, naked, paint-daubed natives, and Fawcett simply walked straight into them, waving his neckerchief and shouting "Friend, friend, friend" in one of the native dialects. Miraculously, the fusillade stopped. Fawcett was grabbed by the natives and pulled back into the jungle. Murray and the others waited for over an hour, not knowing what to do. Eventually, Fawcett returned with a group of the Indians, one of them now wearing Percy's Stetson atop his naked body, all of them carrying presents of bananas, yuccas, fish, necklaces, and parrots for the British explorers.

Unfriendly Indians were only one of the many problems they faced. Murray, like the rest of the team and its mules, was attacked by vampire bats. Soon all had blood and putrid matter dripping from their wounds. Maggots and worms began growing inside Murray's body, with the inch-long worms poking their heads up from his skin, then quickly retreating before they could be grabbed and killed. Flies swirled around him as if he were already a corpse. On top of this Fawcett clearly believed Murray a thief, a coward, a malingerer, and a cancer on his beloved expedition. Murray mutely listened as the others, led by Fawcett, discussed abandoning him in the jungle. In the end, the leader took pity on him and set off to find him help. He found a frontiersman with a mule whom he paid to return Murray to civilization. It was a long, difficult journey, but the sick explorer was eventually nursed back to health in the outback.

He made it to La Paz and back to England where he made furious accusations against Fawcett. An acrimonious battle was fought behind the closed doors of the RGS. How precisely it was resolved was never revealed. The recent feature film *The Lost City of Z* postulates that Fawcett grudgingly apologized to Murray for his treatment of him in the Amazon.

Two years later Murray, ever the glutton for punishment, joined Vilhjalmur Stefansson's star-crossed Canadian Arctic expedition. This one, as we have seen, was even more messed up than Fawcett's. After their ship, the *Karluk* became locked in ice, Murray eventually mutinied and set out, somewhere north of Wrangle Island, for Siberia. If he was rebelling against Stefansson, one might suspect he was perhaps the hero of the mutiny. But Stefansson had by now himself abandoned the ship, and the ill-fated expedition was being run by Bob Bartlett, the skilled and sane Newfoundland captain. It is safe to assume that Bartlett was probably in the right and Murray in the wrong. Regardless, this time Murray would not have an opportunity to plead his case before the RGS. He disappeared—presumably drowned, frozen, or eaten by a polar bear.

Murray was thus involved in three of the most difficult and discombobulated expeditions of this period, in three of the worst places on earth—Antarctica, Amazonia, and the Canadian and Siberian Arctic. He deserves some sort of prize, perhaps the Booby Prize, as the most unfortunate, batshit explorer in this book.

Fawcett didn't find the Lost City of Z in 1911, and further explorations were interrupted by WWI, during which he commanded a battery of men fighting on the Western Front. He fought in some of the bloodiest battles of that gruesome war and he was very lucky he didn't die in any of them. His personality continued to get very mixed reviews in the hellish conditions of the war. Some admired his stamina and ability, others not so much. One fellow officer called him, "probably the nastiest man I have ever met in this world."

Following the war, Fawcett discovered he now had a competitor in the Amazonian lost city racket—Alexander Hamilton Rice, the man who traveled with Hiram Bingham in 1907. He was now working the same territory as Fawcett and he had several advantages. He was a trained medical doctor. He sometimes performed operations on ill or injured Indians, which certainly increased his standing with the remote tribes. He even once performed an operation on himself, plunging a scalpel into his infected body without benefit of anesthetic. His biggest advantage was that he had virtually unlimited funds. He was the wealthy grandson of the former mayor of Boston and governor of Massachusetts and he had married the widow of one of the richest men in America who, conveniently for Rice, had died in the sinking of the *Titanic.* Rice was also perhaps the first truly twentieth century explorer, equipped with all the latest gadgets, including new kinds of clothing, boots, boats, generators—even the newfangled inventions of shortwave radio and a collapsible flying boat airplane to survey the territory from above.

Fawcett resented the fact that Rice could outfit his expeditions with all this gear and hire a large team of assistants, whereas he was "born without the proverbial silver spoon." He also despised Rice's antagonistic actions against the Indians, shooting at them with guns and even dropping bombs on them from his plane.

Fawcett's very limited funds meant he could only manage for his next outing a very modest expedition into the Xingu region, with only two assistants—an Australian boxer named Lewis Brown and an American naturalist named Ernest Holt. Brown upset the sexually repressed Fawcett before they left by indulging himself in a Latin American whorehouse. The boxer could not see the damage. "I'm flesh and blood like the rest!" he retorted to the sanctimonious and outraged Fawcett. Holt, like Murray, grew feeble on the difficult trail. Fawcett, even though at age fifty-three no longer quite the invincible traveler he used to be, began mocking his assistant, calling him "the cripple." Eventually Fawcett fired him while admitting that Holt was "convinced I am sure that I am a lunatic." In turn, Holt reported that "after close association with Colonel Fawcett [Fawcett was not really a Colonel, but, like KFC's Colonel Sanders and Elvis' Colonel

Tom Parker, he called himself one] for a period covering one year, I find that the lesson most clearly impressed upon my mind is: Never again under circumstances form any connections with any Englishman whatsoever."

Fawcett came up with a new idea. Screw all these useless, malingering, mutinous assistants. He would make a last, final attack on Amazonia with his own kin, his strapping son Jack, now eighteen. Knowing this idea might not pass muster with long-suffering Nina, he approached the idea slowly and carefully. He was even distracted from it for a while when the famed explorer and desert spy T. E. Lawrence, better known as Lawrence of Arabia, volunteered to join him on his next trip to the Amazon. Fawcett considered the offer, but decided he did not need another egomaniacal explorer, especially one unused to the difficulties of the jungle, arguing with him in the outback. In any case, he could not afford to pay Lawrence. By 1923, Fawcett was so poor he could not afford even his annual three-pound membership fees at the RGS. Jack, if Nina would allow him to go, would be free labor.

While waiting for this scheme to unfold, Fawcett railed against the money "wasted on these useless Antarctic expeditions" and began again to associate with spiritualists, asking them to use Ouija boards and other claptrap to identify the location of his lost city. Members of the RGS began calling him "a trifle unbalanced."

But things began looking up for Fawcett when he met a classic swashbuckling 1920s character named George Lynch, a man of supposedly "unimpeachable character and high repute" who offered to act as his agent to raise the money for a new expedition. Lynch sailed for New York and within days had convinced the North American Newspaper Alliance to buy story rights to the venture. NANA was a consortium of the biggest, flashiest newspapers of the day, including the *New York World,* the *Toronto Star*, and the *Los Angeles Times*. The papers in the alliance liked to mix up stories about local murders and bank robberies with lurid reports from exotic parts of the globe. The *Star,* for instance, had Ernest Hemingway report for them from the front lines of the Spanish Civil War. Explorer Percy Fawcett's tales of his search for a Latin American lost city were right up its alley.

The break was enough to get Fawcett to ask Nina to let their son, Jack, accompany him. When she somewhat surprisingly agreed, father and son boarded a ship to sail for New York to meet up with Lynch. On arrival Fawcett was shocked to find that his agent had already squandered the first grand of the $5,000 he had raised by extravagantly entertaining a group of hookers in a suite at the Waldorf-Astoria Hotel. Still, Fawcett and Lynch agreed to continue the search for money and got an additional $4,500 out of John D. Rockefeller Jr., heir to the Standard Oil fortune. The expedition was on its way. Rockefeller's $4,500 was less than the cost of just one of Alexander Rice's short-wave transceivers, but it was enough for Fawcett.

Jack enlisted his childhood friend, Raleigh Rimell, who at the time was flailing at his goal of becoming a silent movie actor in Hollywood. He was glad to join his pal for the romantic Amazon adventure. The trio sailed for Rio. After posing for newspaper photos—"THREE MEN FACE CANNIBALS IN RELIC QUEST"—they traveled 1,000 miles by train into the interior of Brazil. They next took a small decrepit river boat up the Paraguay and São Lourenço rivers to the distant outpost of Cuiabá, described by Rimell as "a God-forsaken hole . . . best seen with the eyes closed."

Fawcett acquired native guides, bought horses and mules, soaked up any rumors he could about lost cities and jungle ruins, sent missives off to the NANA newspapers, and eventually headed north into the wilderness. He didn't have much to go on. Few Europeans had preceded him into this wilderness. There were few records to consult. Whatever evidence the sixteenth-century conquistadores had gathered about Incan cities, roads, temples and buildings, the government and the Roman Catholic Church had destroyed or withheld. "It was difficult," wrote Fawcett, "for an administration steeped in the narrow bigotry of an all-powerful Church to give much credence to such thing as an old civilization." To make matters worse, whatever physical evidence remained had been taken back by the jungle in the intervening centuries.

The Fawcetts and their sidekick, Rimell, made slow progress up to the spot Percy called Dead Horse Camp, because on an earlier expedition one of his horses had died there. From there, nothing is known. They probably headed into the land of the Xavante Indians, an area no Brazilians would enter. The Xavante had been colonized in the eighteenth century. After years of being brutalized by Brazilian soldiers, abused by the church, and devastated by epidemics, they had rebelled and returned to their wilderness. One German chronicler wrote that "from that time onwards the Xavante no longer trusted any white man. . . These abused people have therefore changed from trusted compatriots into the most dangerous and determined enemies. They generally kill anyone they can easily catch."

That's the best guess at what befell Percy and Jack Fawcett and Raleigh Rimell. Nobody knows for certain, but what is known is that their disappearance set off the greatest lost-explorer hunt since the search for Franklin had begun seventy years earlier. There were Italian expeditions, German ones, Russian ones, even an entry from New Zealand. Another (poorly organized, utterly unsuccessful) was led by Peter Fleming, the older brother of Ian Fleming, creator of James Bond. A University of California graduate student ventured out and lost her life. An anthropologist on the trail of the Fawcetts was found hanging in the jungle, a possible suicide. It is believed that close to 100 people died searching for Percy Fawcett.

The echoes of the Franklin search were amplified by the actions of Fawcett's wife, Nina, who, like Lady Jane Franklin, became obsessed with the whereabouts of her husband and would remain so for the rest of her life.

The Fawcett story would also echo Stanley's search for Livingstone. A multimillionaire Brazilian newspaper publisher named Asis Chateaubriand sent one of his star tabloid reporters into the jungle to search not for Fawcett, but for a phantom "child of Fawcett," a legendary white Indian supposedly sired by Fawcett after he was captured in the jungle. The reporter found the boy, dubbed him "Dulipé, the White God of the Xingu," and brought him of the wilderness. He was paraded around Brazil as a freak explorer-child, although doctors determined he was simply an albino. After his fifteen minutes of fame were up, he was abandoned on the streets of Cuiabá, where he reportedly died from alcoholism.

One of the most celebrated searches was led by Royal Geographical Society explorer George Miller Dyott. With Fawcett missing for two years, the NANA newspaper chain decided the story still had legs and while the Lost City angle was a lost cause, he himself was not. THE SEARCH FOR THE LOST CITY OF Z was now replaced with THE SEARCH FOR COLONEL FAWCETT. It would be, the newspapers told their readers, "Adventure That Makes the Blood Race—Romance, Mystery, and Peril!"

The alliance also helped Diott publicize his search for assistants: "Must be single, quiet, and youthful." Twenty thousand responded, from all over the world. Dyott chose four, who assembled with him in February of 1928 at a dock in Hoboken, New Jersey. They had a massive send-off, attended by flamboyant New York mayor Jimmy Walker, and Elsie Rimell, Raleigh's mother, who arrived from California with a present for Dyott to give to her son once he found him in the jungle.

In Brazil, the expedition grew to twenty-six members with seventy-four oxen and mules carrying more than three tons of food and gear. The Brazilians derided it both as a "Cecille B. DeMille safari" and a "suicide club." The top-heavy expedition of course turned into a shitshow. Thousands of Indians showed up out of the jungle, demanding presents from the Fawcett-searchers. When they didn't all get everything they wanted, they began acting aggressively toward the interlopers. The Americans were lucky to get out of the forest with their lives. Dyott at least got a book out of it, *Man Hunting in the Jungle*, then starred in a Hollywood B-movie about the adventure called *Savage Gold*.

When physical attempts to find Fawcett failed, people tried other methods. His wife and some leaders of the RGS attempted to ascertain what had happened by consulting psychics and soothsayers. Eventually Nina died, demented and penniless. As one observer said, she had "sacrificed her life to her husband and his memory." Her younger son, Brian, who had been working in the railroad business in Peru through all this nuttiness, did not give up. He attempted to mount his own search party, applying to the British Embassy in Brazil for assistance. The embassy officials, who thought Brian "just as mad as his father," refused to facilitate what they called his "suicide." The younger Fawcett went anyway, dropping thousands of leaflets from a plane into the jungle, reading "Are you Jack Fawcett? If your answer is yes, then make this sign holding arms above your head. . . .Can you control the Indians if we land?"

There is an ancient proverb that Fawcett liked to quote: "Those whom the Gods intend to destroy, first they make mad."

*

After the Fawcett debacle, an American weekly newspaper, the *Independent*, sarcastically noted, "perhaps if there were a sufficient number of jungles available and enough expeditions to go round, we would see the spectacle of our whole population marching off in search of lost explorers, ancient civilizations, and something which it vaguely felt was missing in its life."

It turned out there were more jungles available, only 2,000 kilometers or so north of the one Bingham, Rice, and the Fawcetts had been slashing through. And yes, many more people lined up to explore them.

La Mosquitia is the massive, unfortunately named jungle in the south-eastern corner of Honduras. It has lots of mosquitoes. Lots of poisonous snakes. Lots of rain. Very few people. From time to time, massive hurricanes come ashore from the Caribbean and blow all the leaves off the trees. Today, it has a few drug-smuggling trans-shipment air strips. Generally, La Mosquitia is an unpleasant and dangerous place. It also has its share of legends, most especially the legend of The Lost City of the Monkey God, a spot people started looking for around 1900 and are still looking for today.

In the 1920s, an itinerant rubber tapper described to Luxembourgian explorer Eduard Conzemius a ruin of a city he had seen. It was made of a stone that looked like white marble. The rubber tapper soon disappeared and local Indians added to the mystery by telling Conzemius that he had died because "the devil killed him for looking at this forbidden place."

In 1927, the celebrated, soon-to-be controversial aviator Charles Lindbergh claimed to have seen the *Ciudad Blanco*, or White City, while flying over Mosquitia. He called it, "an amazing ancient metropolis."

The Smithsonian's Bureau of American Ethnology sent archeologist William Duncan Strong to investigate. Strong had the usual battles with insects, snakes, and the jungle, and also managed to blow a finger off with one of his boomsticks. Nevertheless, he did confirm the local stories of lost cities, and made the new claim that they were not created by the Maya people who lived further north in Guatemala and Mexico, but by an entirely different culture.

Conzemius, Lindbergh, and Strong were followed by a collection of con-men and charlatans who made Percy Fawcett look tame and sane by comparison. Puffing on a big stogie at all times, George Gustav Heye was a larger than life (six-foot-four and 300 pounds) Indian artifact collector who created the Museum of the American Indian on New York's Broadway. He sent a number of adventurers down to La Mosquitia to help stock his museum. The first was a dude named Frederick Mitchell-Hedges, who played the explorer role to the hilt. He had the double-barreled name, the plummy British accent, the briar pipe, the tweedy explorer duds. He claimed to have already discovered the Maya city of Lubaantun in Belize and like to show off the "Crystal

Skull of Doom" he had found there. He also claimed he had eight bullet wounds and three knife scars, he had fought with Pancho Villa, and he had searched for sea monsters with Sir Arthur Conan Doyle's son in the Indian Ocean.

At Heye's behest, Mitchell-Hedges charged off to Honduras and returned with more tales of the Lost City of the Monkey God, but with no proof, since he, perhaps sensibly, did not go far into the jungle. Instead, he hung around the much more pleasant beaches and coast islands that Honduras has to offer. He also produced ancient pottery he claimed to have pulled from the Caribbean and a ludicrous tale that he had discovered Atlantis, which he said was "the cradle of the American races." He then wrote a book about his travels called *Land of Wonder and Fear*. One archeologist wrote, "To me the wonder was how he could write such nonsense and the fear was how much taller the next yarn would be."

Mitchell-Hedges, not surprisingly, turned out to be a fraud and con-artist on a spectacular scale. He had not discovered Lubaantun. His "Crystal Skull of Doom" was revealed as a fake. He had not fought with Pancho Villa and did not have eight bullet wounds. As for Atlantis, well, if it does exist, it is somewhere in the Mediterranean, not off the coast of Honduras.

Realizing that he had been bamboozled, Heye, for his next hire looked for someone a little more professional. He wasn't entirely successful, landing on another explorer who had invented a fancy, phony title for himself. "Captain" R. Stuart Murray was a Canadian journalist who had never served in the military, although he once did cover a two-bit revolution in Santo Domingo as a newspaper reporter. The captain led two expeditions for Heye in 1934 and 1935. "There's supposedly a lost city I'm going to look for," he told the New York press, "which the Indians call the Lost City of the Monkey God. They're afraid to go near it, for they believe that anyone who approaches it will, within the month, be killed by the bite of a poisonous snake."

Murray did not find the city, but he did find a few artifacts, including an interesting carving of a monkey covering its face with its paws.

Two trips into the jungle were enough for him and he next took a gig as a guest lecturer on an elegant cruise ship, the *Stella Polaris*.[40]

On Murray's travels on the *Stella Polaris*, he fell in with the editor of the ship's newspaper, Theodore Morde. The pair traded war-stories —Morde's of his reporting from the frontlines of the Spanish Civil War, where he claimed to have rubbed shoulders with Hemingway, and Murray's of his search for the lost city in Honduras. Murray said he was done with the Honduran jungle but offered to introduce his new pal to Heye to see if the impresario could be suckered a third time.

Heye indeed was interested and in March of 1940 sent Morde and his friend Lawrence Brown with a thousand pounds of equipment and supplies to look for the fabled white city. There was a little thing called World War II brewing in Europe, but America was not in it yet, and the public was still jazzed about Latin American adventure.

Morde and Brown returned in August to great fanfare. In a radio interview for CBS, Morde spilled all the details about his fabulous adventure:

> We went to a region of Honduras that had never been explored. . .We spent weeks poling tediously up tangled jungle streams. When we could go no further, we started hacking a way through the jungle . . . after weeks of that life, we were starved, weak and discouraged. Then, just as we were about to give up, I saw from the top of a small cliff, something that made me stop in my tracks . . . it was the wall of a city—the Lost City of the Monkey God!

Morde breathlessly described the masks and artifacts he had found in the city and its fabulous setting: "The towering mountains provided the perfect backdrop. Nearby, a rushing waterfall, beautiful as a

40 These Chautauqua-at-sea lectures are still popular. I've done a few myself, including one on a trans-Atlantic crossing of the *Queen Elizabeth II*, another on a transformed Russian spy ship turned into an expedition vessel crossing to Antarctica, another off Greenland.

sequined evening gown, spilled down into the green valley of ruins. Birds as brilliant as jewels flitted from tree to tree, and little monkey faces peered inquisitively at us from the surrounding screen of green foliage." He even claimed to be able to know the population of the once-grand city. "Probably 30,000 people once lived there. But that was 2,000 years ago."

Theodore Morde

Morde got a huge amount of attention for finding the Lost City. There were dozens of newspaper articles. He was even featured decked out in his explorer garb in a Camel cigarette ad with the copy reading "When I'm trekking through the wilds of Honduras, I like to take a break and smoke a Camel." The only trouble was that his wonderful story, however much everyone wanted to hear it, was balderdash.

Morde kept detailed day-by-day journals of his travels in Honduras but shared them with no-one. It was later said that they had been destroyed or had somehow disappeared. In fact, they were hiding in plain sight (in possession of his family) and when they finally came to light in 2016, the truth came out. Morde and his geologist friend Brown had not only not found the Lost City, but they had also not even bothered to look for it. The journals revealed that the Lost City adventure was merely a cover for their real goal—to search in Honduran rivers for gold. They were looking for another Klondike. This search took them miles from the area of the Paulaya and Plátano rivers where the lost city was supposed to be and where Morde had claimed to have found it. On the distant stream they were on, they did manage to find some gold flecks and set up a dam, sluice boxes and other panning paraphernalia. A flash flood washed out their mining site, however, and the wicked rainy season was soon threatening their lives. They headed back to the coast and either dug for or, more probably, bought a few pieces of pre-Columbian pottery and returned to show them off and tell their fanciful story to the American press.

His journals prove that Morde's "discoveries" were a complete fraud. On the last page of one volume, he concludes, "We are convinced no great civilization ever existed up there. And there are no archeological discoveries of importance to be made."

EPILOGUE

And so ends our story. But why here? And why now?

Morde, in a sense, was the last of the old-time explorers, chasing one of the five quests, supporting himself independently. Unfortunately, his escapades took this school of exploration from the sublime or, at least, the impressive, to the ridiculous. He corrupted exploration. Other explorers had their faults. Baker may have been a racist, Cook at times a charlatan, Livingstone and Franklin failures, but at least they were not total frauds. Morde was an outright liar.

Morde might have redeemed himself by returning to Honduras and actually finding the Lost City of the Monkey God, as he claimed he wanted. However, WWII shut down that plan and all the other plans people may have had to find lost cities, challenge mountains, or explore deserts, barrens, or other neglected parts of the world. WWII did see a lot of inventive, crazy, "out there" adventuring, but it was in the service of either the Allies or the Axis, not for the amorphous cause of exploration.

Morde himself was caught up in the new military adventure. All the publicity he received after returning from his Honduran explorations led to a call from Washington inviting him to work for the Office of Strategic Services, precursor to the CIA and one of the crucibles of proto-James Bondian skullduggery. They didn't have to ask twice. Morde thought the opportunity sounded even more exciting than searching for lost cities in Latin America and jumped at it. He was sent off on several top-secret missions to Europe, Africa, and the Middle East. The details of most of them have never been revealed, although one that was uncovered involved a wild scheme cooked up between Morde and Franz Von Papen, vice-chancellor of Germany under Hitler from 1933–1934 and German ambassador to Turkey during the war. Morde surreptitiously met with Von Papen in Istanbul and proposed a radical plan to either assassinate Hitler or snatch him out of Berlin and abscond with him to London.

With Von Papen's blessing, Morde took the outrageous proposal to his boss at the Office of Strategic Services, William J. "Wild Bill" Donovan, who approved it and took it to President Franklin Roosevelt for consideration. Roosevelt's defense advisor Robert Sherwood warned the president that Morde was a "rogue agent." The president got cold feet and nothing came of the proposal.

Morde went back to Europe and spent the rest of the war as an OSS chief in Italy, running a covert patrol boat that inserted agents behind enemy lines, conducted sabotage, and chased submarines. After the war, he talked about returning to exploration and even wrote a letter to The Explorers Club outlining his intentions, but he never did. The world had changed. People had changed, overdosing on drama through two World Wars and the Great Depression. The flight to suburban prosperity was on, even if it entailed a certain monotony. Stories of lost cities, ancient civilizations, and geographic mysteries receded from the headlines.

In 1954, Morde was found naked but for a bath robe, hanging in the shower of his parents' Dartmouth home. The official cause of death was suicide, but not all agreed. "I want to believe it was a rival spy," said his nephew, Dave Morde. "He had some very bad enemies. It just doesn't make sense otherwise." Morde's mother believed that he had been cursed by Honduran Indians in retaliation for his exploring (or, in fact, not exploring) sacred sites because that's what her son told her.

Another reason 1940 has been chosen to end this chronicle of nuttiness was that that was the year of the United States Antarctica Service Expedition, a quintessentially batshit attempt to get to the South Pole by driving to it in comfort. Thomas Poulter, who had nearly died on one of Admiral Richard Byrd's Antarctic expeditions of the 1930s, came up with a bold plan to create a huge 56-foot-long snow cruiser to take a team of four to the Pole. He managed to convince the American government to fork out $150,000 ($3 million in today's money) to construct the massive vehicle. It seemed doomed from the start. At 25 feet wide and weighing 37 tons with an airplane mounted on its roof, it could barely fit on American roads, and managed to crash off one of them and get stuck in a creek en route to the Boston docks. On its arrival in Antarctica on January 12, 1940, it crushed the ramp taking it off the transport ship, and almost killed leader Richard Byrd. It was quickly determined that its slick tires and elaborate diesel and electric drivetrain would barely move it. The crew took to driving it in reverse, which gave it slightly more traction, but eventually the team gave up and the madcap behemoth, designed to have a range of 8000 miles, never moved more than one or two over the white continent. It was abandoned on a section of the Ross Ice Shelf, which years later broke off from the continent, floated away, and presumably eventually sunk to the bottom of the ocean.

The kind of exploration that came into vogue in the 1950s was very different. The most celebrated expedition of that decade was the British assault on Mount Everest. It differed from pre-war efforts in several ways. First, unlike the often-slapdash efforts that proceeded it, it was extremely well organized. Second, it was successful: the first ascent of the world's tallest mountain. Third, the leader, Sir John Hunt, set aside his ego and did not ascend to the summit himself. Instead, he allowed two other climbers to take the prize, something few (if any) explorers from the 1800–1940 period would have done. Further, neither of the climbers was British. Edmund Hillary was a Kiwi. Tensing Norgay was a Nepalese Sherpa. Some nineteenth-century RGS pooh-bahs must have turned over in their graves.

The closest the post-war period saw to old-style expeditions was Thor Heyerdahl's sail across the Pacific from South America to the Tuamotu Islands in a hand-built raft. The ostensible purpose of the voyage was to prove that the South Pacific had been first populated by people from South America. This has been ridiculed as diffusionist hogwash. The highly respected Canadian anthropologist (and *National Geographic* "Explorer-in-Residence") Wade Davis says that Heyerdahl "ignored the overwhelming body of linguistic, ethnographic, and ethnobotanical evidence, augmented today by genetic and archeological data, indicating that he was patently wrong." So Heyerdahl was mistaken, but no-one would call the Norwegian adventurer or his skilled companions batshit.

Nor, of course, could anyone accuse the most ambitious explorers of the post-war period—the astronauts and cosmonauts of the American and Soviet space programs—of any kind of crazy. The expeditions, culminating in the landing of two men on the moon in July 1969, were obviously run with a degree of significant scientific rigor and engineering precision that had never been seen before in the field of exploration. The post-war era was very different from all that had preceded it.

Yet another reason that 1940 is the end point of this chronicle is that it saw the launch of the career of an explorer who serves as a counterweight to all the wild-ass characters in this book. A man who, in my opinion, qualifies as the greatest explorer ever. A man who really did discover for the people of Earth a whole new world.

Jacques Cousteau was an explorer, an inventor, a filmmaker, an environmental activist, and a visionary. Almost singlehandedly, he gave us the opportunity to see the underwater world. Before he could do that, he had to invent or improve much of the technology that made it possible. In the 1940s, Cousteau worked with engineer Émile Gagnon to create the Aqua-Lung,

Jacques Cousteau

a twin-hose demand regulator system—the first breathing apparatus that permitted independent, untethered and extensive undersea exploration. He also created one of the world's first underwater camera housings so that he could make his first film, *Par Dix-huit Mètres de Fond* (*Eighteen Meters Deep*).

His activities, and those of all his compatriot Frenchmen, were interrupted by the Nazi occupation. Cousteau became a fighter for the French Resistance and an officer in the French Navy. He was involved in hair-raising dangerous secret missions for which he later received the *Légion d'Honneur* and the *Croix de Guerre*.

When the fighting stopped, Cousteau embarked on a fifty-year exploration of the entire undersea world on his two ships, both named *Calypso*. He transmitted his experience and knowledge through dozens of books and personal appearances but it was his camera that most caught the public imagination, turning the movie screens and television sets of the world into portholes into ocean life. His first film, *The Silent World*, won both the Palme d'Or at the Cannes Film Festival and an Academy Award, the first of three he would win, along with forty Emmy nominations. His television shows through the 1960s and 1970s totally changed how the public saw the ocean and, indeed, the entire planet. He was winner of the US Presidential Medal of Freedom among many other awards and distinctions. He was voted the "Greatest Frenchman ever" seventeen years running and was the recipient of an 800,000-signature petition that he run for the presidency of France.

The extent of Cousteau's influence can't be understated. That an estimated 40,000 new underwater explorers are certified as divers every month is due to him more than any other individual. He also played a leading role in the growth and popularization of environmentalism.

When Cousteau began exploring the world's oceans, they were in relatively pristine shape. In the course of his travels, he began to notice their destruction by pollution, nuclear waste, acidification, warming, and over-fishing. We have seen how the explorers of Africa contributed to the slaughter of wildlife; how the explorers of South America contributed to the decimation of the land and people of the continent. They ignored or denied their culpability. Cousteau did not. He grew from being someone who explored for pure adventure to someone who explored to reveal new environments to the world to someone motivated primarily to protect these places. He became a fierce advocate for the planet and, especially, the ocean and in doing so gained recognition as a dedicated activist and global citizen.

In the 1990s, Cousteau realized that diesel-fuel-powered ships like his own beloved *Calypso* were harming the world's oceans. His inventive mind developed a ship powered by a spinning wind turbine rather than an engine. It was a more efficient form of propulsion than conventional sails yet, like them, completely green.

More important than the technology Cousteau gave to the world were his ideas. "We don't influence future generations only by our genes," he wrote. "We also pass on our 'memes'—our ideas." Among his most challenging was the idea that the ocean floor could be a human habitat for extended periods of time. That was the inspiration for his lifelong experiments in building the underwater villages—his Continental Shelf projects.

Cousteau was also, uniquely, an explorer who thought deeply about the nature of exploration. He asked the question, "What inspires an explorer to undertake a voyage with no destination, to search with no objective, to travel with no itinerary other than the uncharted, the unfathomed, the unexpected?" As a child he had observed how the wisteria shoots creeping up garden walls turned away from the shade and searched out the best direction for growth. "I wondered if nature endowed all forms of life—animals, even plants—with an exploration instinct."

Ultimately, he confessed that he had no answers: "I could not hope to explain the drive to explore, although I have readily recognized its telltale signs of unrest in the eyes of explorers I have been privileged to meet." He also noted that "we, the new explorers for the modern age, must rely to the fullest on the traditional explorer's greatest asset: the human intellect."

Unlike most of the explorers chronicled in this book, Cousteau thought deeply about the nature of risk in exploration. Danger is not something one wants to dwell on. When asked about it during the expeditions I have been on, I usually give the flippant counsel, "Always Remember—Safety Third!" Cousteau had a wry sense of humor but couldn't afford to be so jocular: he was often engaged in deep technical diving in cold, fast-flowing, unknown waters, sometimes experimenting with treacherous rebreather technology. It's a dangerous business yet Cousteau didn't lose people the way Franklin, Burton, or Fawcett did.

That's not to say there were no tragedies. In 1952, one of his crew, Jean-Pierre Servanti, died in a diving accident. In 1979, Cousteau lost his own son, Philippe, when his seaplane crashed at a dive site. In neither death was the explorer to blame, but, as leader, he took responsibility. He grieved and worked hard to prevent future tragedy. He was instrumental in the development of rules and dive-tables that if properly followed prevent embolism, nitrogen narcosis (the so-called "rapture of the deep"), decompression sickness ("the bends"), and other dangers of deep diving.[41]

Unlike some of the befuddled characters and their supporters whose adventures we've followed in this book, Cousteau rejected the notion of "heroism." He felt the public's fascination with recklessness was misplaced. "When a braggart boasts in headlines that 'danger is my business,'" he declared, "it seems to me he may as well add, 'and stupidity is my specialty.'"

---

41 Cousteau also helped create some of the protocols for cave diving. I've done a bit of cave diving in Mexico's Yucatan Peninsula. It's one of the scariest things you can do. I was grateful for Cousteau's advice. "Suppress fear," he wrote in one of his many books. "Risk itself is only a threat. Fear is an enemy. In the face of a danger that requires clear-witted reaction, fear clouds judgement." I did. He was right.

In so many ways, Cousteau is almost an antidote to the batshit adventurers of the 1800–1940 period. He is a quintessentially modern explorer—brave, humanist, technically skilled, fiercely intelligent, and above all, a man who transformed the world through his travels. It may be a fool's errand to name the world's greatest explorer, but my vote is for Jacques Cousteau.

CHAMPIONS AND PROMOTERS OF INDIE EXPLORATION

Explorers did not spring from the green hills of England or the smoky cities of America by chance. Throughout the Victorian and Edwardian eras there were novelists, memoirists, and numerous organizations that inspired boys and men and the occasional woman to jump into the exploration racket. What follows is a non-comprehensive, slightly idiosyncratic guide to the most important of these influences, at least to my mind.

Even at the beginning of the nineteenth century, when books were much harder to access, the journals of explorers like Captain James Cook were the equivalent of science fiction in a later century to young readers. "The reading of voyages and travels occupied all my leisure moments," wrote Alexander Gordon Laing. "*The History of Robinson Crusoe*, in particular, inflamed my young imagination. I was impatient to encounter adventures like this—nay, I already felt an ambition to signalize myself by some important discovery springing up in my heart."

There were many novelists in the nineteenth century who celebrated the world of exploration. Their books usually didn't get the stamp of approval from uptight literary critics of the day, but they were bought and read in huge numbers by the exploration-obsessed public. The first of the century was also perhaps the most extraordinary and unique, and it is still famous today, more than 200 years after it was initially published.

Mary Shelley's *Frankenstein*

On April 5, 1815, Mount Tambora, a stratovolcano in Indonesia, exploded. It was (and still is) the largest volcanic eruption in human history. Its ash cloud covered the world, producing what was known as "the year without a summer." A terrible famine resulted in North America, Europe, and Asia. More than 71,000 died.

Mary Shelley

In June 1816, three celebrated British writers, Lord Byron, Percy Bysshe Shelley, and Shelley's teenage lover, later his wife, Mary Shelley, holidayed together in a villa on the shores of Lake Geneva. The Tambora explosion had left a constant cloud and rain over all of Europe, so the trio could not indulge in its planned outdoor activities, mostly sailing. Instead, Byron—famously described as "mad, bad, and dangerous to know"—proposed a threesome. Once he tired of that, he suggested they pass the time by each trying to write a gothic horror tale to match the grey mood of the summer. Mary's effort, *Frankenstein*, was by far the most successful.

Remarkably, the dark tale is framed by the story of an independent explorer attempting to sail to the North Pole. In the opening pages we are introduced to young Captain Walton whose ship gets trapped in Arctic ice to the dismay of his mutinous crew. While they are stuck, Walton and company witness a strange creature crossing the ice, followed by a man who they bring aboard and learn is Dr. Victor Frankenstein. The doctor tells the captain the long story of how he created what we all know as Frankenstein's monster from discarded dead body parts animated by new-fangled electricity. In the final chapters, Frankenstein chases his monster across all of Russia until he finally reaches the frozen Arctic Ocean, which he proceeds to traverse by dogsled. With his dogs dying and the ice breaking up beneath him, he thinks he is doomed until he spies the explorers, who save him.

When he arrives aboard the ship, the good doctor finds Walton's crew threatening mutiny unless the captain frees the ship from the ice and returns to England. Frankenstein, from his sick bed, gives an impassioned speech about the glory of seeking new lands, encouraging the men to support Walton's obsessed quest for the pole.

Shelley's literary foresight is not only remarkable but also somewhat mysterious. The first serious known attempt on the North Pole was by William Parry, in 1827, eleven years after she wrote the book. As for her fictional mutinous ice-bound battles between crew and captain, they would be enacted for real by future expeditions to the North and South Poles but not for another fifty years.

Frankenstein dies. Then the monster appears, described by the shocked captain as being "loathsome with appalling hideousness," he confesses to his past ill-deeds, promises to burn himself to death on an ice floe heading north for the pole, then leaps from the cabin window and disappears into the Arctic night. Chastened by the frightening experience and recognizing the dangerous similarity of his own obsession to get to the pole to Frankenstein's desire to create life, Walton frees the ship and heads back to England.

Although she was very much the junior member of the trio of writers in that Lake Geneva villa, Mary Shelley created by far the most successful of the books written there. *Frankenstein* was published within two years to a chorus of the usual dickish naysaying. The *British Critic* bleated that "even if our authoress can forget the gentleness of her sex, there is no reason why we should. We shall therefore dismiss the novel without further comment." Nevertheless, it was generally well received. None other than Sir Walter Scott praised it as "an extraordinary tale, in which the author seems to us to disclose uncommon powers of poetic imagination."

It is now considered a classic and the world's first piece of science fiction. It is certainly the most celebrated novel written by a teenager. It is also the most amazingly prescient novel about polar exploration, a field that did not exist in 1816. Whether or not *Frankenstein* encouraged explorers to set out for the Arctic is not certain, but it definitely had the effect of interesting the public in wilderness travels.

R. M. Ballantyne's *The Coral Island*

More directly influential on exploration was Scottish writer R.M. Ballantyne's juvenile novel *The Coral Island*. First published in 1857, it has never been out of print. I don't know whether twelve-year-olds still read it today, but I remember devouring it at that age.

Ballantyne was something of an explorer himself. After a minimal education, he shipped out to northern Canada to work as a fur trader for the Hudson's Bay Company. Back in Scotland in 1856, he banged off his first novel, *The Young Fur Traders*, then followed the next year with his mega-hit *The Coral Island: A Tale of the Pacific Ocean.*

Though he had never visited the islands of the South Pacific, he was able to paint a convincing picture of them. He made a few crazy errors, like placing penguin colonies in the tropics and, of course, every shark that appears is a man-eater and every native a cannibal, but, in general, his portrait of a South Pacific coral island is fairly accurate.

The story is of three teenage sailors, marooned on what they first think is an uninhabited island. The author tells us they feel they have hit the jackpot, then throws in a little gratuitous racism to buoy them further. *"Do you know what conclusion I have come to?"* said Peterkin.

"I have made up my mind that it's capital—first-rate—the best thing that ever happened to us, and the most splendid prospect that ever lay before three jolly young tars. We've got an island all to ourselves. We'll take possession in the name of the king. We'll go and enter the service of its black inhabitants. Of course, we'll rise, naturally, to the top of affairs: white men always do in savage countries. You shall be king, Jack; Ralph, prime minister; and I shall be-"

"The court-jester," interrupted Jack.

The book reads as though written to inspire (primarily) boys to head out into wilderness and explore the world. It includes a scene in which two of the three main characters jawbone about the role and usefulness of books in prepping people for the great outdoors:

"I say, Jack, how does it happen that you seem to be up to everything? You have told us the names of half-a-dozen trees already, and yet you say that you were never in the South Seas before."

"I'm not up to everything, Peterkin, as you'll find out ere long, replied Jack with a smile; "but I have been a great reader of books of travel and adventure all my life, and that has put me up to a good many things that you are, perhaps, not acquainted with."

"Oh, Jack, that's all humbug! If you begin to lay everything to the credit of books, I'll quite lose my opinion of you," cried Peterkin with a look of contempt. "I've seen a lot o' fellows that were always poring over books, and when they came to try to do anything, they were no better than baboons!"

"You are quite right," retorted Jack; "and I have seen a lot of fellows, who never looked into books at all, who knew nothing about anything except the things they had actually seen, and very little they knew even about these. Indeed, some were so ignorant that they did not know that cocoa nuts grew on cocoa-nut trees!"

Jules Verne's *Around the World in 80 Days*

Within a few years of Ballantyne's classic an even more influential author burst onto the scene. At age eleven, Jules Verne, inspired by adventure books he had read, including *The Coral Island*, attempted to stow away on a ship headed for the Indies in order to bring back a coral necklace for his cousin, Caroline. At the last moment, he was caught by his father who made him promise that he would in future travel "only in his imagination."

Verne did that, creating many of the great works of imaginative travel fiction—*20,000 Leagues Under the Sea, Journey to the Center of the Earth*, and, especially, *Around the World in 80 Days*. His books were spectacularly successful. He is now considered the second-most translated author in the world, behind only Agatha Christie.

Around the World in 80 Days inspired many people to attempt to emulate Verne's fictional journey. Most famously, investigative reporter Nellie Bly attempted to best the eighty-day voyage in 1889. Bly was a pioneering journalist who had been beaten down for years by dimwit male editors. She finally broke through by feigning madness and getting herself admitted to New York's Women's Lunatic Asylum and writing a dramatic undercover exposé of conditions in that hellhole. For her next adventure, she proposed to her editor at Pulitzer's *New*

York World the idea of beating the eighty days in Verne's fictional journey. She traveled alone, with almost no luggage.

Eighty was not an easy number to beat, but Bly did it. Since then, the eighty-day circumnavigation has inspired people to take on the challenge in many ways—on bicycles, in sailboats, and, in one particularly wacky attempt, on foot while wearing an iron mask.

Robert Louis Stevenson's *Treasure Island*

Perhaps the most famous travel-adventure novel of the nineteenth century was Robert Louis Stevenson's *Treasure Island*, first published in 1881. Again, the book was successful in its own time and remains popular today. It has been made into dozens of film versions—silent ones, Italian ones, Disney ones, animated ones, even one set in space.[42]

H. Rider Haggard's *King Solomon's Mines*

H. Rider Haggard, who published *King Solomon's Mines* in 1885, felt there were flaws in *Treasure Island* and determined to one-up Stevenson. His beat was Africa, where he had worked in the British colonial administration of the Transvaal and Natal (both now part of South Africa). He set his wild treasure-hunting yarn there, rather

---

42 I have contributed to the genre myself, writing and directing a version in 1997 starring Jack Palance, Kevin Zegers, and Patrick Bergin. My version was originally to be based on an old unproduced screenplay by Orson Welles, but when the producers decided that it presented too many potential legal problems with the litigious Welles estate, I was assigned to write a totally new script based on Stevenson's original book. (Good thing too—Welles' version was lame.) At the time, I considered myself something of an expert on kids' drama. My first maxim —the kids get themselves into trouble, and out of trouble, on their own, without the help of adults, especially of adults in authority. I took some liberties tightening up the original, which I considered (and still do) to break this central rule and to be meandering and unfocused. Some critics approved, but I was savagely trolled on the internet and learned that there are a large group of T.I. zealots, especially in England, who consider every word of the tale to be near gospel and not to be messed with. Who knows how these purists reacted to *Muppet Treasure Island*, in which Captain Smollett is played by Kermit the Frog and Ben Gunn by Miss Piggy.

than Stevenson's Caribbean. He banged it off in six weeks and, at the last moment, refused a flat fee of £100 from his publisher, requesting instead 10 percent royalties from the book's sales. The move set him up for life. *King Solomon's Mines* was a runaway bestseller, modestly advertised as "THE MOST AMAZING BOOK EVER WRITTEN."

Narrated by the hero, Allan Quartermain, it is a rollicking adventure, full of arduous treks, battles with hostile natives, evil witch doctors, comely maidens, with large dollops of gory, grisly discoveries. Today's readers will be offended by the douchey British imperialist condescension toward the Africans in the tale, however common it was in its day. The book inspired many to consider jumping the next mailship for Zanzibar or Cape Town. As Quartermain tells the reader:

> There is no journey upon this earth that a man may not make if he sets his heart to it. There is nothing, Umboba, that he cannot do, there are no mountains he may not climb, there are no deserts he cannot cross, save a mountain and a desert of which you are spared the knowledge, if love leads him.

Haggard followed *King Solomon's Mines* with an even wilder tale of African exploration. *She* is also considered a classic of imaginative literature. To date, it has sold over 80 million copies. The book has a convoluted set up and a complicated plot, and it is a bit hard to imagine twenty-first-century teens picking it up, but it has served as the basis for numerous films (1908, 1911, 1916, 1917, 1925, 1935, 1954, 1965, 1984, and 2001) and even a rock opera. The story follows the adventures of two plucky British explorers who head to Africa looking for treasure and end up discovering a lost kingdom, a primitive race of natives, and a mysterious white queen, Ayesha, "She Who Must be Obeyed."

In addition to sending wannabe explorers to Africa, *She* inspired other others—writers from Rudyard Kipling to Henry Miller to Margaret Atwood have said they were influenced by it. Of course, it has been re-evaluated in recent years in light of changing sensibilities.

Haggard, like most of these other writers of Victorian adventure literature, is accused of archaic attitudes toward all but the alabaster-shaded heroes of his book. Indeed, Kenyan author Ngũgĩ wa Thiong'o, in his book, *Decolonising the Mind*, characterizes Haggard as "one of the geniuses of racism."

Victoria's Secret Literature

While Haggard, Stevenson, and Ballantyne aimed their books at adolescents, other writers of the era used exotic travel as a subject for a far different genre of scribbling and a far different market. The Victorian era has a well-deserved reputation for prudishness, but it also produced a quantity of salacious pornography. One of the most familiar tropes of these erotically charged books and journals, nearly as popular as evening shenanigans in girls' boarding schools, was the sailing voyage to Turkey, the Orient, or Africa, or a lush Caribbean plantation setting, in which wild threesomes or orgies, often involving gorgeous slaves or harem girls, would occur during the hot tropical nights. The stories were uncredited, but it is believed they were mostly written by publisher William Lazenby and the acclaimed decadent British poet Algernon Swinburne.

These lurid tales had by necessity a limited readership, so it is unknown whether they actually convinced anyone to head off to the tropics in hopes of lusty adventure. Swinburne himself hated to travel, although, according to gossip of the day, he had a long-standing crush on Sir Richard Burton and imagined himself having slippery S&M trysts with the famous African explorer.

Charles Darwin's *The Origin of Species*

Charles Darwin was probably the most important explorer-scientist of the nineteenth century. In 1831, he embarked on a five-year sail around the world aboard the HMS *Beagle,* studying the biology and geology of the planet and coming up with an earth-shattering theory that challenged all scientific and religious dogma about man's place in the universe.

His book, *On the Origin of Species by Means of Natural Selection, or the Preservation of Favoured Races in the Struggle for Life,* has been voted the most influential academic book ever and hailed as "a book that changed the way we think about everything." Alfred Russel Wallace writes that Darwin "wrought a greater evolution in human thought within a quarter century than any man of our time—or perhaps any time."

Darwin delayed publication for twenty years, first conceiving of the theory of evolution in 1839 and not releasing his book until 1859. The reasons for the delay are not fully known, but it is believed he feared upsetting both his naturalist friends in the clergy and his pious wife Emma.

The title might suggest to some that the book promoted racism, but the term "races" was used in the nineteenth century as a synonym for "varieties." The book did promote the idea of the "survival of the fittest" and was later used by promoters of racism and the faux-science of eugenics.

Did it also encourage further exploration? Marginally. Darwin was a globe-circling explorer who had a profound influence on the world, but only a peripheral one on other travelers. He did popularize what is now one of the favorite destinations of adventure travelers, the Galapagos Islands.

Darwin is commemorated in geographical features around the world, including Darwin Sound and Mount Darwin, both in South America, and the city of Darwin, now the capital of Australia's Northern Territory. He is also one of the very few explorers whose name has been turned into an adjective: Darwinian. Columbus is another, with his name used to create the word Pre-Columbian.

Edgar Rice Burroughs's *Tarzan of the Apes*

Known by most as a movie or television character, *Tarzan of the Apes* originally appeared in a 1912 novel written by Edgar Rice Burroughs.

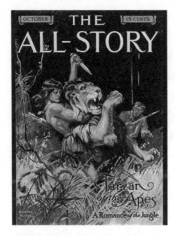

Tarzan

Tarzan became a cultural icon largely because Burroughs, against the advice of his conservative publishers, capitalized on the character's popularity by featuring him in dozens more books and syndicating him to comic books, movies, and merchandisers.

Ray Bradbury wrote in the *Paris Review*: "Edgar Rice Burroughs would never have looked on himself as a social mover and shaker. But as it turns out—and I love to say it because it upsets everyone terribly—Burroughs is probably the most influential writer in the entire history of the world." He continued: "By giving romance and adventure to a whole generation of boys, Burroughs caused them to go out and become special."

Burroughs is also one of the very few writers who has had not one but two municipalities named after his most famous creation —Tarzana, California, and Tarzan, Texas. If you're not up for exploring Africa, you might at least consider a visit to these Tarzan-themed towns.

Royal Geographical Society

While Burroughs, Stevenson, Haggard, Swinburne, and the others were promoting adventure and exploration in their books, organizations like the RGS and The Explorers Club were championing and promoting it in a more institutional manner. The RGS was not the first geographic society—we have already seen how the African Association and the Société de Géographie sprang up in the early 1800s to promote European discovery of Timbuktu. But after its formation in 1830, the RGS became the most influential and important of the lot and arguably remains so to this day.

It was originally made up of the crustiest of upper-crust Londoners. The founders included three dukes, nine earls, twenty-four peers, twenty-four baronets and knights, thirty-two naval officers, and fifty-five army officers. Of course, all were white, penis-equipped, and determined to glorify exploration and spread British values and attitudes around the world. The biographer of Sir Roderick Murchison, president of the RGS for four long terms between 1843 and 1871, writes: "the explorer acted out the European longing to be challenged by nature in a wild and exotic setting. In so doing, he simultaneously verified the superiority of European civilization, opened new frontiers for expansive capitalism, and provided an outlet for emotional impulses stifled by industrialisation and urbanisation." The RGS actively supported explorers or, at least explorers it approved of. Speke and Livingstone were liked; Burton less so. Scott was a favorite, but not Shackleton, and certainly not that foreigner Amundsen.

Women were not allowed as members until the twentieth century and then only after a long bitter battle within the organization. The matter had been brought up in 1887, but after eight months of debate was dropped due to the outrage it had caused. In 1892, the governing council voted to admit the fairer sex, but a cabal of military fuckwits managed to overthrow the decision. As Earl Curzon of Kedleston, who later would become president, thundered in the *Times*, "we contest in toto, the general capability of women to contribute to scientific, geographical knowledge. Their sex and training render them equally unfitted for exploration, and the genus of professional female globetrotters with which America has lately familiarized us is one of the horrors of the latter end of the 19th Century." Take that, Nellie Bly.

A referendum held in the 1890s in which the "yes" votes outnumbered the "no" votes by a margin of 1,165 to 465 was again overturned by the reactionaries. It was not until 1913 that the opposition was overcome and females finally admitted, to the dismay of Curzon, now Lord Curzon, 1st Marquess of Kedleston, KG, CGSI, bunch more fancy titles. He next turned his attention to founding and leading the

Anti-Suffrage League, which aimed to prevent women from voting in British elections.

When the RGS finally allowed women to join, Isabella Bird Bishop was part of the first cohort of fourteen and the first to give a paper at the society. She had lived as a near invalid for the first forty years of her life. Ironically, it was her afflictions that turned her into an adventurer. Told by doctors she had to escape Britain's climate, she traveled, first to America, then to Australia. She despised Australia and so jumped on a rat-infested paddle steamer, which she loved, for the Sandwich Islands, now Hawaii, which she loved even more. The erstwhile invalid climbed giant Mauna Loa and described its "liquid sea of living fire" in one of her many books about her travels. She spent seven months in the islands, observing with interest the joyful, hedonistic ways of the Hawaiians. She then left for Colorado, where she took up with a shaggy one-eyed outlaw named Rocky Mountain Jim, who was eventually shot dead in a gunfight. She wrote a book about him, calling him "a man any woman might love but no sane woman would marry." On its publication, she expressed relief that "the critics have not scented out impropriety," then set off for more adventures—in Japan, Malaya, Tibet, India, and Morocco.

National Geographic Society

Fifty-eight years after the formation of the RGS, thirty-three gentlemen assembled in Washington to explore the possibility of creating an American version of it. Among them were Arctic explorer Brigadier General Adolphus Greeley; John Wesley Powell, the one-armed explorer of the Colorado River and the Grand Canyon; and Gardiner Greene Hubbard, representing his famous son-in-law, Alexander Graham Bell, who was then cooking up new inventions on Cape Breton Island. Bell would eventually become an important and active member of the society.

The National Geographic Society struggled until Bell took over the presidency with the goal of broadening the organization's appeal so that "the janitor, the plumber, and loneliest lighthouse keeper [can] share the fun with kings and scientists of sending an expedition to Peru or an explorer to the South Pole." Before long, the society rapidly outstripped its British forebear in membership and fame, largely due to its renowned yellow-trimmed magazine. The journal did not start off with a bang. The first issues were full of extremely dry, academic papers, and were described as "dreadfully scientific, suitable for diffusing geographic knowledge among those who already have it and scaring off the rest." That all changed with the November 1896 issue, which included a photo of a half nude Zulu bride and her groom, along with the somewhat bizarre text: "These people are of a dark bronze hue, and have good athletic features. They possess excellent traits but are horribly cruel once they have smelled blood."

Editor Gilbert Grosvenor was uncertain about running the photo, but his mentor Bell advised him that prudery should not influence the decision. Bare breasts (always, of course, of a "dark bronze hue," never white) became an almost monthly feature of National Geographic. As Tom Buckley would write in an article in the New York Times: "So unquestionably genteel was the magazine, and so patently pure its anthropological interest, that even at a time when nice people called a leg a limb it never occurred to anyone to accuse Grosvenor of impropriety."

Until the arrival of Playboy in 1953, National Geographic was the only mainstream source of photographic nudity. Almost unwittingly, the magazine inspired boys to dream of lives of travel, exploration, and adventure in the early twentieth century.

In fairness, the magazine did publish a lot of ambitious photojournalism, such as its coverage of the 1903 eruption of Mt. Pelée in Martinique. National Geographic became the world's leading source of information about extreme natural phenomena, exploration, and expeditions of discovery. And the bare tits didn't seem to hurt (although changing sensibilities mean they've been phased out in our century).

When editor Grosvenor died in 1954, his magazine's circulation was over five million, a number that the magazine described, in characteristic fashion, as equivalent to a stack of magazines 25 miles high. Circulation peaked at twelve million in the 1980s and still hangs in at more than two million today (with a substantial online audience).

The Explorers Club

The National Geographic Society's goal of popularizing exploration was laudable, but in 1904 a group of men decided they wanted a more exclusive organization comprised not of plumbers and lighthouse keepers but actual explorers. There are strict requirements for membership in The Explorers Club. Originally the club was Manhattan-centric. While still based in the Big Apple, it now also has thirty-two chapters in the United States and around the world.

The club's headquarters is styled exactly as one would expect: a stone, five-story, faux-Tudor mansion on the Upper East Side, chock-a-block with stuffed cheetahs and gazelles, relics of expeditions past, as well as books, maps, and photos. A giant polar bear greets visitors to the second floor. A brass plaque lists the "Famous Firsts" of club members: First to the North Pole, First to the South Pole, First to the Summit of Mt. Everest, First to the deepest point in the ocean, First to the Moon. These are somewhat misleading. None of the men who the plaque commemorates were members at the time of their famous firsts. Robert Peary, Roald Amundsen, Edmund Hillary and Tenzing Norquay, Don Walsh and Jacques Piccard, Neil Armstrong and Buzz Aldrin, were all offered honorary memberships after their great achievements. A university can give out as many honorary degrees as it likes, but it can't then claim the honorees as famous alumni.

The club's early years were tumultuous. Of the first six presidents, three left under cloudy circumstances. Frederick Cook ended up in jail, Robert Peary was accused of having fudged his North Pole triumph, and Vilhjalmur Stefansson's reputation was marred by the tragedies of his Arctic expeditions. By the club's teenage years, things had largely settled down and by 1930 it could rightly consider itself "the world center for exploration."

The club developed some long-standing traditions, most famously an annual dinner with members in black tie or "native dress," in which unique culinary offerings are presented—fried cockroaches, invasive lionfish, and, on one occasion, slices of meat that claimed to be from a 20,000-year-old mammoth recovered from the Arctic permafrost. It also has a tradition of permitting members to carry an Explorers Club flag on certain recognized expeditions.[43]

Women were not admitted to the club until 1981. This was a highly contentious issue, even though it was 1981, not 1881, for chrissakes. Some dinosaurs threatened to resign if women were allowed in, but the "let them in" crowd was better organized and more eloquent. Among them was then-president Charles F. Brush III, who commented that "it is highly bizarre to call ourselves an explorers club and exclude half the world."

Faanya Rose became a member in 1994 and was elected the first female president in 2000. Her reign included a devastating fire in the headquarters and the 9/11 attack on the World Trade Center. There was also an incident at the annual dinner in which a guest ate a tarantula and wound up in hospital with a serious allergic reaction. Rose acquitted herself admirably during these crises.

Scouts, Guides, and Public School Exploring

In 1908, one of the most powerful promotions of wilderness exploration began with the publication of Robert Baden Powell's book *Scouting for Boys*. It inspired the Boy Scouts and Girl Guides movements and got thousands of teenagers interested in exploration,

---

43 I am a fellow of the club (so, you see, it's no longer that exclusive), and I have successfully applied to carry a flag on five expeditions—to Brazil's Rio Roosevelt, Mexico's Naica Crystal Cave, the Caño Cristales river in Colombia, on an underwater expedition off Eleuthera, and on a submersible off Curacao. I am also a part of a relatively small group of multi-generational members. My daughter is a member and sits on the club's board of directors.

"woodcraft," wilderness travel, and survival. By 1909, the first Scout rally (or Jamboree, as they were called), was held at the Crystal Palace in London with 11,000 boys and a few brave girls dressed as Scouts in attendance.

By the following year, there were 100,000 Scouts. By 2019, there were 46 million registered Scouts and nine million registered Guides. Younger scouts are called Wolf Cubs and younger Guides are called Brownies (or they were until 2022 when it was decided the name was potentially offensive). Many adult explorers have attributed their interest in exploration to Scouting or Guiding. And in the movie *Indiana Jones and the Lost Crusade*, the most famous fictional explorer ever, Indiana Jones, finds his life mission when as a Scout he discovers the "Cross of Coronado."

A similar but more ambitious program, the Public Schools Exploring Society, was created in 1932 by George Murray Levick, known in exploration circles for his discovery of the depraved "hooligan cocks" subset of Adelie penguins during the ill-fated Scott Antarctica expedition.

The organization was designed to toughen up England's public school boys for wilderness exploration. (One of England's quirks is that its so-called public schools are in fact private schools: expensive, very elite joints such as Eton and Harrow.) With the spread of bolshie egalitarianism in the twentieth century, the Public Schools Exploring Society changed its name and mission several times, winding up with the British Exploring Society. In 2011, it suffered a tragic accident when a group of its teenage members were attacked by a polar bear on Norway's Svalbard Island. One was killed and four others badly injured.

Memoirs, Chautauquas, and Travelogues

Few things got people fired up about charging off into the wilderness like reading memoirs or biographies of those who had done it already. There are scads of them. Someone with nothing better to do once counted 185 biographies of David Livingstone.

Sailing to distant places is a popular sub-genre. (A sailor I know jokes that he was the only one ever to sail around the world and not write a book about it.) One of the first, most influential, and perhaps still the best of these is Joshua Slocum's *Sailing Alone Around the World.* Slocum was a Canadian-born sea captain who, with the end of commercial sail, decided to do as his title suggests. He departed from Fairhaven, Massachusetts in 1895, rounded the globe, and returned to Newport, Rhode Island three years later.

Slocum may have been alone at sea but was seldom alone on land. He had a number of wives and lady friends. One of them was Mabel Wagnalls, the young heiress to the Funk and Wagnalls publishing house, who helped secure him a publishing deal. He published his wonderful book in 1900, and it is still in print today. British poet and journalist Sir Edwin Arnold claimed that "I do not hesitate to call it the most extraordinary book ever published."[44] Slocum singlehandedly started the vogue for long-distance exploring under sail, which inspired new designs, techniques, and equipment that made it possible to take on the world's oceans either alone, with family, or with modest short-handed crews.

One of Slocum's contemporaries was Theodore Roosevelt, president of the United States from 1901 to 1909. Roosevelt met Slocum on a few occasions. Each man inspired the other. Roosevelt was unquestionably the most adventurous man to call the White House home. He lived under canvas for at least a month a year, including the years he served as New York governor and president.

Theodore Roosevelt

---

44 In 2000, I turned the story into a film that has now been seen by well over a million viewers on TV, DVD, and YouTube. The appetite for armchair adventuring continues. (Various distributors and pirates have released the film under different titles, so just search YouTube for "Joshua Slocum documentary" and you'll find it.)

Roosevelt's safaris to Africa are famous, but his climactic antic was his descent of Brazil's previously unnavigated Rio da Dúvida (River of Doubt), now renamed the Rio Roosevelt. It was a wild, hairy trip with lost boats, hostile natives, dangerous animals, a murdered man, and the near death of the former president from an infected cut, malaria, and starvation. It is remarkable that Roosevelt survived this wild adventure, although in a sense he didn't. His health never fully recovered. He died five years later but not before writing a book about his adventure: *Through the Brazilian Wilderness* was another of the many tomes that got armchair adventurers out into the outdoors.[45]

Richard Halliburton

While Slocum (sea captain) and Roosevelt (politician) had day jobs, Richard Halliburton was a professional writer who adventured to provide grist for his mill. He led an extraordinary life and produced dozens of bestselling adventure travel books through the 1920s and 1930s. He made no bones about his bohemian lifestyle, dedicating his first book to his Princeton roommates, "whose sanity, consistency, and respectability . . . drove [him] to this book."

When his father advised him to return home to Memphis, get a proper job, and get his life on "an even tenor," Halliburton replied that, "I hate that expression and as far as I am able, I intend to avoid that condition. When impulse and spontaneity fail to make my way uneven then I shall sit up nights inventing means of making my life as

45 In 2014, I organized and led an expedition to try to find one of Roosevelt's abandoned boats. We experienced the (still) utterly remote and dangerous wilderness through which he traveled, kayaking though wild rapids and ending up covered in hundreds of South American bug bites only a few feet from the snapping jaws of a large, agitated caiman.

conglomerate and vivid as possible. . . . And when my time comes to die, I'll be able to die happy, for I will have done and seen and heard and experienced all the joy, pain and thrills—any emotion that any human ever had—and I'll be especially happy if I am spared a stupid, common death in bed."

Halliburton got his wish, drowning in a sinking Chinese junk in a vicious storm in the Pacific Ocean in 1939. But before that awful day, he had a lived his life of adventures. Most famously, he swam the length of the Panama Canal, paying the lowest tariff ever charged for the privilege—thirty-six cents. He was the only non-Chinese to witness and document the extravagant wedding in the Forbidden City of the last Chinese emperor and empress, who were both sixteen at the time. His book *The Glorious Adventure* recounted his retracing of Ulysses' travels through the Classical Greek world. He also re-enacted the explorations of Hermán Cortèz in Mexico and the fictitious travails of Robinson Crusoe. His flight around the world in an open-seater biplane with aviator Moye Stephens included the first aerial photographs of Mt. Everest and an illicit swim in the reflecting pool of the Taj Mahal, for which he was arrested. It wasn't Halliburton's only run-in with the police. While preparing to copy Hannibal by crossing the Alps by elephant, he was arrested in Paris for homosexual activities. Essayist Susan Sontag appropriately described Halliburton as a writer specializing in "the theatricalization of experience."

As well as writing about his travels, Halliburton spoke about them, sometimes in Chautauqua tent shows. These wildly popular summer venues began in the 1890s, hit their height of popularity in the 1920s, then dwindled until about 1940. The movement started in Chautauqua, New York, a picturesque lakeside village 70 miles west of Buffalo (today famed as a summer citadel of the arts, the home of Bill and Hillary Clinton, and the site of the attempted onstage assassination of Salman Rushdie in 2022 by a fuck-nut extremist).

The original Chautauqua movement was highbrow—spiritual, educational, cultural—and so successful that other places adopted the name to their own purposes, creating a circuit. This cheapened the movement, at least in the eyes of the New York founders. Gone were the Methodist moralists who held sway on Lake Chautauqua, replaced with popular speakers (Halliburton), firebrand orators (William Jennings Bryan), controversial politicians (socialist Eugene Debs), women's rights activists (Susan B. Anthony), and explorers (Vilhjalmur Stefansson).

The combination of the Chautauqua venues and the growth of photography, cinematography, and worldwide steamship travel created a new form of entertainment—the travelogue. The first to master this new medium was John Lawson Stoddard, who used a stereopticon to entertain audiences with stories of his travels through Europe, India, China, Japan, Egypt, and other locales. It was once said that Stoddard's "rise to fame was spectacular and unprecedented in the annals of American entertainment. No American lecturer, musician, or actor has ever won as large a following in so short a time. From his second season, almost every lecture was sold out. . . . He filled Daly's Theatre, one of the largest in New York, fifty times a season for ten years . . . this would mean that Stoddard alone drew approximately 100,000 persons in New York each year."

When Stoddard retired, his mantle passed to Burton Holmes, who abandoned the stereopticon in favor of the exciting technology of moving pictures. He also quit the summer tent shows, realizing that summer was the best time to travel and shoot new material and winter the most lucrative time to fill large indoor venues. Usually with the help of local civic groups like Rotary and Kiwanis, Holmes created a huge circuit of theaters and auditoriums across North America that ran the travel programs he and his acolytes produced. The format was standardized: ninety minutes of footage from some exotic part of the world with the filmmaker standing beside the screen, giving live commentary from a lectern. Holmes is believed to have crossed the Atlantic and Pacific over fifty times and to have shown his films over 8,000 times. For better or worse, he also developed some of the clichés of the format, including the ubiquitous ending, "and, as the sun sets in the west, we leave the peaceful natives of (fill in the blank) island."

The growth of Discovery, Outdoor, and Travel channels, not to mention YouTube, has diminished this once-thriving travel-adventure theatrical circuit, but it survives. I joined it myself some years ago, editing together a film of the twenty-two volcanoes I had by that time climbed and photographed. I got myself a California-based booking agent and went on the road just as Burton Holmes had 100 years earlier. I presented the film in cities big and small—Philadelphia, Seattle, Portland, Poughkeepsie, Grand Rapids, and North Bay. I had some good shows, but it was obvious that the genre that had electrified audiences in 1912 was on its last legs in 2012.

In 2015, I photographed on top of another volcano, the then-very-active Marum lava lake in Ambrym, Vanuatu. Natives of other islands in the archipelago call Ambrym the "Black Magic Island," both for its spooky volcano, its traditional, primitive culture (almost no vehicles, electricity, or plumbing, lots of betelnut-chewing) and its history that supposedly (and as recently as 1950) included cannibalism.

Black Magic Island lived up to its reputation. While there, I ingested sulfuric acid from the hydrogen sulfide and sulfur dioxide gases swirling out of the volcano. The incident sent me into a year of serious hospital treatments and managed to destroy one of my vocal cords (you have two—I've now got only one), effectively ending my brilliant career on the live-presentation circuit. It also means that if you ever hear me on radio or TV plugging this book with a raspy whisper, you'll have to turn up the volume.

BIBLIOGRAPHY

Adams, Mark, *Turn Right at Machu Picchu*, New York, Penguin Books, 2011.

Ballantyne, R. M., *The Coral Island: A Tale of the Pacific Ocean*, London: T. Nelson & Sons, 1857.

Berton, Pierre, *The Arctic Grail*, Toronto: Anchor Canada, 1988.

Berton, Pierre, *Prisoners of the North*, Toronto: Doubleday Canada, 2004.

Bovill, E.W., *Missions to the Niger*, Cambridge: Cambridge University Press, 1966.

Burton, Sir Richard, (translator), *Arabian Nights*, London, 1875. Reprinted in Orange, Connecticut: Samizdat Express, 1974.

Caravantes, Peggy, *Marooned in the Arctic: The True Story of Ada Blackjack, the Female Robinson Crusoe*, Chicago: Chicago Review Press, 2016.

Cobham, David, *Race to Antarctica* (YouTube).

Conan Doyle, Arthur, *The Lost World*, London: Hodder & Stoughton, 1912.

Cousteau, Jacques, and Susan Schiefelbein, *The Human, The Orchid, and The Octopus: Exploring and Conserving our Natural World*, New York: Bloomsbury USA, 2007.

221

Crocker, Kathleen and Currie, Jane, *Chautauqua Institution 1874–1974*, Charleston, SC: Arcadia Publishing, 2001.

Diubaldo, Richard, *Stefansson and the Canadian Arctic*, Montreal & Kingston: McGill-Queen's University Press, 1978.

Dugard, Martin, *The Explorers*, New York: Random House, 2014.

Fawcett, Colonel Percy, *Exploration Fawcett*, London: Hutchinson & Co., 1953

Geiger, John, *The Third Man Factor*, Toronto: Penguin Canada, 2009.

Geiger, John and Mitchell, *Alana, Franklin's Lost Ship*, Toronto: Harper Collins, 2015.

Gramm, David, *The Lost City of Z*, New York: Doubleday, 2005.

Haggard, Sir H Rider, *King Solomon's Mines*, London: Cassell & Co., 1885.

Haggard, Sir H. Rider, *She, A History of Adventure*, London: Longmans, 1887.

Heaney, Christopher, *Cradle of Gold*, New York: St. Martin's Press, 2010.

Henson, Matthew, *A Negro Explorer at the North Pole*, New York: Frederick Stokes, 1912.

Howgego, Ray, *The Book of Exploration*, London: Weidenfeld & Nicholson, 2009.

Hutchison, Gillian, *Sir John Franklin's Erebus and Terror Expedition: Lost and Found*, London: Adlard Coles Nautical/Bloomsbury Publishing, 2017.

Jeal, Tim, *Explorers of the Nile*, New Haven: Yale University Press, 2011.

Jeal, Tim, *Livingstone*, New York: William Heinemann Ltd.., 1973.

Jennings, Ken *Maphead*, New York: Scribner, 2012.

Keay, John, *The Mammoth Book of Explorers*, New York: Carroll & Graf Publishers, 2002.

Kryza, Frank, *The Race for Timbuktu*, New York: Ecco/Harper Collins, 2007.

Lowe, Lara, *The Great Adventurers: Scott of the Antarctic*, Cromwell Productions (Amazon Prime).

McGoogan, Ken, *Fatal Passage*, New York: Carroll & Graf Publishers, 2001.

McGoogan, Ken, *Lady Franklin's Revenge*, Toronto: Harper Collins, 2006.

McLynn, Frank, *Hearts of Darkness: The European Exploration of Africa*, New York: Carroll & Graf Publishers, Inc., 1992.

National Geographic Expeditions Atlas, Washington, D.C.: National Geographic Society, 2000.

Nickerson, Sheila, *Midnight to the North*, New York: Jeremy P.Tarcher/ Putnam, 2002.

Niven, Jennifer, *Ada Blackjack: A True Story of Survival in the Arctic*, New York: Hyperion, 2003.

Ondaatje, Michael, *Journey to the Source of the Nile*, Toronto: Harper Collins 1998.

Plimpton, George, *As Told at The Explorers Club*, Guilford, CT: Lyons Press, 2003.

Preston, Douglas J., *The Lost City of the Monkey God*, New York: Grand Central Publishing, 2017.

Riffenburgh, Beau, *Shackleton's Forgotten Expedition: The Voyage of the Nimrod*, New York: Bloomsbury Publishing, 2005.

Roberts, Jason, *A Sense of the World*, Toronto: HarperCollins Publishers, 2007.

Roosevelt, Theodore, *Through the Brazilian Wilderness*, New York: Charles Scribner's Sons, 1914.

Sancton, Julian, *Madhouse at the End of the Earth*, New York: Crown Random House, 2021.

Schonfield, Hugh, *Richard Burton Explorer*, Tuningen, Germany: Texianer Verlag, 2013.

Shelley, Mary, *Frankenstein, or A Modern Prometheus*, London: Lackington, Hughes, Harding, Mavor & Jones, 1818.

Slocum, Joshua, *Sailing Alone Around the World*, New York: The Century Company, 1900.

Stefansson, Vilhjalmur, *My Life with The Eskimos*, New York: Macmillan, 1913.

Stevenson, Robert Louis, *Treasure Island*, London: Cassel & Co, 1883.

Stewart, Christopher S., *Jungleland*, Sydney, Toronto etc.: HarperCollins Publishers, 2013.

The History Makers: Shackleton (Amazon Prime).

The Race for the Poles (Discovery/Times Video).

Verne, Jules, *Around the World in Eighty Days*, Paris, Pierre-Jules Hetzel, 1873.

Whyte, Ken, *The Uncrowned King: The Sensational Rise of William Randolph Hearst*, Toronto: Random House Canada, 2008.

Wilkinson, Alec, *The Ice Balloon*, New York: Alfred A. Knopf, 2012.

Winters, Kathleen C., *Amelia Earhart: The Turbulent Life of an American Icon*, New York: Palgrave Macmillan (St. Martin's Press), 2010.

INDEX

ACKNOWLEDGEMENTS

My great thanks to my initial über-editor Phillippa Baran. Thanks also to my early beta-readers, Richard Wiese, Ron Base, Christopher Heard, Jason Schoonover, Keith Ross Leckie and Geordie Ryan. Most especially, thanks to the great team at Sutherland House Books - Publisher Ken Whyte, Managing Editor Shalomi Ranisinghe, Marketing Director Serina Mercer, Publicist Sarah Miniaci, and Designer Lena Yang. Thanks to Don Miller Photography for the author photo. And as always thanks to the A, B, and C of my life - Ashley, Brianna and Carolyn Rowe.

THE AUTHOR

Peter Rowe's long career as a filmmaker includes producing and filming the 49-part series *Angry Planet*, shot on all seven continents. His previous books include *Music vs the Man*, *Adventures in Filmmaking*, and *Ablaze—Ten Years that Shook the World*. He is a fellow of the Royal Geographical Society, The Explorers Club, and the Royal Canadian Geographic Society. Notwithstanding the scurrilous, profane, and outlandish nature of this book, he has not (yet) been blackballed from any of these organizations.